£3.50
24/23

The Selfish Altruist

RELIEF WORK IN FAMINE AND WAR

Tony Vaux

publishing for a sustainable future

London • New York

First published in the UK and USA in hardback in 2001 and in paperback in 2004 by Earthscan Ltd

Reprinted 2004, 2009

ISBN: 978-1-85383-879-8

Typesetting by Composition and Design Services, Belarus
Cover design by Andrew Corbett

For a full list of publications please contact:

Earthscan

2 Park Square, Milton Park, Abingdon, Oxon OX14 4RN

Simultaneously published in the USA and Canada by Earthscan

711 Third Avenue, New York, NY 10017

Earthscan is an imprint of the Taylor & Francis Group, an informa business

Earthscan publishes in association with WWF-UK and the International Institute for Environment and Development

A catalogue record for this book is available from the British Library

Library of Congress Cataloging-in-Publication Data

Vaux, Anthony.
    The selfish altruist : relief work in famine and war / Anthony
        Vaux.
        p. cm.
    Includes bibliographical references and index.
    ISBN 1-85383-879-9 (cloth)
    1. Humanitarian assistance. 2. Altruism. 3. Oxfam. 4. Food relief.
    5. War relief. I. Title.

HV544.5.V38 2001
363.34'988–dc21   2001023348

At Earthscan we strive to minimize our environmental impacts and car-
bon footprint through reducing waste, recycling and offsetting our CO_2
emissions, including those created through publication of this book.

Contents

Foreword

In this book Tony Vaux speaks with disarming honesty about the dilemmas – personal and institutional – of 'aid management' in humanitarian emergencies. The guiding principle he proposes in dealing with these dilemmas is 'humanity', interpreted as 'concern for the person in need'.

The term 'humanity' is perhaps a trifle ironic, since humankind is unlikely to strike an independent observer (say a visiting alien) as a paragon of concern for human needs. More likely, it would appear as a species of exceptional brutality and cruelty. This feature is most evident in the history of war, which has no parallel among other species. During the last 100 years alone, more than 250 wars have been fought, with at least 100 million casualties. In contrast, war is virtually unknown in the animal world, notwithstanding metaphors such as 'fighting like cats and dogs'. One has to look far along the biological scale, for example among particular types of ants, to find anything resembling war among non-human species.

Nevertheless, looking to the future, there is some hope that humankind will learn to practice the values commonly associated with the term 'humanity'. Humanitarian work is an important part of this learning process. As this book shows, however, humanitarian work is fraught with dangers and dilemmas.

To propose 'concern for the person in need' as a guiding principle in addressing these dilemmas may not seem adequate. Indeed, it is easy to think of situations where this principle would offer insufficient guidance on its own. Consider, for instance, the predicament of aid agencies in Sudan in the 1980s where, as Tony Vaux observes, 'providing a few sacks of food was virtually the same as providing a Kalashnikov rifle [as] they could be exchanged for each other within hours of delivery'. Concern alone does not solve this dilemma. Similarly, concern alone does not tell us how to prioritize relief programmes in famine situations where resources are too short to ensure everyone's survival.

Yet, the more one becomes absorbed in this riveting book, the more one realizes that 'concern for the person in need' does have a sharp edge as a principle of humanitarian action. The reason for this is that, contrary to popular perception, humanitarian action is often compromised, or even corrupted, by very different motives. We are not talking here of humanitarian action on the part of national governments, which is quite often a thinly-veiled instrument for the pursuit of commercial, strategic and other interests. What Tony Vaux points out is that even the actions of non-governmental organizations (NGOs) of impeccable repute, such as Oxfam, are often influenced by motives and emotions far removed from humanitarian concern. These may include ideological prejudice, personal feuds or ambitions, institutional rivalries, fundraising imperatives, the intoxication of power and even racism.

It is disturbing, for instance, to read that 'the desire to help so easily becomes the desire for power'. Yet the author's account of humanitarian work in war-torn Mozambique provides telling illustrations of this elementary truth. As he takes us on his lifelong journey from emergency to emergency (in Sudan, Afghanistan, Rwanda, Kosovo, Azerbaijan, Somalia and elsewhere), many 'humanitarian dilemmas' come alive with a force that no amount of academic analysis can convey.

These revelations are bound to disturb those who are used to the fundraising-poster image of Oxfam and other humanitarian agencies as benign, concern-driven enterprises. Yet they are necessary to bring about greater accountability in this field. It is often said that humanitarian agencies should be more accountable to the people or communities they are helping. But the ground-reality is that the latter typically have no power whatsoever over the former, making it very hard to foster this kind of accountability. In practice, humanitarian agencies are accountable primarily to the donors, who hold the purse strings. In this situation, it is important to promote a better understanding of the dilemmas – and political economy – of humanitarian intervention among donors (and this includes the general public). That, to my mind, is one of the chief contributions of this book.

The book can also be read as a useful rejoinder to extremist critiques of humanitarian agencies. Exposing the 'disaster relief industry', as it is sometimes called, goes down quite well with sensation-hungry readers, and a little bit of sensation is perhaps necessary to draw attention to the issues involved. But this adversarial approach does not do justice to the complexities of humanitarian work, and also carries a danger of strengthening isolationist tendencies in Western countries. It is to

Tony Vaux's credit that he has presented his own critique in a constructive spirit.

I cannot resist mentioning a few specific themes of the book that have a strong personal resonance. One of them is the pervasive role of propaganda in contemporary Western societies, particularly when it comes to war situations. Based on my own experiences in Iraq in 1990–1992, I am not surprised to read Tony Vaux's impression of Bosnia in 1993: 'The difference between what the European public believes and what happens on the ground is extraordinary.' The same could be said, I am sure, of most of the other emergencies discussed in this book.

On a more positive note, the book has strengthened my conviction that the expansion of democracy (not only in authoritarian countries, but also in those that are perceived today as 'democratic') is, ultimately, the most effective way of defeating the forces of militarism in the contemporary world. It is often argued that people 'enjoy fighting', but this claim is at odds with wide-ranging personal testimonies from war zones across the world. As Tony Vaux wrote in Azerbaijan in 1993: 'When asked what were their priority needs, people invariably replied: "Stop the war. Stop the war".' In a community of genuinely democratic societies, this popular revulsion against war is likely to receive a much stronger hearing than it does today.

Finally, many stories and anecdotes in this book suggest that 'humanity' is a universal value. This, again, reminds me of the solidarity and compassion I have witnessed among disaster-stricken people in many different places, from the squats of London to Iraqi homes and Kashmiri villages. As I write these lines, a wave of solidarity for earthquake victims in Gujarat is sweeping across India and beyond – another demonstration of the pervasive role of 'concern for others' in social life. Of course, human beings are also capable of extreme selfishness and cruelty, as other stories and anecdotes in this book indeed illustrate. But there is hope in the fact that compassion and concern can flourish in very diverse environments, including the most trying. In this hope, perhaps, lies the answer to Tony Vaux's poignant question, 'how can an aid worker be happy?'

Tony Vaux has another reason to feel happy, namely that at the end of this arduous (even harrowing) journey he has been able to share his thoughts with the public in this highly enlightening book. That, too, is a contribution to the cause of 'humanity'.

Jean Drèze
Delhi School of Economics

Acknowledgements

I would like to thank Oxfam for a grant towards the sabbatical year in which I wrote this book. In particular Stewart Wallis, David Bryer and Paul Smith-Lomas supported the idea with little assurance of the result. Nicola Reindorp provided encouragement and penetrating analysis of the draft. Joan Turner and Ros Buck in the Oxfam library gave every possible assistance while Rosie Dodd tirelessly sought out archive material.

Underpinning this book are the thoughts of a remarkable group of academics (all of whom I worked with while at Oxfam): Alex de Waal, Mark Duffield, David Keen, Nick Leader and Hugo Slim. Throughout the book I find Amartya Sen's thoughts like a ghost at my elbow, starting with his breathtaking analysis of famine and leading on to the concept of development as freedom, which I have turned to in my search for an alternative to metaphysics in Chapter 9, where there are also strong traces of the influence of Richard Rorty.

Rather than clutter the text, I follow the lead given by Michael Ignatieff in *The Warrior's Honor* and offer a descriptive guide to the sources at the end of the book, rather than exact footnotes and references. This gives the opportunity to acknowledge influences even where there are no direct references or quotations. Anyone wanting exact citations can contact me by email at vauxt@aol.com.

Among personal friends who have helped and encouraged me I would like to equally thank Douglas Saltmarshe. This book would have foundered in confusion without the wise guidance of David Turton of the Refugee Studies Centre at the University of Oxford. For no good reason, he always believed that I had something to say, and made me believe so too.

Finally, I would like to thank the Earthscan team. Jonathan Sinclair Wilson for showing confidence and encouragement when there was little to justify it, Pascale Mettam and Martha Fumagalli for enthusiasm in the production process and Akan Leander for patience with my revisions and brilliance in reading my handwriting.

There are others who deserve thanks, too close to me or too numerous to mention.

List of Acronyms and Abbreviations

A-FOR	Albania-Force: NATO in Albania
AIDS	acquired immune deficiency syndrome
AGRICOM	Mozambique's state agricultural marketing company
CAP	Common Agricultural Policy
CDR	Coalition for the Defence of the Republic (Rwanda)
DPCCN	Departmento de Prevencao e Controlo das Calamidades Naturais (Department for the Prevention and Control of Natural Calamities)
DFID	Department for International Development (UK)
ECU	European Commission currency
EEC	European Economic Community
EU	European Union
FRELIMO	Frente para Liberacao de Mocambique (Mozambique Liberation Front)
GNP	gross national product
HDI	Human Development Index (UN)
ICRC	International Committee of the Red Cross
IMF	International Monetary Fund
KLA	Kosovo Liberation Army
MSF	Médecins Sans Frontières
NATO	North Atlantic Treaty Organization
NGO	non-governmental organization
ODI	Overseas Development Institute
PTSD	post-traumatic stress disorder
RAF	Royal Air Force
RENAMO	Resistencia Nacional de Mocambique (Mozambique National Resistance)
RPF	Rwanda Patriotic Front
RRC	Relief and Rehabilitation Commission
SABC	South African Broadcasting Company
SCF	Save the Children Fund

SPLA	Sudan Peoples' Liberation Army
TPLF	Tigrayan People's Liberation Front
UN	United Nations
UNHCR	UN High Commission for Refugees
UNITAF	UN Task Force (Somalia)
UNPROFOR	UN Protection Force (Bosina)
USAID	United States Agency for International Development
USSR	Union of Soviet Socialist Republics
3WE	Third World and Environment Broadcasting Project
WFP	UN World Food Programme

Introduction

What are our feelings when we see the victims of famine and war: the starving child, the distraught mother, the old person whose way of life has been destroyed?

We experience not just one feeling, nor purely a sense of altruistic concern, but other feelings of which we would rather not be conscious. Maybe a little smugness because the same thing has not happened to us. Perhaps even a sense of superiority, crediting ourselves with cleverness because we have protected ourselves against such terrible misery. Such feelings give a pleasant sense of self-confidence and we feel even better as we roll out our prescriptions for solving the world's problems.

Having made a donation to charity or written to an MP, the viewer turns to other issues, while the aid worker is left with the task of converting public response into practical action. Yet the same mixture of motives and feelings persists. A feeling that 'I have been clever and they have been stupid' may convert itself into a tendency to treat people as if they have no worth or ability at all. It reinforces helplessness and makes those who are being helped feel all the more inferior and dependent. The victims of terrible tragedy, surrounded with loss and bereavement, are treated simply as bodies to be fed, nuisances in the global economy. They are not people worthy of concern – people whose thoughts and lives are valued in themselves. Disaster is compounded by a sense of being devalued. The body suffers physical want, while the mind suffers from a sense of worthlessness.

Most aid workers have learned to recognize this danger and avoid the most extreme behaviour. But the problem of selfishness still creeps in, perhaps in more subtle ways. Altruism is a difficult feeling to maintain and a shaky concept in a postmodern world, without given beliefs and morality. In any case, our natural tendency is to think of ourselves first and to bring our own perceptions, prejudices and principles into our expression of concern for other people. We feel that because they are powerless we have the right to impose, and enjoy, our own power.

One purpose of this book is to bring these issues into the open and to explore them dispassionately. For aid workers, there is plenty of scope to develop our own ideologies, to choose whom to help and whom to ignore, to enjoy a sense of power and to overlook the capacity of those we help. We may project our own sense of victimization onto those we are supposed to help and may fight our battles through their suffering. We boost our own confidence by being optimistic. But if we protect ourselves by simply believing that all humans are 'good', we cannot cope with what we then have to call 'evil' when we find it in ethnic cleansing and genocide. We try to separate ourselves from our altruism but our altruistic concern is an expression of our self and of our feelings.

For most of us there are no religious or social norms that fix our standard of response. We struggle with our selfishness, trying to find something outside to guide our response. It is not easy to have few moral values and plenty of wealth, relative to the rest of the world. We are free to choose whether to feel concern for another person or not. No one tells us what to think or to do. We are alone with ourselves and an aged concept of responsibility.

Personally, when confronted by someone begging, I rely on my feelings to decide whether and how much to give. The decision reflects my mood at that moment. I have found no rational way of doing otherwise. But I remain suspicious of my mood. If there were 1000 beggars and they all faced starvation, I would have to analyse my feelings.

This book is about the paradox of altruism as an expression of the self, and the consequences in humanitarian aid. It argues that altruism is not something we choose as an alternative to selfishness but a value that we aspire towards – an escape from the more selfish influences of the gene and the past. We have to learn how to understand and then make a proper place for ourselves, realizing that it is the same 'self' which makes the choice. I call 'concern for the person in need' the principle of humanity. It is not a simple concept. It is as complex as the person for whom we feel concern, and includes their entire social, economic and political context. To do justice to our concern we have to know everything, and because we cannot do this, altruism is an aspiration, not a fact.

The book also looks at the issues in a linear or historical perspective. It is about the shift in responsibility for humanitarian response from private aid agencies, which enjoyed their heyday during the Cold

War, towards Western governments which, free from the constraint of superpower conflict, are now much more active and influential in providing emergency relief and in searching for solutions to poverty and conflict. The problem in the past may have been the idiosyncrasy of aid agencies and their personnel. But what happens when the initiative switches to government? And what, finally, are the challenges facing humanitarianism today?

The book deals with assumptions and cultural norms. I will try to describe hidden biases and perceptions in the process of aid work, including my own. To some extent, these hidden biases refer to a specific set of people. But although I may often speak as a British person talking about British aid workers (usually working for a specific agency, namely Oxfam) and addressing a British public, I hope that other readers may be able to interpret what I am saying according to their own culture and set of assumptions. Indeed, the contrast may throw light on their own circumstances. This book is a kind of postmodern history in which the personal viewpoint interacts with the issues under discussion. I form my perceptions from the issues I deal with. Because there is no fixed morality that can be applied globally, this is inevitable when examining global issues; but it is especially appropriate today as we try to form new concepts about what people are and how they are affected by the principles of science, the spread of technology and the global economy. We are groping for a global culture to match our global economy, global science and global technology. The issue of care for others is absolutely fundamental to that culture. From the perspective of the reader, the question might be: 'Who am I today?'

* * *

As a preliminary question, we need to ask whether there is any agreed moral basis for modern humanitarianism? There may be little guidance (for most of us) from established religion and there is also a diminishing sense of fixed public morality. Old concepts of 'duty' and 'social responsibility', which perhaps reached their height (in the UK, at least) during World War II, have been deeply eroded. The socialist ideology of the 1960s and 1970s no longer offers significant numbers of people a philosophical basis for their relationship with the world's poor and suffering peoples.

Is there guidance from within the humanitarian tradition? Since the Crimean war, the issue has been dominated by the question (of concern to generals as much as to humanitarians) of how to limit the effects of war to what is publicly acceptable. In the 19th century, and more famously during World War I, the levels of human destruction became so great that governments and military leaders feared mutiny and rebellion, and could not continue without making some concessions to the needs of their soldiers. After World War II, the effects of 'total war', including the mass aerial bombardment of cities, threatened to make civilians reject war as a solution to any political problem. Through a series of Geneva conventions and other agreements, the practice of war has just kept ahead of public acceptability.

The process was based on making a distinction between combatants and non-combatants and on agreements between consenting governments representing nation states (the 'high contracting parties' to the conventions). Wounded soldiers earned the right, in so far as the conventions were applied, to be treated as non-combatants. Methods of war that target civilians have been prohibited. But the process has begun to stall because combatants and non-combatants cannot be distinguished from each other in the wars typical of the post-colonial, post-Cold War era. Pressures that had been held in check by outside forces are now unravelling against a context of rapid global change. These wars are not between states or even between recognizable military entities, and they rarely have a recognizable objective of peace; they are chronic wars of political control, of marginalization and of access to resources.

The organization entrusted with upholding international humanitarian law is the International Committee of the Red Cross (ICRC), which has recently tried hard to provide an ideological framework for humanitarianism, realizing that a chaotic situation will undermine even the most deeply held principles, such as the right to give assistance to those in need. For most of the last century the principles were considered self-evident; but in the 1960s the ICRC identified seven underlying principles: humanity, impartiality, neutrality, independence, universality, voluntary service and unity. Nevertheless, these have failed to make much impact on the ever-increasing numbers and ideologies of private aid agencies. One problem is that they do not clearly differentiate between important principles, such as 'humanity' on one hand, and those such as 'voluntary service' on the other, which appear relatively trivial. In any case, actions cannot be guided simultaneously by seven different principles.

Instead of simplifying the principles and exploring more fundamental values, the tendency in the last two decades has been to expand

and elaborate the principles, making them ever more pragmatic. In the late 1980s, several aid agencies (I admit that I was one of those involved in the drafting) worked together to produce the Red Cross Code of Conduct which listed 10 practical principles and 12 recommendations. In the 1990s, the Sphere Project laid down hundreds of professional standards for humanitarian responses. There are several other influential codes that aid agencies can sign up to if they wish such as the 'Providence Principles' drafted in the USA and individual sets of rules for other countries, among them Sudan and Liberia. But all of this obscures the fundamental question: what is humanitarianism? With the end of the Cold War, when Western governments began flexing their political muscle, it has become increasingly important to decide what is fundamental and what is peripheral. Or to put it another way, what are values and what are simply working mechanisms.

What I argue in this book is that the principle of 'humanity' represents the fundamental moral value of humanitarianism. It takes precedence over all others.

What does it mean? I define the principle of humanity as 'concern for the person in need'. Impartiality is an essential quality of humanity because it means that we do not distinguish between persons. In other words, we are fair. The experience described in this book demonstrates that we need to pare away personal prejudice and preconception in order to reach a comprehensive understanding of 'the person in need'. Otherwise, for the serious altruist at least, there can be no real concern, only a superficial and selfish relationship. This concern is an immensely demanding concept, requiring constant self-questioning, good communication and relentless analysis.

In my view, the other Red Cross principles, with the exception of impartiality are negotiable and must always allow for exceptions. For example, the objective of the principle of humanity is not served by remaining 'neutral' in relation to genocide (as the ICRC now acknowledges in the case of the Holocaust). I do not think it is necessarily true that voluntary action is preferable to the intervention of governments. Voluntary action has its place; so too does paid and accountable political action. The new world order in which governments now operate may be better at exerting greater political power upon humanitarian issues. What I have learned is that, in terms of helping people, all the wisdom of principles, codes and standards is superseded by the simple concept of humanity, applied impartially and to the best of our ability. Governments will struggle to come to terms with this, just as aid agencies have done.

* * *

The fact that Western governments are now in the ascendant over voluntary aid agencies became clearer to me during 1993–1999 when I was regional manager of Oxfam's programmes in Eastern Europe and the former Soviet Union – especially when the North Atlantic Treaty Organization (NATO) intervened in Kosovo. NATO's intervention was performed in the name of humanitarianism, but was so obviously bound up in political issues and the personal interests of politicians that I felt the meaning of the word desperately needed to be clarified. If voluntary agencies are to hand over the torch of leadership to governments, let us at least take stock of what we have learned during the Cold War, and of our own failures and successes.

I realized that I had not yet thought through the issues because I had not needed to and had never been challenged. That in itself was a chilling revelation. Did no one actually care enough about humanitarian work to ask such questions? Was it all a conspiracy of silence with the aim of keeping the poor out of the minds and hearts of Western people who wanted to get on with their own lives? Suddenly I saw it all in a new light.

I was also alarmed that I too had been swept along on an uncontrollable tide created by NATO and the leading politicians of NATO states. It was as if I had suddenly become a part of NATO's agenda. Profound changes in Oxfam's own ways of working at the same time also demanded my attention. Oxfam was being reborn as a new organization; it was more business oriented, corporate and pragmatic than before. Was this good or bad? The 'old Oxfam' in which I had worked for over 25 years was being replaced and modernized. What was 'new Oxfam'? Was all this good or bad?

This book is the outcome of a year of catharsis and reflection at the Refugee Study Programme (later renamed the Refugee Study Centre) at Oxford University, under the kindly and encouraging guidance of David Turton. I asked myself what was the fundamental principle that had guided my better actions over the course of the years. I thought as deeply as I could about the ten years from 1984 when I had been Oxfam's emergencies coordinator, assessing humanitarian crises and organizing responses in conjunction with colleagues in field offices and in the Oxford headquarters, where I was based. I tried to make sense of it by looking back at old records and my own reports. I read some of what others had written, especially those academics who had themselves been engaged with Oxfam and had similarly stepped back to think about what they had experienced. I began to assemble my most striking memories of Ethiopia, Sudan, Mozambique, Afghanistan, Somalia and the collapse of communism in Eastern Europe and the former Soviet Union. All of these recollections have been reworked and now form the chapters of this book.

I felt I could not ignore what had happened in Rwanda in 1994, the greatest and most shameful cataclysm of humanitarianism. I was not directly involved, fortunately, because I had already shifted responsibility and was dealing with Bosnia where – after three years of detachment by the West – ethnic cleansing had been stopped. In Rwanda, however, ethnic cleansing proceeded to the direst of all human consequences: genocide – the attempt to obliterate an entire race of people. Many of my colleagues working in Rwanda said they had lost faith in humanity and in humanitarian work. I felt an obligation to think myself into that event and to explore the capacity of the imagination to explain the unexplainable. The result is unsatisfactory, but my point is that it is better to try than to pretend it does not exist.

It is selfish not to think deeply about the person in need. It is selfish just to feed a few children and save their lives without knowing what else is happening, what others are doing, what happened in the past and what will happen in the future. In order to understand the person in need and his or her full social, economic and political context, we need to obliterate our own self. It is not a pleasant process because we have to question ourselves relentlessly. The advantage is that we will have a better chance of making the right decisions. If we allow ourselves to intrude on that judgement, we will believe that we know the answers before we really do, and mistakes will be made. Humanitarianism needs to move towards pure altruism. This applies to aid workers in voluntary agencies as well as to those in government who are now assuming greater power. The issue is about 'minimizing' the self and increasing awareness of the 'other'.

Humanity does not mean concern for physical well being only. Aid that simply provides calories for the stomach and water for the throat is a reduction of people to things. How can there be human concern for such a mean objective? 'Concern for the person' entails concern for the whole being, including a person's state of mind, sense of loss and the devaluation of life. The suffering of the body and the mind cannot be distinguished from each other. It is concern for every aspect of a person including their loss of relatives and way of life, their disability, their love of children, their past and their future. Humanitarian concern is a demanding concept because it has no limit. It involves the aid worker infinitely in deeper and deeper understanding, and it is never satisfied. The aid worker constantly balances the physical and the emotional and can never reach a sense of perfect fulfilment. The aid worker is condemned to live with dissatisfaction and uneasiness.

One reason for this is that aid workers are not questioned generally by society at large and have to make up the questions for themselves. It would be better if people who saw others starve on TV and consequently sent in a donation were much more demanding about what should happen. The media generally allow aid agencies to get away with any sort of response on the premise that public confidence should not be undermined by criticism. But this simply allows for mistakes and sloppy thinking. The problem is not really the lack of reflection by aid workers, but the lack of genuine interest by the public. It is too convenient to just 'trust' the aid agency. But in cases where thousands of people are dying, is that really enough?

The great fault of aid agencies in the last 20 years has been the lack of introspection, or rather the inability to deal seriously with situations. This has allowed a superficial optimism to develop. In order to express concern for other people, we have to believe that they are good. In effect, aid agencies have preserved the concept of the 'deserving poor'. The idea is that people deserve our help because they are innocent victims. But this is not always true. And if it is not, are we supposed to withhold aid? The public response to the camps in Goma in 1995, which were full of people who had been involved in the Rwanda genocide, was exceptionally large, possibly because the public failed to appreciate that their aid was mainly going to those who caused the problem, and not to the victims themselves. But this self-deception was not possible for aid workers. The issue of helping murderers caused great stress to aid workers.

Aid workers began to wonder whether they had also become imbued with a notion of the 'deserving black'. It was hard to avoid the conclusion that aid agencies had protected African governments from criticism and allowed them to be considered part of the group that deserved humanitarian concern. Allied with the mistakes of humanitarianism is racism. Aid agency staff find it hard to accept that black people exploit each other and tell lies just as white people do, and that greed is not the sole preserve of cigar-smoking white men who run the World Bank or are in charge of large corporations. The victims of tragedies in Africa are often the victims of African greed, of merchants and politicians who may be abetted by the West but who could have chosen to behave in other ways. Overlooking such facts is really an insult and shows no real concern for the truth about other people's lives.

A survivor of the Rwanda genocide told me that she felt insulted by Western people asking her to forgive and forget. What they mean, she said, is that they want to be able to forget their own failure and to ignore their reactions to an event that they felt unable to understand. They want to just carry on in their own way as if nothing had happened, and so, she said, 'They preach to me that I must forget also.'

There are no easy answers in this book, and certainly no recipes for simple changes that will put everything right. I am rather tired of glib pronouncements. Aid agencies are too fond of calling for minor adjustments as if proposing solutions were almost as good as achieving them. I lived in India for seven years and had to conclude that people were just as poor when I left as when I arrived. Every day as I stepped out of my house I had to walk past, and sometimes over, the bodies of poor people who might be either alive or dead. During 1984–1994 I worked as part of a huge team of aid workers, donors and celebrities on resolving famine in Ethiopia. Recently I returned to find another famine and people starving in the same way and in the same places as they did in 1984 – with the same arguments and discussions taking place about the solutions.

What have we achieved? There needs to be space and time, at least, for reflection, and yet aid managers, in my experience, do not have that time. They simply respond to a relentless sequence of events, which wears them out over time – just as I was worn out by my own experiences and inability to take charge of what was happening to me.

* * *

I am not sure whether we are born with a sense of 'concern for the person in need'. I suspect it is more important that we have the ability to sympathize with the emotions of other people; this develops as our experience of humanity widens. The difference in people's response is not necessarily a result of a 'caring nature' that some people have and others lack, but a difference of imagination – the ability to see into another person's experience. I happen to have a strong imagination to which I largely attribute my humanitarian concern. This is not necessarily a good or bad thing. It just happens that way. I find it easy to think myself into the situation of someone in need, and can easily terrify myself by doing so. It is a powerful enough motive to have kept me in humanitarian work for nearly 30 years.

The level of imagination may be relatively fixed, but what varies over the course of time is our confidence that we can do something about our concern. Time and again I have seen hopefulness turn to despair and brilliant plans degenerate into muddled actions. But the determination never disappears, even though energy may be lacking.

The person telling this story needs a little introduction. When I came to Oxford University as a student in 1968, the 'buzz' was that the world could be a better place: more equal, more caring. Everything was going to be all right and we were going to have everything, whether we worked for it or not. We were shaking off the gloom and restrictions of the war years and the limited satisfactions of an older generation who still worried about switching off the lights and spreading the margarine a little more thinly. In our ears was the siren music of Joan Baez and Bob Dylan calling us to enjoyable protest. And to our surprise, the world told us we were good. The Beatles quietly made fun of the materialistic middle classes, and the middle classes enjoyed it, in a mildly embarrassed, suburban sort of way.

The message from the radicals was not to worry too much about silly foibles such as work and possessions. And having got to Oxford through a fierce process of competition, I felt that I could now relax. Optimism was bred into me by the combination of academic success and good company.

The ageing middle classes, still scared by the turmoil of war, were remarkably indulgent. Employers, still influenced by a touch of 1930s Woosterism, liked the idea of recruiting a young graduate who had had a fling or two, even if it was with socialism. On the streets of Oxford we met American students escaping the draft for the Vietnam war. They were escaping evil 'out there'. We were high without needing to take drugs. We were going to change the world by staying in bed. It was a great time.

But the attempt to caricature wears thin. My perspective changes as my mood changes, for there were both good and bad times, and my concepts were shaped by the impressions of friends, happiness and state of mind. The point is that, to some extent, aid work in its heyday in the 1980s was an expression of that 1960s radicalism.

In the chapter on Ethiopia I explore how optimistic socialism, otherwise known as developmentalism, made us slow to respond to famine because we believed that poor people were so wonderful they could cope with anything. The mistake I now notice most is that we ignored the universality of the human desire for power. It was in ourselves, and in the poor, but we were only interested in people within certain limits and stereotypes.

I sometimes wonder if all idealism is a myth or a mistake. Sometimes the very notion of an ideal seems out of place in our modern world. But we cannot help trying to make order out of chaos. We have brains that have evolved to do little else, remorselessly converting visual images to meaning and experience to philosophy.

Why do we react to distress? As long as I can remember, I had a strong sensitivity towards suffering. The lingering death of a pet tortoise, decaying upwards from a maggot-infested leg, preyed on my mind as a child; and at school I was banned from blood donation after fainting at the sight of my own blood. Freud tells us that we build up our sensitivity in our formative childhood years. I cannot remember many of my early childhood experiences; but boarding school exacted a high price for A-level grades and developed my sensitivity towards suffering and violence. I form my objective opinions of the world from subjective experience.

I sometimes wonder if I became a humanitarian out of sheer pride. At Oxford a new organization had just formed called Third World First. I cannot remember how I got into it, but I do recall going from room to room collecting money to relieve starvation. I remember one scene vividly. I had fallen into a routine of jokingly saying 'I'm after your money' and expecting a polite and friendly response because it was a good cause. To my astonishment, someone told me to 'get out'. Even now I can picture my outstretched hand offering the covenant of charity which I expected the lofty young public-school man to sign. I don't remember which charity it was. All the charities were good, all the same. Practicalities were a rosy blur, and maybe that was the problem. I had assumed too much.

'Get out,' he said.

I can recall the white light falling like a slab from the window, which seemed to flatten me as he said those words. I did not know what to do. A young man of my own age, who seemed somehow older, superior, lounging lazily with a friend, taking tea in his college rooms, was sitting higher than me, as if on a plinth – or maybe that is just a trick of memory. I hated snobbery.

The scorn in his eyes turned to disgust. My nervous optimism was suddenly converted to humiliation and anger. I was angry with myself for not being prepared, for not knowing what to do if someone did not smile. He seemed to tell me that I was simply buying a few signatures to save my own conscience. I was just as superficial and pretentious as all the rest. It was my 'road to Damascus' experience. I concluded that the issue of world poverty must be taken seriously or not touched at all. What I discovered, perhaps, was that for me the worst thing was to be called shallow and superficial. Was that pride? I ask because it is something I have often found to be a block to humanitarian aid. In Afghanistan, Oxfam staff declared that they would stop all aid programmes until the Taliban allowed women to participate in the programmes on a more or less equal basis with men. The Taliban would not give way, nor would Oxfam, and hundreds of thousands of people were affected because neither side would back down.

I hope that by exploring the way in which personal motive interacts with practical response, I will stimulate more self-awareness among aid workers. Recognizing our own internal bias enables us to suddenly see the world in a different way. In Rembrandt's portrait of the great King Belshazzar in the National Gallery in London, the king's fatty hand rests enquiringly on the flesh and luxury around him as he tries to comprehend the blinding light and the shadowy finger writing chill words on the wall. I still feel like that sometimes, almost absurdly exposed in a moment of ecstatic contemplation, with a sense of having to look at something that I do not want to see. What am I doing here? Where does the bright light come from? Can't I stay here and eat? Why the pull of the starving millions? Why humanity? Why should this obsession fall on *me*?

I learned recently and by chance that Rembrandt's portrait is not as Rembrandt intended. The way in which we see the king stare at the trailing finger spelling his doom in letters on the wall is itself a distortion. Someone in the past considered that the king was too defiant in his pose and decided to 'spin' the portrait anticlockwise so that the king appears to reel backwards from the writing on the wall. This involved cutting away triangular slices of the canvas and turning it in the frame. In Rembrandt's original, the king must have appeared to lean forward as if he wanted to drive his head into the pointing finger.

It would have been a far more disturbing painting. Man confronting God. Me declaring that I was going to have nothing to do with all these problems.

It is strange how big issues such the relationship of Belshazzar and God can be altered by a man with a pair of scissors. And for me the change was brought about by a sense of boredom and a bit of paper.

* * *

My life changed in a few seconds on a tube train in London in 1972. I was returning from work in the City during my brief spell as an international banker after leaving Oxford. My colleagues and I had been examining the prospect of making a large loan for a dam in Brazil. The room looked out directly onto the wedding-cake grandeur of the Bank of England and I kept a picture of the Lake District on my desk to keep myself sane.

We wrote a briefing for the regional manager. I never met him but imagined him as the archetypal businessman who would take the client out for lunch, and over brandy and cigars quietly offer a loan, on profitable terms, of course, before reverting to talk of the stock exchange and golf. Ironically, I became a regional manager myself many years later at Oxfam, not the bank, and found that staff viewed me in the same sort of way. I was a distant and wealthy eminence living in the lap of luxury and inclined to put on too much weight. Time holds the present as a mirror to the past and makes us learn what we have experienced all over again.

That evening, as the train darted to the suburbs between darkened walls, I watched as passengers clutched at handrails or hunched themselves over books, holding handbags and umbrellas, furling shoulders over their bodies protectively, as if each held a secret. My thoughts trailed over the map of the underground to an advert for jobs with the Brook Street Bureau. I was dressed in a pinstripe city suit, carrying *The Economist*. Bored, I opened it and saw that Oxfam wanted someone to write about world poverty. In a flash I realized that it was the chance to get serious. I applied for the job thinking that it was better to work as a packer in Oxfam than to be the most exalted manager in the City. I seem to remember that I read Matthew Arnold's poem the 'Scholar Gypsy' to reinforce my decision to give up the prospect of a conventional life. I was 22.

My boss asked me to write a two-page summary of world statistics on poverty and then tore apart what I wrote. It was not the cosy friendliness I had expected. The exacting boss treated poverty seriously. It was a good lesson; good intentions are not enough.

* * *

This book may seem like a book about Oxfam because I have always worked with Oxfam (until this year at least), and it may be useful to indicate what sort of bias that may create.

Certainly, Oxfam brings its own set of expectations to the analysis. It still surprises me that Oxfam was founded as a response to problems in Greece and the Greek islands, where today people go for their holidays. During World War II, German-occupied Greece suffered a famine as terrible as the one in Ethiopia in 1984. In the winter of 1941, 2000 Greek children died every day and the final death toll is estimated to have been around a quarter of a million. The cause was an Allied blockade intended to weaken the Germans. Many people in Britain were horrified and protested to the government. There was a special resonance with classical scholars, one of the most prominent being Gilbert Murray in Oxford who became, in effect, the founder of Oxfam. A national famine relief committee was established to focus attention on the famine, and subgroups were subsequently formed in several cities, including Oxford, with Murray taking the lead.

For many months Prime Minister Winston Churchill held firmly to the view that winning the war was more important than anything else, including the death of the Greeks. The arguments in the House of Commons were eloquent and covered most of the moral issues which humanitarians still debate today. It set a standard for Oxfam of always being ready to challenge the government when it put political interests above humanitarian ones. That sharp political edge remains just as relevant today as aid agencies are challenged by the increasing involvement of government in emergency relief.

In this case, the Allies relented and allowed food to enter the famine areas. The Oxford Committee for Famine Relief (which became Oxfam) sent food and by a series of chances (connected with the determination and commitment of certain individuals) became the only committee to survive long after the war. The founders worked passionately until they had created an international aid agency, and ultimately the largest international charity in Britain.

During the 1950s, Oxfam was a tiny organization running a single second-hand shop in Oxford, where it gathered clothes and money to send to an office in Vienna. The focus was helping refugees after the war – the sort of people we see in old newsreels, wheeling a pram across the map of Europe.

In the 1960s, the spread of TV brought the emotional impact of humanitarian disaster directly into people's homes. Oxfam rose to national prominence during the Biafra war, which was the first humanitarian disaster to be seen by millions of people and also the first to be the subject of systematic distortion. Overwhelmed by images of starvation and by public outcry, Oxfam's director ordered a plane of relief supplies into Biafra without undertaking a proper investigation on the ground. The truth behind the Biafra famine proved murky. The secessionists had used a public relations company to exaggerate the suffering. Oxfam found itself accused of fuelling a pointless conflict. Since then, Oxfam has learned to rely only on making its own assessments in conflict situations, and using advice from people on the ground. From this bitter lesson Oxfam became, in the 1970s and 1980s, the listening aid agency.

There was also a strand of Quaker influence that tended the same way. Oxfam has no formal religious connections but at least, until the 1980s, individual Quakers had a powerful impact on the ethos and philosophy of Oxfam – particularly the concept of respect for individuals in their own right. My own concept of the principle of humanity owes a good deal to the Quakers, and may be seen by some as a restatement of old values. I greatly enjoyed my early years with Oxfam because people felt welcomed even though the demands were heavy. When people feel valued they are better able to tackle the human biases which become so troublesome if they have to fight for their own dignity and principles through the lives and deaths of those they are supposed to help.

I do not think the concept of humanity, 'concern for the person in need', is the individual property of Quakers, of Oxfam or of Britain. It is not culturally specific. There can be variants of it which better reflect other values held in high esteem in societies. The concept of Ubuntu, described here by Archbishop Tutu, is more socially orientated but still recognizable as humanity:

Ubuntu *is very difficult to render into a Western language. It speaks of the very essence of being human. When we want to give high praise to someone we say, 'Yu, u nobuntu': 'Hey, he or she has ubuntu.' This means they are generous, hospitable, friendly, caring and compassionate. They share what they have. It also means my humanity is caught up, is inextricably bound up, in theirs. We belong in a bundle of life. We say, 'a person is a person through other people'. It is not 'I think therefore I am'. It says rather: 'I am a human because I belong.' I participate. I share. A person with* ubuntu *is open and available to others, affirming of others, does not feel threatened that others are able and good. For he or she has a proper self-assurance that comes from knowing that he or she belongs in a greater whole and is diminished when others are humiliated or diminished, when others are tortured or oppressed, or treated as if they were less than who they are.*

Oxfam's key policy paper on disasters contains a very simple statement of what is at the heart of humanity. It says: 'Field staff should identify and build on local rather than external resources, with consultation and involvement of the affected local population.'

In the end, that remains the most basic lesson that I have learned and relearned. Everything else may seem questionable, transitory and subjective. But that simple concept has, for me at least, withstood all the tests of time. Still, it is not as easy at it looks: our own self stands in the way.

Chapter 1
Kosovo: The Loss of Impartiality

D oes NATO's Kosovo intervention mark a new global era in which Western power promotes the concept of humanity? Or does it show Western military power seizing hold of humanitarian principles and distorting them?

I suspect that there is nothing quite as definite as a new world order, and we are still in the modes of the past; but the tendency of the post-Cold War period seems to create winners and losers. The casualty of the new world order, if Kosovo is anything to go by, is likely to be impartiality. The main purpose of this chapter is to explain more fully why impartiality is an essential attribute of humanity.

If humanitarian responsibility rests primarily with government, as it does today, it becomes embroiled in political interests and ideology. Aid managers find the concepts of altruism and selfishness conflicting; but instead of being an issue of conscience, it now cuts into the nature of government and forces people to think clearly about their balance of interests. This may be just as well. Not all political decisions are self-interested. Ideals appeal both to politicians and to their voters. But how do politicians and governments balance their own interests with those of the people they seek to help? The lesson from Kosovo seems to be that governments are much less concerned than aid agencies about impartiality. They intervene, on one hand, and demonize on the other. Is this a reflection of our 'first-past-the-post' democratic system? Perhaps politicians can only cope with situations where there is a winner and a loser, a right and a wrong. If so, there will be difficult lessons to be learned. Humanitarian crises, in my experience, are never that simple, and often the reality is very different from what we first perceive. In this chapter I will analyse this problem through Oxfam's experience in Kosovo and show that concern for 'the person in need' must include all who are in need, not just those we happen to favour.

* * *

I changed my views about NATO when one of its bombs nearly killed one of Oxfam's staff in Belgrade. On 30 April 1999, as manager of the regional programme in Eastern Europe, I received this message:

> *The rocket landed 6 feet in front of the building where Gordana Rajkov lives. Gordana (Oxfam's disability adviser) needs assistance to get out of bed since she suffers from muscular dystrophy. Luckily, one of our staff, Mimica, was staying with her during the night with her little son. Otherwise Gordana would not have been able to move at all.*
>
> *Mimica and Gordana heard the rocket flying over their building and then heard the detonation. The power supply was immediately cut, the window panes burst. A part of the ceiling landed on Mimica's head. The walls of surrounding buildings were severely hurt and cries were heard from the rubble. Mimica went out to help the neighbours pull some people out. Since Gordana is a wheelchair user, she could not use the elevator and they had to stay in the flat until the morning when friends called in to carry Gordana down the stairs.*

When Gordana was bombed by NATO, I suddenly had the feeling that I might be on the wrong side. And then came the more chilling realization that I should not be on any side at all. All the arguments of the past began to unravel. Having worked on the problems of Kosovo since 1993 and having witnessed the brutality, I had felt relieved when the Western powers declared that enough was enough and they were going to force President Milosevic to stop violating human rights. But as the threats involved the reality of bombing, and as the bombing became more and more indiscriminate, I realized that I was not on the side of the poor and suffering but of an awesome punitive power with its own objectives, and with personal and organizational interests ravelled up in what purported to be a principled stand. This was not a cool, calculated pressure to uphold humanitarian values but an increasingly desperate attempt by NATO to preserve its own name and the credibility of Western politicians.

As President Clinton said: 'Our mission is to demonstrate the seriousness of NATO's purpose – to deter an even bloodier offensive against innocent civilians in Kosovo.' As shown on Alan Little's documentary for the BBC, *The Death of Yugoslavia*, Clinton paused halfway through the sentence, perhaps marking at that point the real reason for the mission.

Similarly, at the outset of the Kosovo action, UK Prime Minister Tony Blair spoke of 'a new internationalism where the brutal repression of whole ethnic groups will no longer be tolerated'.

This seemed to be a categorical imperative in support of humanitarian objectives. But a few days later in Chicago, on 22 April 1999, Blair qualified his earlier words significantly: 'The mass expulsion of ethnic Albanians from Kosovo demanded the notice of the rest of the world. But it does make a difference that this is taking place in such a combustible part of Europe.' The 'but' makes all the difference.

When NATO could not achieve its objective by bombing purely military targets, it gradually widened its scope. The target in Gordana's case was, ostensibly, a military headquarters not far from Gordana's flat. But as everyone in Belgrade knew, it had been out of use for some time, and all other military installations in the city had been evacuated. Despite NATO's wonderful technology, the aim was surprisingly imprecise. I began to wonder if the people in NATO had perhaps become personally involved and were turning an action in support of humanitarian values into an opportunity to punish 'the Serbs' – who had been demonized throughout the Bosnia war – and were conducting a personal vendetta against Milosevic. And it was all in the name of humanitarianism. How had we got to this point?

There was no doubt about the evil nature of the Serb paramilitaries. They were groups of thugs licensed by the state who offered guns to Serbs and encouraged violence against the majority Albanian population of the tiny province. They flaunted themselves in the Grand Hotel in Pristina and unceremoniously ejected one of our partner Albanians from the lobby when he tried to meet me there. I was inside, politely attended by the waiters, and did not know why he had not arrived. After an hour or so I gave up and drove to the Oxfam office. I happened to see him on the way, walking along the street, head down. He told me that despite being roughed up he was determined to repeat the experiment and assert his rights. He was a lawyer who specialized in human rights and who risked his life every day. Over the six years before NATO's bombing I had become increasingly angry, having seen so much suffering. I visited two old disabled men in Kosovo who lived in a squalid room with the dead, damp smell of unchanged air. Because of their fear of the Serb police they had not been outside for two years. It made me angry that the West took so little notice of this tragedy, and I had been among those who called for the threat of force. It all seemed reasonably obvious at the time.

It would have been easy, and perhaps natural, to focus on the Albanians of Kosovo as symbols of humanitarian concern. If so, we might not worry too much about the bombing of Belgrade. But we would also have to ignore the Albanian paramilitaries, who were beginning to put pressure on the Albanian community long before NATO launched its offensive. They were carefully orchestrating international horror, and may have organized events including the massacres that caused the international intervention. Naturally, people inside Kosovo did not like to talk about such things, and there was a difference between the image projected to outsiders and the reality. Perhaps it was these 'enforcers' who so rapidly expanded the Kosovo Liberation Army (KLA) under NATO's protective onslaught. After their victorious return to Kosovo, they began to copy the Serb paramilitaries and to enact the same violations of human rights against similarly vulnerable Serbs.

As I discovered when I returned to Kosovo in September 1999, three months after NATO's victory, the Albanian leadership in Kosovo had quickly cornered the markets, and prices had shot up in Kosovo. The rich and powerful were exploiting the poor and weak. The price of petrol in Pristina was double the price in Macedonia, a couple of hours' drive away. But the new officials protected the racket and kept the price up. As Oxfam staff told me from the experience of their relatives, all paid jobs were being reserved for supporters of the KLA, and employers who did not contribute to the KLA would find themselves in deep trouble. It was not the victory of the Albanian people but of a new elite, which began to create its own apartheid under the protective arm of Western power.

I found my sympathies changing and began to realize that it was not simply a matter of recognizing the needs and rights of individuals from the 'other side', but also of viewing these individuals in relation to their interests. Impartiality means distinguishing one person from the next, and being aware that many people have an interest in the vulnerability of others. Indeed, humans appear to be a good deal more interested in exerting power over others than in anything else. Therefore when analysing needs, we have to see them as being at the centre of a mass of predatory interests, including some that may come from within ourselves.

* * *

It puzzles me now that I was not more cautious about advocating the use of force. But when I think of the sequence of events, each stage seems to make sense. Perhaps it was the same for the Western politicians and NATO's generals.

A year before the NATO bombing, in mid-1998, Serb security forces moved from sporadic harassment to large-scale destruction of Albanian homes. Over 200,000 people, 10 per cent of the population, were displaced. Most went to live with relatives in places that were less devastated, but some fled across the borders to Albania, Montenegro and Macedonia. Staff at Oxfam were deeply worried about the prospect of people being homeless and cold in the winter. The opportunity to use military force was irresistible. In August, Oxfam released a statement regretting that 'the threat of military force by NATO over the summer has not prevented major offensives or the systematic abuse of civilians... Oxfam believes action to enforce a ceasefire must be taken'.

There was considerable debate. Some felt that Oxfam should never call for the use of force in any circumstances. But Oxfam had done so in the case of Somalia in 1992, breaking with a long tradition of pacifism which had been part of the Quaker influence from the earliest days. Although the Somalia intervention had been a failure (as I describe in Chapter 6) NATO's intervention in Bosnia in 1995 had finally brought an end to three years of appalling war. We expected something similar in Kosovo.

In August 1998, Oxfam wrote to UK Foreign Secretary Robin Cook, asserting the need to use the threat of force: 'As Dayton demonstrated, after all diplomatic initiatives have failed, this is the only remaining option to uphold citizens' rights in war. This may not be an ideal option, but from Oxfam's perspective, it is the least worst option.'

Staff members in the region were uneasy about this position. They pointed out that the immediate effect of a NATO intervention would be to push Milosevic to extremes and might make matters far more difficult for people in Kosovo. Oxfam and other aid agencies would have to withdraw. The mood in Kosovo itself was more buoyant; staff believed that NATO could force Milosevic to back down. Part of the argument for favouring the threat of force (and I was one who used it) was that NATO's power was so obviously overwhelming that it would never have to be used.

Initially, this seemed to have been proved right. On 13 October 1998, a crisis was averted when US envoy Richard Holbrooke signed an agreement with President Milosevic that promised an end to violence and the deployment of an international monitoring mission. But as time went on it became apparent that the violence had not stopped and that NATO's threat was being flaunted. By the spring of 1999, Western politicians were conscious that they had been cheated, not for the first time, by Milosevic; there was an element of personal pride in the confrontation. British and American representatives Robin Cook and Madeleine Albright made no secret of the fact that they were very angry. In his BBC documentary *The Death of Yugoslavia*, Alan Little stated: 'high ideals walked hand in hand with revenge.'

As well as the personal pride of Western politicians, there was NATO's pride too. Coming up to its birthday celebrations, NATO was being ridiculed. In the early months of 1999, the peace talks dragged on interminably at Rambouillet in France. The last straw was the massacre at Racak in March 1999. Images of a scattered line of mangled bodies in a gully above the village and the remains of people shot repeatedly as they tried to flee shocked the world. But there was an air of stage management about the filming of Racak, and it later transpired that the head of the Kosovo Monitoring Mission had been on the phone to Washington and NATO while still viewing the bodies. There is doubt today about whether the KLA deliberately provoked the Serb forces and created the highly publicized conditions for war. Alan Little is among those who have questioned whether it was deliberately given prominence by those in the West who wanted an excuse to launch the NATO offensive.

Having made a threat, NATO and Western political leaders found it extremely difficult to back down. The momentum of events pushed them forward into escalating their threats. Similarly, Oxfam found it difficult to reconsider the basis of its statement in August 1998. Throughout the early months of 1999 there was intense debate in Oxfam about the issue of force. However, retreat was difficult not only because it is always difficult to reverse a previous decision, but also because the grounds for doing so would have to question whether all diplomatic means had been exhausted. Since the actual proceedings at Rambouillet were held in secret, this would entail calling into question the truthfulness of senior politicians such as Robin Cook. This would be difficult for Oxfam in that highly-charged political environment.

Eventually the Rambouillet talks broke down and on 24 March the inconceivable use of force became high-level bombing. Oxfam found itself, rather unusually, unable to agree a public position. Although various policy statements were drafted that supported the use of force but with various riders and qualifications, they were not released. It was clear by this time that the press would only want to know 'does Oxfam support NATO' and a 'cadged' statement expressing concern might not be reported accurately.

Oxfam realized that any hint of opposition to the bombing would put it in direct confrontation with the political establishment on its most crucial issue of the time. And rather late in the day, on the insistence of field staff, Oxfam also realized that any statement in favour of the bombing would endanger staff in Kosovo (still under Serb control) and Belgrade. Two staff members from another aid agency CARE were arrested in Belgrade and accused of spying. Oxfam's regional representative described the situation there:

> We have seen a steadily deteriorating security situation and an increase in the paranoia of security and government authorities. This includes all forms of communication being tapped and monitored, most international NGOs being removed from the country or asked to leave, people being arrested and held without cause or notice, and charged with acts of sedition ranging from taking notes in the street to reporting bomb damage over the Internet. An increase in civilian hostility to the international community and local people who worked for international agencies has also been experienced... To date, Oxfam has had to hand over six vehicles to the authorities and has had 100,000 deutschmarks appropriated from our bank account. Several of our staff have been called in for information interviews, and one associate of Oxfam was held and questioned over three separate periods of up to 72 hours for having parked an Oxfam vehicle in his yard.

The problem beginning to emerge for Oxfam was that the attempt to express its views impartially and objectively was impossible because it operated from Britain, and Britain was part of NATO. Public opinion itself was so polarized that a qualified view would antagonize both sides. In particular, anything less than enthusiasm for the bombing might have been taken as an attack on the government. In some parts of the organization there was dismay that the UK's biggest international charity, with a long history in the region, was silent on what was probably the greatest humanitarian event of the decade – especially with a British prime minister declaring that concern for the people of Kosovo was a prime issue of national policy.

Interestingly, no other UK agency, as far as I am aware, made any direct comment on the rights and wrongs of the situation. The initiative on this massive humanitarian issue was taken up by the government and NATO. The impossibility of articulating a public position left Oxfam, and other agencies, unusually pragmatic in their humanitarian responses. Everything became a matter of what works, and what is funded. To my great regret, Oxfam did not take stock of its relationship with NATO and Western governments but simply responded as events proceeded.

The immediate consequence of the NATO bombing was as Oxfam field staff had predicted. The Serb forces conducted a vicious campaign of ethnic cleansing against the Albanians. Instead of stopping human rights violations, NATO's actions had made them worse. Suddenly the question being debated in the press was a different one. 'Was the NATO bombing a terrible mistake?' journalists asked Oxfam, wondering if Oxfam would challenge NATO. Staff in the field began to ask: what principles does Oxfam stand for? By this time refugees were arriving in Macedonia and Albania, reporting the terrible violence and atrocities of the Serb forces. But the debate was about military strategy. Should the West deploy ground troops as the only way to stop ethnic cleansing?

Oxfam felt uneasy about challenging military tactics. Military experts were always ready to pour scorn on the advice of amateurs. NATO's bombing campaign had triggered a humanitarian disaster, but Western aid agencies could not make loose comments or even express concern without finding themselves opposing their own governments and many of their supporters.

Because NATO would not back up the bombing by action on the ground, they had to increase the range of bombing targets. The aim was also to turn the people of Serbia against the war by devastating Serbia's economy and causing fear. The infrastructure of Serbia was attacked on the grounds that it was pro-military. NATO's policy was within a whisker of being an attack on civilians and illegal under the Geneva Convention. This was what led to Gordana being bombed.

Inside Oxfam the debate continued to be dominated by pragmatic considerations. What could Oxfam add which was not already known? Finally, Oxfam's directors decided that Oxfam could not engage in the public debate 'without endangering some of our colleagues'. Security became the paramount issue and Oxfam remained silent until after the bombing had finished.

* * *

In 1942 when Oxfam's founders tried to stop the famine in Greece, there was no Geneva Convention covering the targeting of civilians in order to achieve military purposes. Oxfam's stand contributed to the formulation of those conventions that were agreed after the war had ended. It is thus at the core of Oxfam's history that a principled position may have a long-term outcome, however unpopular at the time. It is interesting to speculate whether Oxfam would have been able to take such a stand if it had then relied on widespread public support. One thing I discovered during the Kosovo crisis is that a nation at war does not respond to public comment in the way that a nation at peace does.

The basic problem for Oxfam was that any divergence from the dominant view would have been hugely expensive. Oxfam's staff in Belgrade urged Oxfam to condemn the bombing. They sent a detailed analysis of the consequences, pointing out, for example, that because of the deliberate destruction of the electricity supply through the use of graphite bombs there was 'no bread, which is the staple food for many people impoverished by the economic situation, and no cooking – the vast majority of people use electric cookers; gas is mostly unavailable and black market prices have made the cost go up to two average monthly salaries'.

They argued that, as in Greece during 1942, the effect of Allied action was to cause famine. However, it would be difficult to reconcile the fact that Oxfam had argued for the threat of force and was now against the use of graphite bombs. Military experts would ask how Oxfam proposed to decide which sorts of bombs should be used. If Oxfam had reservations about NATO's actions, what was its solution?

One of the staff in Belgrade wrote:

My own feeling is that in its policy Oxfam has mirrored the international community. Policy analysis has been scanty, often based on the drive of one or two people, lacking depth and foresight, with either too little or too much advice from the field, depending on the situation. I work for Oxfam because I believe in its good intentions and willingness to listen, because I thought it had more foresight than others. I find myself wondering about this more and more.

Basically, I think the cause of the problem was that Oxfam could not disentangle itself from its position as a British charity, and was unable to escape from the fact that it was part of a British establishment that was engaged in war. This may have been a 'just war', but even if it was not (and there were doubts), Oxfam would have been in the same situation.

After analysing and reflecting on these issues for over a year, I still feel a kind of numbing of the mind that tells me there is unfinished business. For the most part, aid workers pack away their unpleasant experiences and move on to the next challenge. But Kosovo pulled me up with a jolt. It also coincided with massive changes inside Oxfam in which my own job as regional manager for Eastern Europe and the former Soviet Union disappeared, and this may have coloured my own responses. The subjective, mingled with the objective, had undermined my ability to make a strong stand on an issue which troubled me a good deal but which I could not resolve.

A series of emotional pulls – as people from different parts of the region or within the organization in Oxford got in touch and gave their impassioned views – all made sense but could not be reconciled. Local staff members in Kosovo, with whom I had worked for many years, were left behind when the NATO bombing began and expatriates were evacuated. These staff members themselves became victims of the ethnic cleansing and arrived at the borders as refugees, were put into camps and had to live on open ground behind barbed wire. Strangely enough, some of them still had mobile phones and could call us in Oxford and tell us what they were experiencing. I would sympathize with them, feel anger against the Serb forces and then get a call from Belgrade. Everyone wanted to know what Oxfam's position was and many said they felt betrayed by the silence. 'How can you not condemn what I have just suffered?' they asked. And the calls came from both sides.

* * *

Nearly a million people fled from the ethnic cleansing in Kosovo. When I visited Korca in southern Albania in June 1999, Oxfam staff members were working closely alongside NATO troops, building a new camp and putting up tents and water systems for the refugees from Kosovo. No one had told them not to. There had been no statement distancing Oxfam from NATO's actions and they simply assumed that there was no problem about working with the military. What troubles me is that I did not even realize this myself. I visited the base of the French forces, took tea with the soldiers and chatted about humanitarian issues. Strangely enough (as I see it now), I quickly adapted to this as the normal way of coping with the situation. So did everyone else. Oxfam's coordinator in Albania, Toby Porter, had a similar experience but was one of the first to comprehend what we had done. He reflected on the contrast with Oxfam's practice elsewhere: 'Would aid agencies working with refugees from the Democratic Republic of Congo accept travel on a Rwandan military helicopter from Kigali to Gisenyi? Or would agencies working with refugees from Sudan transport material on an SPLA (Sudan Peoples' Liberation Army) truck between Nairobi and Lokichoggio?'

When the war was 'won' there was jubilation among the aid agencies. Describing the day NATO sent its troops into Kosovo, Porter wrote:

Anyone present at the UN/NGO meeting in Tirana on 14 June where the commander of A-FOR [NATO Forces in Albania], General Reith, was greeted with a rapturous standing ovation by NGOs may have had difficulty in offering credible arguments in support of the impartiality of the humanitarian community in Albania... It is hard to escape the rather disturbing conclusion that impartiality is very much easier in a context of geographical and political difference. When your own nations (and donors) are involved, international agencies seem to have struggled with their own impartiality.

Porter suddenly made us realize that we had suffered a sort of madness and forgotten who we were. We had not behaved as impartial humanitarians but as if we were a part of NATO. For years I had trained staff in the importance of being impartial, and above all to distance themselves from military forces engaged in conflict, however much Oxfam might sympathize with their cause. The danger was that if we were perceived as sympathizers by their enemies, we could be considered as targets ourselves. Moreover, it could make it impossible to reach people who were in opposition to those military forces. There had been a few occasions, as in Mozambique (see Chapter 4), when we had decided to break the rules, but only after carefully weighing up the consequences. The normal mode was strict impartiality until proven otherwise.

Porter himself had been filmed for TV in an interview with Michael Ignatieff while flying in a military helicopter to the refugee camps on the Kosovo border. I had watched it without considering at the time whether it was the right thing to do. But would it not have been legitimate for Serb forces to shoot the helicopter down? If that had happened, what grounds would humanitarian organizations have for protest? How would they justify their presence on a military flight in a combat zone? If such an event occurred Oxfam might also expect to be thrown out of Belgrade and our staff there might be badly harassed because their employers were so clearly taking the side of the people who were bombing the city.

I later reflected that the same might have happened if I (as manager of Oxfam's Belgrade operations) was shown on TV in Serbia, taking tea with the French soldiers and enjoying a joke with the British squaddies while they erected the (clearly labelled) Oxfam water tanks at Korca. We began to realize that we had been viewing everything through NATO-tinted spectacles.

Another of Oxfam's most senior managers, Marcus Thompson, rushed out in an RAF Hercules to join a British government, Department for International Development (DFID), assessment when the first refugees started to emerge from Kosovo. On arrival in Albania he met NATO generals and attended a confidential military briefing. Months later, Thompson reflected:

> We were naive to think that to be involved with DFID in this context would not involve us with the British and NATO military (they were handling all our air freight anyway)... In Macedonia [where Oxfam worked alongside NATO troops], I rationalized this as a coincidence of humanitarian interest between us and NATO in that particular situation... NATO had seized the humanitarian lead. Indeed A-FOR (NATO) in Albania had only a humanitarian brief, though that looked a bit thin when squadrons of strike helicopters arrived. I accepted that we were obliged to engage with them in the humanitarian field.

Thompson had written many of the main policy documents concerning Oxfam's work in conflict and was surprised, like the rest of us, that the discrepancy of policy and practice was not more obvious to him at the time.

My conclusion today is that NATO's power over information affected the way we thought and this made Oxfam behave in a partial manner. We became subjective, and our subjective position was that of NATO's. And it was easy to do so because we had not sat down and worked out our own position in relation to all of the pressures and interests. Therefore we gave no guidance to others. As one of the locally-based British managers told me: 'We were listening to what Bill Clinton and Jamie Shea were saying all the time, not to Oxfam' – because Oxfam had said nothing at all.

What were the consequences? If we had taken a 'principled' position (as, in fact, the French agency Médecins Sans Frontières (MSF) did over the issue of working with the military), Oxfam's representatives would simply have missed free flights and Oxfam would have paid a lot of money for air freight rather than having things sent free with the RAF (Royal Air Force). Our ability to respond to need would have been reduced. We would not have taken tea with the French but simply delivered equipment to them and left them to it without expert advice. They would have managed in the end but there would have been a few delays and mistakes. We would have refused lifts on helicopters. Other aid agencies with fewer scruples and perhaps less ability to help would have taken our place.

The reality is that it was a lot more convenient not to worry about such things, and it was a competitive environment in which plenty of others were even less thoughtful than Oxfam.

What we should have been much more conscious of was that, in the wider scope of things, our ability to work in Belgrade was probably more important than anything else. There was no shortage of aid agencies willing to help the refugees from Kosovo. In fact, they were competing for funding from donor agencies. But there were over half a million people in Serbia who were displaced during earlier wars, especially from the Krajina region of Croatia and from Bosnia. The economy was in a terrible state, largely due to Milosevic's corruption. In terms of poverty and suffering, Serbia should have been the central focus for any aid agency working in the Balkan region. Of course, the million people who fled from Kosovo needed help, but Oxfam's real strength was its history of work in Serbia, where there were very few other aid agencies in operation. The problem was that donors were unwilling to fund work there, and after the NATO bombing the funding ceased completely. Despite its principled stand about working with the military in Albania, MSF was refused permission to work in Belgrade. It appeared that this was because they had not been there during the bombing. A different kind of logic operated. Oxfam was given high regard for its 'loyalty' in staying on when so many other agencies either left or had nothing to do with Serbia.

By contrast, the aid operations for the Kosovo refugees in Albania and Macedonia became obscenely elaborate and overfunded. According to a UN report, 17 government delegations visited Albania every week. The response was like an international sporting event with each country urging its team to greater achievements. In order to achieve greater and greater profile, most of the effort went into showpiece camps where a particular nation could display what it was capable of. As the competition escalated, camps were set up where three hot meals were served every day and there were hot showers, air conditioning and laundries. The 'best' camps were like hotels; the only difference was the barbed wire around the perimeter, designed not to keep people in but to keep out those individuals who had not been chosen for this special treatment.

Nevertheless, 70 per cent of the refugees did not live in camps but with 'host families', where most of them paid for their accommodation and received very little aid. Many preferred to do this because it maintained their personal freedom and self-respect. But it did not fit into the picture which Western aid needed of people utterly dependent upon NATO and grateful for its help. It paid to behave as a beggar, and this became the image which people in the West saw. Sadly, it reinforced their image of Eastern Europeans as 'asylum seekers', and the concept of refugees as scarcely distinguishable from 'scroungers'.

It was also a wasteful and inefficient system. The camps increased the risk of crime and disease. There was no integration with local people and little possibility of jobs because the camps were distant from any town. But because of their heavy funding, camps became the magnet drawing people away from private homes. The funds raised for Kosovo could have helped local families to help refugees, as many of them wished to do. But what would there be to show to the journalist, the general and the minister?

The real question is why did not the journalist, the general and the minister query this? It was perfectly obvious to anyone visiting Albania. Perhaps there was a feeling that any criticism of NATO might amount to undermining its war objective, which by this time was the defeat of Milosevic. Perhaps because journalists, too, relied on NATO for transport and information.

The issue became increasingly demoralizing for aid workers on the ground. The standards in most refugee camps were far higher than anything that aid agencies could normally afford. Those who had been drafted in suddenly from camps in Africa were astonished to find such a contrast. Furthermore, aid workers in Africa felt appalled by what they were reading about Kosovo. Nina Galbe of the ICRC was quoted in the *Times* (21 May 1999) as saying:

Here in Africa we see people who have walked naked without a thread on their back, who don't have a grain of rice. With all due respect to the horrors the people of Kosovo have suffered, they are dressed in their winter clothes; the babies are kept in their blankets. They are not malnourished.

The same article contrasts the prefabricated houses being flown out to Kosovo with the fact that 'typically, Africans sleep out in the open, or under makeshift shelters made from branches, leaves or mud or from plastic sheeting provided by an aid agency'.

Some of these comparisons are not exactly fair. It is not reasonable to expect Kosovo Albanians to suddenly live like Somali or Sudanese pastoralists. The real problem is not what the Kosovars got, but what Africans did not get. No one would have worried about the three-course hot meals except that rations in Africa were so very much lower, and often below the basic requirement for survival. At best they consisted only of a basic cereal and some beans, whereas in Kosovo there were, according to the same article, 'tins of chicken, foil-wrapped cheeses, fresh oranges and milk. In some ready-made meals there is even coffee and fruit tarts.'

Nearly 100,000 Kosovar refugees were flown to destinations in the rich countries of Western Europe. Such a solution had never been considered in Africa. Oxfam field offices around the world began to express alarm at the 'double standards'. One aid worker quoted in the press found the camps in Macedonia 'far superior' to those he had seen in Africa and asked 'What's the difference?', replying to himself: 'There are white people here.'

In *The Guardian* on 13 August 1999 John Vidal wrote:

Kosovo is skewing emergency and humanitarian aid and is now redefining global responsibilities, possibly for many years to come. The accepted principle of extending a minimal hand to the most helpless is being replaced by an undignified new global politics of self-interest and expediency that sails close to moral irresponsibility and racism.

* * *

All of these issues are essentially about impartiality and show (or should show) the difference between independent organizations and government. In a situation of conflict, it is the task of political leaders to make us support their side, and therefore to blot out our concern for those on the other side. Ironically, the essence of conflict is to create or heighten a sense of identity, and with it goes a sense of exclusion towards those deemed to be 'the enemy'. This is achieved by blotting out aspects of the enemy that are admired. The easy way is to blot out all communication and to control information entirely. As a result, wars determine and consolidate national identity more than anything else.

But a characteristic of NATO's bombing of Belgrade (technically not a war, because war was never declared) was that communication persisted. John Simpson doggedly reported for the BBC from Belgrade, despite many British government protests that he was creating sympathy for the enemy. People in Belgrade watched the BBC and CNN. What is particularly interesting is the way in which the Internet enabled people in Belgrade to exchange views among themselves. One individual described what happened when a NATO bomb finally hit the old army building next to the flat of Oxfam's Gordana Rajkov:

At night when the shizela *sounds, the wall of ironic popular spirit that protects us crumbles, and all the wounds made by bombs hurt us.*

They continue bombing empty buildings. When the air strikes began, I bid farewell to the army headquarter's pink building built in the best spirit of social-realism in the first days of the war, but its destruction astounded me nevertheless. Why destroy a building where everything has been taken, from furniture to the light fixtures? The only thing they could not take out were two arty glass panes (8 metres by 20 metres) which were reduced to smithereens, and their author, now already an old man, wept over them as if one of his relatives had died.

NATO has finally learned something about the Serb mentality and immediately applied it against us. They realized that our set of values are different from theirs. That is why they invented 'bombing with delays'. Once they realized that Serbs – the moment something explodes – run to the scene to see whether they can help in any way, they started coming back 15 minutes later to target already hit sites.

Immediately after the left wing of the army headquarters was destroyed, the whole neighbourhood flocked to the street or stayed on their balconies. The ambulance came immediately, the firemen and the police. During this time I was on the phone with my godmother, Olja... And then I heard the whizzing of a missile. This isn't whizzing. It rather resembles the sound made by a car driving at full speed over wet silt. I had enough time to tell Olja to get away from the window and to slowly, without panic, throw myself down to the bathroom when two explosions destroyed the second wing of the army headquarters. The noble people who at the time were taking people out of rubble lost their legs, arms or heads.

Strangely, crises create similarities between opposing sides. Values of care and concern – and the lack of them – are emphasized. NATO justified its actions on humanitarian grounds. Citizens of Belgrade developed their sense of resistance by portraying NATO as lacking in humanity. The implication for professional humanitarians is that their values are likely to be coopted, and so will their organizations.

No doubt, this has always happened in conflicts where agencies such as Oxfam funded local partners. But the Kosovo experience affected Oxfam itself and altered its behaviour. By failing to take a principled stand it became coopted. I do not say this as if it were a fatal flaw in Oxfam. On the contrary, Oxfam grappled more seriously with the issues than many other organizations. But there is a very important lesson. If Western governments are becoming more active in humanitarian issues, voluntary agencies must be much clearer about their principles, and must make time to analyse the interests that will otherwise coopt them.

* * *

During the Cold War, if Milosevic had undertaken ethnic cleansing in Kosovo, Western governments might have left aid agencies simply to get on with it. They would have been too afraid of offending the former Soviet Union to intervene. But today, they do not leave aid agencies alone – certainly not in places where they have any interest other than to placate public feelings of humanitarian concern. Kosovo may be an extreme case, but it shows what is really happening in the emergence of a new world order.

I will end this chapter with some (rather lengthy) reflections on the ways in which opinions and values within aid agencies can be shaped and distorted by society and society's politicians. If we say, as NATO did, that Milosevic is the cause of trouble in the Balkans (and he is democratically elected), we are conceding that politicians can wield immense power, and therefore should examine the way they use it. As I said earlier, they can use their power to polarize opinion during conflict; however, in other situations they can use their power to promote a sense of detachment. What they are really doing is employing language, information and influence to promote the view that they have chosen to adopt.

Throughout the Kosovo crisis I had a strong feeling that my views were not my own but were being shaped for me. For personal reasons I did not make a strong enough stand against that process. I had the same feeling earlier, while managing Oxfam programmes during the Bosnian war. Having had more time to reflect on that, perhaps I can use those examples as a warning that when humanitarian and political issues mingle, appearances can be deceptive. The only answer is to hold tightly to humanitarian values and engage in deep and serious analysis.

In order not to be tedious, I will recount a very complex history in a glib and opinionated manner. At the outset of the Bosnian war in 1992, the US had considered the possibility of intervention but decided to leave the issue to the Europeans. It therefore needed to detach itself from a sense of responsibility. US Secretary of State Warren Christopher said in February 1993:

> *The death of President Tito and the end of communist domination of the former Yugoslavia raised the lid on the cauldron of ancient hatreds. This is the land where at least three religions and a half dozen ethnic groups have vied across the centuries. It was the birthplace of World War I. It has been a cradle of European conflict, and it remains so today.*

There is a great deal of 'spin' in this apparently innocuous statement. It is true that communism had disappeared, but this happened early in the 1980s and Tito died in 1979. What about the 13 years in between? There was no sudden lurch into conflict. The images are interesting: 'cauldron of ancient hatreds', 'birthplace of war', 'cradle of conflict'. Aren't these metaphors for witchcraft? Are there meant to be overtones of *The Crucible* that strike a particular terror into the American psyche? And 'a half dozen ethnic groups': isn't there a feeling of primitivism, lack of civilization, something we want to keep away from?

The subtext is that the Balkans is a place of black magic and primitive peoples not worth spending time or money on, let alone a place in which to risk American lives. The reality of the cosmopolitan Europe-loving Yugoslavia of my experience in the early 1990s is totally different. I doubt if Christopher's words are a reflection of his real opinion but rather a clever use of emotive language to achieve a specific political aim, which was to persuade Americans to support his policy of non-intervention. Later, after the US chose to intervene, Clinton reversed the language, speaking of Kosovo as Europe's backyard.

At the same time, British Foreign Secretary Douglas Hurd and Minister of State Douglas Hogg referred repeatedly to 'ancient hatreds' in the Balkans as if the people there had a specific racial or genetic characteristic. This kind of language feeds on and reinforces a racist stereotype. Having put the stamp of 'ancient hatred' on the region, Hurd and Hogg felt justified in taking no further action. This allowed thugs in the region to stir up hatreds for their own purposes, perpetuating the Hurd–Hogg myth. Perhaps it allowed Hurd and Hogg to sleep peacefully, having absolved themselves of a sense of responsibility.

The Balkan stereotype was a way of deflecting public concern. An alternative, if things had gone the other way, might have been to characterize the Serbs as doughty wartime allies and to recall their loyalty against the Nazis. Instead, the Serbs were characterized as violent bullies and the Bosnian Muslims (in order to forget that they were Muslims they were often simply called 'Bosnians') earned British sympathy as the 'underdogs'.

A second method of manipulating opinion was through the use of specialized information, especially military information. After a shocking visit to Bosnia in January 1993, I urged Oxfam to call for Western military intervention. But in discussions with the UK Foreign Office, and personally with Douglas Hurd, Oxfam was warned that impossibly large military forces would be required to defeat 'the Serbs'(250,000 was the figure quoted). We were told that during World War II, 'seven [German] army divisions' had been unable to contain them. Their war record was now turned against them as evidence of their extraordinary ferocity. But it was impossible to argue with the military's own analysis. Any aid agency suggesting action would be asked how it could make a better assessment of military strategy than the chief of staff. If the agency argued that the situation was too serious to ignore, it was asked how it would justify the body bags (predicted to be thousands) to the grieving families. But, just two years later in 1995, and after 200,000 unnecessary deaths, NATO suddenly stopped the war with negligible losses. The mistaken military assessments of 1993 were never explained. It is a sad reflection that if these had been assessments made by, say, Rwandan or Ethiopian governments, Oxfam would not have worried nearly so much about challenging them. The fact is that flatly opposing the UK's own government is a very different thing from opposing the government of another country.

Some Balkan leaders went a good deal further in managing information to suit their purposes. When I visited Croatia during the war in

1992, I got into an argument with a Catholic nun about the need to distribute relief goods impartially, not according to ethnic or religious preferences. She suddenly thrust the papers aside, told me I just did not understand and began her own story. At the beginning of the war her family (all Croats) was living in a village where there was a majority of Serbs. One night Serb paramilitaries secretly killed a Serb man. They left in the night leaving no trace. When the murdered Serb was found everyone assumed that the Croats had done it. So the Serbs killed the Croats, including the nun's own mother. Later I heard very similar stories told by other ethnic groups.

I gradually came to question practically all information about the Balkans. The predominant Western view of recent Balkan history is characterized by the BBC documentary *The Death of Yugoslavia* which has also been turned into a book. This relies on a series of interviews with politicians who, despite admitting to all sorts of lies in the past, are generally assumed to have spoken the truth to the BBC. Quite why this should be assumed I do not know. Their view of history becomes a political perspective about Milosevic (their chief enemy) trying to keep hold of and extend his power (which is exactly how they wanted history to be seen). Slovenia, Croatia, Bosnia, Kosovo and Montenegro are all straining to get away from oppression and to promote democratic cosmopolitan societies. The BBC version thus tends to support the NATO view of Milosevic as the enemy. Undoubtedly, that is a very important element of recent Balkan history but it conveniently absolves the West of any responsibility.

A different view, which I will label 'Yugoslav' because I heard it so often in the region, is that the West missed the chance to support the multicultural state of Yugoslavia. They 'Balkanized' the Balkans. Milosevic was powerful in Yugoslavia, but did that mean that the concept of Yugoslavia was wrong? Was it not the only concept that would have prevented war? When the Berlin Wall came down in 1989, Yugoslavia was suffering serious economic problems. The 'command economy' of communism was under severe strain as Yugoslav consumers became more and more eager for Western goods rather then the dull junk produced under the 'central plan'. But Yugoslavia was still a sovereign state protected by the UN charter. Yugoslavs assumed that, despite Milosevic, there was no serious threat to their nationhood, and relied on the West to uphold the UN charter.

Milosevic ruthlessly played the card of ethnicity. By abolishing the autonomous status of Kosovo he secured support from nationalist

Serbs, but created fear in Slovenia, Croatia, Bosnia and elsewhere. This enabled regional politicians to make a grab for power. Western politicians could have intervened by applying strong diplomatic and economic pressure to prevent a fragile situation from sliding into disaster. Instead, when Slovenia declared independence it was given international sympathy (especially from Italy) and encouraged to make a bid to secede. When Tudjman in Croatia did the same, he received immediate support and offers of practical support and recognition from Germany. Obviously this action struck at the safety of the 250,000 Serbs living in Croatia, but they were ignored. Tudjman seized the chance to carve out a personal fiefdom, war ensued and eventually the Serbs were ethnically cleansed.

Britain and other Europeans powers joined Germany in offering recognition. Croatians and others could see a realistic chance of secession because they had outside support. The spread of war throughout the region became inevitable. But without those early offers of recognition, the war might not have started. This was a failure of international diplomacy rather than a case of 'ancient hatreds'.

The result was to change the identity of all those individuals who had been born since 1946 when Yugoslavia became a state, and all those who had adopted that broader identity. Slavenka Drakulic has written very movingly about this change of identity after the Croatian war, from being brought up as a Yugoslav and now finding herself to be a Croat:

Some of my foreign friends... cannot understand that they and I have less in common now. I am living in a country that has had six bloody months of war, and it is hard for them to understand that being Croat has become my destiny. How can I explain to them that in this war I am defined by my nationality, and by it alone... The trouble with this nationhood, however, is that whereas before I was defined by my education, my job, my ideas, my character – and, yes, my nationality too – now I am stripped of all that. I am nobody because I am not a person any more. I am one of 4.5 million Croats.

Why did the European states do so little to protect Yugoslavia? Making a direct analogy with the breakup of the former Soviet Union, they set up the Badinter Commission to analyse Yugoslavia's status at the end of the Cold War. This group of constitutional lawyers decided, on purely constitutional grounds and without regard to the consequences, that the regional entities of Yugoslavia had enjoyed a significant level of independence and therefore Yugoslavia could be classed as a federation rather than a state. This simple piece of legalistic analysis overturned the multicultural Yugoslav 'project' of 50 years' duration.

The destruction of Yugoslavia became a game of influence. Germany led the process of disintegration by recognizing Croatia and then pressurizing other European states to follow. This was the time of reunification with East Germany, and there was a sentimental desire to re-establish old links with Croatia. John Major's UK government went along with Germany in exchange for permission to opt out of the social chapter at Maastricht. The threat of conflict in the Balkans was such a low priority that it could be traded away for an easy time with Conservative backbenchers.

From the 'Yugoslav' perspective, the German action smacked of wartime enmity. In Belgrade, the dismemberment of Yugoslavia is often portrayed on TV as a neo-Nazi plot, and Madeleine Albright has been shown swathed in swastikas. Britain's failure to oppose Germany has been portrayed as the betrayal of an old ally. Thus 'ancient hatreds' are perpetuated. Milosevic has created a climate in which many Serbs have lost confidence in the West.

The danger of all these political manoeuvrings is that they create endless tension, conflict and human suffering. The series of wars in the Balkans stems from the West's inability to deal with the problem of Yugoslavia in 1991. Once this first failure had taken place, all other steps involved compromise and failure. It was not the Balkan propensity for hatred but the failure of Western diplomacy that made war in Bosnia inevitable and led to the final debacle in Kosovo, and the creation of Milosevic as evil personified.

* * *

Political partiality deliberately distorts the situations in which humanitarian actors operate. The distortion of Balkan history may not have direct consequences, but the same process is applied to humanitarian issues. For example, at a later stage in the Bosnian war, those who wanted the West to intervene politicized and distorted the issue of rape. Writing in the Belgrade human rights journal *Temida* (which was supported by Oxfam), Dubravka Zarkov questions the view of certain Western writers (whom she names and quotes) who claimed that: 'The effects of rape are exceptionally severe in Muslim communities where the religion emphasizes virginity and chastity before marriage.'

She points out that this stereotype of Muslim women is completely false in Bosnia, where the label 'Muslim' is little different
from the label 'Christian' for most young people in England. She
comments:

*After reading these texts I could not help but ask how much that imagery of
ethnic chastity corresponds with the situation of Bosnia today with educated, urbanized and modern Muslim women who are by no means different
from educated, urbanized and modern Croat, Serb, Yugoslav or any other
women living in Bosnia for whom pre-marital sex is a fact of life? Or how
different are Muslim women who cherish the importance of virginity, and
for whom life without marriage and children is not worth living, from
Croat and Serb women who think the same... Finally, why is the Bosnian
Muslim community singled out as the one that will stigmatize, ostracize
and further victimize rape victims?*

The rape of Bosnian women, picked up by US women's organizations and exploited by newspapers as a source of sensational stories,
became a major factor in the argument whether the West should intervene in Bosnia. Perhaps it is not surprising that women in the US
might imagine that they were dealing with a Muslim fundamentalist
society in which rape might have extraordinary social consequences.
Journalists living in Sarajevo would have been aware that this was a
distortion of the truth but did very little to dispel the myth that, in
some sense, rape was a particularly dreadful experience for Muslims.
The evening stroll or 'fashion parade' along the city's main street had
been famous for years and continued even during the war. A 'Muslim'
youth group, in particular, that Oxfam supported in Tuzla asked for
support to organize a fashion show. These were active young women,
for whom rape was a terrible event, but not particularly because they
were Muslims.

From a humanitarian perspective, what harm does this do? Western intervention was necessary, and maybe a few lies don't matter.
But they do. For one thing, they compounded the misconception of
rape in war as a crime of one individual against another instead of its
reality as a method of pursuing war aims. As Zarkov and many others
have demonstrated, rape in wartime is less to do with sexual gratification
than to do with the struggle for dominance between different groups of
males. Zarkov comments:

Rape (in war) is not only an assertion of masculine power over feminine vulnerability. It is also a competition between two specific masculinities: that of the rapist and that of the raped woman's menfolk. As such, rape is a message passed between men – vivid proof of victory for one and loss and defeat for the other.

Instead of being a phenomenon exclusive to Muslim women, rape was used as a method of war by all factions, for similar purposes and with similar results. Failure to realize this resulted in mistaken aid projects aimed at the counselling of individual rape victims. There was no recognition that rape may have been intended as a means of attacking other people, especially the husband, through women's humiliation.

Rape of Muslim women was no different from rape of Serb and Croat women. But such rapes were not reported and became invisible to the West, so much so that statistics for rape in other territories were not collected. The UN commission examining the issue of rape did not interview victims in Serbia, and out of 223 refugees interviewed in Croatia and Slovenia, 100 were Muslims and only one was a Serb. The figures then became the basis for statistics about atrocities across the region, such as those used by the UN's special commission of experts, which concluded that: '90 per cent of the crimes committed in Bosnia–Hercegovina were the responsibility of Serb extremists, 6 per cent by Croat extremists and 4 per cent by Muslim extremists'.

The issue of rape was basically turned into 'evidence' with which to demonize the Serbs. Humanitarian organizations found themselves caught up in the process. Urs Boegli of the ICRC says he was often asked to give a figure for the number of women raped in Bosnia:

I had a meeting with a French politician with the 80,000 figure wanting to know what ICRC [International Committee of the Red Cross] really knew. At that stage it was below 100 cases. Of course there were many cases we didn't know, but she left my office somehow with a figure of 40,000 which became the accepted figure.

Western sanctions against Serbia have tended to prevent Serb perspectives from reaching the outside world. As a simple example, until 1995 the Belgrade journal *Temida* could not be sold abroad because foreign remittances were prohibited under the sanctions regime. It also meant that the *Temida* group of analysts was weakened because it could not buy Western material. The same applied even to the much less politicized issue of disability. Oxfam kept disability organizations in touch with technical developments around the world by (illegally, perhaps) paying their subscriptions to international journals.

* * *

A year before she was bombed out of her flat, Gordana Rajkov and I met at a place called Fojnica, an hour's drive from Sarajevo in the heartland of Bosnia. It was the first time she had been back to Bosnia since the war ended. People had come from all over the region for a conference on disability, to be held in a famous spa town deep among the pine trees of a quiet wooded valley. War-wounded men promenaded on crutches and in wheelchairs by the river as they relaxed between their schedule of treatments. This huge complex of buildings had been the only place we could find where there was access for wheelchairs and good accommodation at a reasonably cheap price. Delegates to the conference, nearly all of whom were disabled, had come from Croatia, Serbia, Bosnia and Kosovo. We were hoping to revive the links and alliances between them that had existed before the war. We sat and discussed during the day and then went our separate ways in the evening.

One night a group, including Gordana, sat up late and began singing sentimental songs from the past. Some were local Bosnian songs. Others were from Croatia and Serbia. They had a few drinks and began to sing more loudly. Suddenly, a former Bosnian soldier in a wheelchair entered and pointed a gun at them. He told them to get out. He could not bear to hear Serb songs; the Serbs had killed all his friends and made him a cripple for life. In the morning the police came and took him away.

Unaware of all this I came down from my room and found Gordana sitting slumped in her wheelchair, very upset. She lifted her head and said: 'I believed it could be like it was in the past. I believed we could live together again, Croats, Muslims, Serbs. But it is not to be. I was stupid to think like that.'

It seems especially sad to me that Gordana, the person with the most goodwill and the most hope for a multi-ethnic society, should have been bombed by NATO. Perhaps the main lesson from all of this is not to take things at face value or to assume that others see things in the same way. In the new politicized environment, we have to relentlessly question what we are doing and how others will react to it. More specifically, Oxfam should have relearned the value of impartiality. In failing to distance itself from NATO, we in Oxfam made it possible and justifiable for Milosevic to accuse us of taking sides, throw us out of Serbia and prevent us from helping the people most in need, where we had most capacity to do so. Luckily he did not, and Oxfam was able to go on and launch extremely valuable programmes to help people in Serbia after the Kosovo crisis was over. The only problem was that Western donors showed little inclination to provide funds, and seemed to consider that punishing Milosevic was a suitable strategy to bring about long-term stability.

Second, we should not have made a calculation that the threat of force would be enough and that actual force would never be needed. It was outside our competence to make that prediction. Our role should have been to analyse what was happening, to ask what interests lay behind any expression of 'concern' or humanity, and to carefully define our relationship with those who claimed our values but also held other interests as well.

Gordana was confronted by a man who was angered by our mistakes but luckily he did not actually shoot. If NATO's bombing had actually killed a member of Oxfam's staff, or if they had been attacked because pictures of John Porter or myself associating with NATO had been shown on Belgrade television... We were lucky, but it is not enough to escape disaster by luck.

Chapter 2

Ethiopia: A Golden Age of Humanitarianism?

W as there a golden age of humanitarianism? Many would say it was during the Cold War when politicians kept out, and charities were free to do what they wished. Aid workers with longer memories talk fondly about the Ethiopia emergency of 1984, when celebrities were called from their rock groups to attend to the so-called 'biblical famine'of Michael Buerk's famous description: 'Dawn, and as the sun breaks through the piercing chill of night on the plain outside Korem it lights up a biblical famine, now, in the 20th century. This place, say workers here, is the closest thing to hell on earth.'

As the world responded, humanitarianism quickly became a popular cause and the status of aid workers rose high. People in towns and villages all over the UK organized fundraising events. The whole world joined in simultaneous pop concerts to express their compassion. Money poured into aid agencies as never before. People demanded that their governments should help, and ministers nodded apologetically. For a brief time the aid agencies seemed to rule the world. Having lived and worked through that period, I feel a deep satisfaction; but is it really justified? Reflection now makes me wonder whether we were all, aid workers and public alike, hiding from the truth.

* * *

More recently, aid agencies have come under a good deal of criticism for failing to take account of politics in Ethiopia and the fact that the country was at war. I basically agree. But it was not the most obvious and devastating failure. The real question is: why was the response six months too late? Why was it a journalist arriving almost by chance who broke the news of famine to the world when hundreds of thousands had already died? There were dozens of aid agencies based in the country; left on their own, without the stimulus of Buerk's documentary and Geldof's energy, it seemed that they might have ignored the famine. What would have happened if there had been no Buerk and no Geldof?

When the avalanche of public donations began, the question was swept away. No one wanted to jeopardize aid programmes that saved lives by asking awkward questions and undermining public confidence. The feeling was that we must not frighten the donors. The intentions were undoubtedly good (although some observers have detected a conspiracy of crude self-interest), but the effect was that the root causes of the famine and the lack of international response were never tackled. As a result, famine occurred again and again. As I write, 16 years later, I have recently returned from Ethiopia where I found that people are starving again in the same places and for the same reasons, and there is no help coming.

I do not want to be unfair to front-line aid workers. They have to cope with enough without armchair critics. A few months after Buerk's documentary, I stood and pondered on the plains of Korem where he had stood – where now there were feeding programmes for children. I watched the same blue light, the same flitting white forms. I watched the smaller children being weighed and measured, felt the withered wrists, the failing pulses and witnessed the little body bags slung into a pit. I turned away and tried to say something cheerful.

After so many deaths in a day, and so much suffering, we retire to a tent and have a cup of tea, talking of what the different agencies are doing, of taps and 'T45' water tanks, hose pipes, plastic sheeting. Technical talk is especially comforting because it gives a feeling of solidity when all else is sliding into death. The weighing instruments and slings for little babies, red plastic beakers and blue plastic for the floor… these are the ritual elements of our religion, the icons in our temple. We do not have much energy for anything else. We reduce the political problems to getting on with the local administration. As the memory of the children fades, we talk of turf battles among agencies and romances, real or likely, between Oxfam engineers and Save the Children nurses. We end up grousing about the problems of supply from HQ – angry that blankets and beakers did not arrive. We dispose of any lingering emotion with the help of a few drinks.

The natural tendency of aid workers faced with unspeakable suffering is to find ways of shielding themselves from the anger and frustration it evokes – the pointless, senseless events over which they have no control. Aid workers try not to probe too deeply into causes and consequences, and are impatient with those who do. The midst of a funeral is not the time to have an inquisition on the cause of death. It is better to celebrate the heroic efforts of the mothers who guard their little children, and the fathers carrying them for miles when they are weak with hunger themselves. Faced with famine, we feel it is a waste of time to complain about the abstract politics that caused it. Instead, we want the world to feel what we feel, a sense of bereavement, the loss of people and happiness, the recognition that we have been diminished by what we have seen.

Very often I have felt that mood myself and been impatient with people who sit at desks and write learned analyses that seem to have no purpose except to say that what we are doing is wrong. It needs to be said that compassion is not a means to an end but an end in itself, and some of the greatest work of aid agencies is not what they intend, but what their staff do out of their own humanity. But when the suffering is unnecessary, and caused by the actions of other people, the principle of humanity should extend towards understanding. If the cause is an act of man, it is better not to call it an act of God. By making that mistake, we limit our ability to prevent the same thing from happening again, and could be blamed by those for whom we feel concern. Aid workers in the front line may not have the emotional energy for the task, but they should make sure that others do, and that they do it seriously. They can then build a chain of concern upwards from the person in need.

So why was the response so late? At the end of 1984 I returned from India and was shocked to find that the famine had been ignored for so long. I offered to analyse the causes for Oxfam and plunged myself into a month of examining papers and records. Over the course of time, I have sifted through those findings in my mind, and now feel that the main issue was the ideology of the aid agencies at that time. Essentially, they were trying to transform the world through development rather than keeping bodies alive by famine relief. They turned opportunistic beliefs into reality, and lived in a 'dream world' from which the famine was a rude awakening.

By the early 1980s, student radicalism had merged with socialism to produce a particular ideology among aid agencies which has been called 'developmentalism'. This focuses on fields, schools and hospitals, but also assumes that the process can lead to the transformation of the state. The idea was revolution through development. This extraordinarily optimistic ideology characterized the golden age and became so strong that aid agencies did not turn away from their developmentalist beliefs, even when poor people were suffering from the effects of famine. It was the 'teach a man to fish' as opposed to 'give a man a fish' school of thought, and it had an inbuilt tendency to ignore situations where relief work – the distribution of fish and food – was actually necessary. There was a firm belief that groups of people involved in development projects would transform economic relationships and ultimately the state itself. In its extreme form, the theory was that small development projects were going to thaw the inhuman hostility of the Cold War. The powerlessness of the Ethiopian people under its oppressive government was ignored. People thought that new forms of ox-cultivation would change everything if only the media and the pop stars would stay away and let them get on with it.

Perhaps people in some parts of Ethiopia were actually being taught to fish while they starved. To belong to the 'teach a man to fish' school carried much greater status than to belong to the 'give a man a fish school'. As the famine developed during 1983 and the early months of 1984, aid agencies continued with their projects of rural development as if nothing unusual was happening. I cannot prove that this is the case for all aid agencies, and many will deny that it bears any relationship to their own experience. But very few agencies have been able to explain why it took a journalist and a pop star to propel them into action. Rather unfairly, I will have to single out Oxfam for scrutiny and as the source of my examples.

Early in 1984, as the famine began to develop, Oxfam's trustees decided (rather astonishingly for an organization that had not so long ago been the Oxford Committee for Famine Relief) that in Ethiopia 'relief projects should be avoided and development projects sought'. This developmentalist approach has been characterized in a slightly different but complementary way by Oxfam's former director in Sudan, Mark Duffield. In Duffield's analysis, aid became confused with leftist views of multiculturalism. People in poorer countries must not be discriminated against and must be understood. This means that focus on weaknesses, such as exploitative governmental conflicts, amounted to racism. It was a slur on black people.

In this well-intentioned project, Duffield explains, aid agencies moved away from the relief of poverty and suffering, ignored analyses of political tensions and focused on cultural understanding and local economic development. From my own memories, I can find resonance with Duffield's thinking. In the 1970s and 1980s, it was politically incorrect to make any negative remark about an African country or a poor person. British aid agencies in the 1980s agreed a code of communication based on 'positive images'. This was drawn up in order to counter 'negative' images of starving children, which were perceived as racist stereotypes. But it meant that when black children actually did starve, there was a reluctance to change the image or the action, or to look at the political causes.

For a long time Oxfam had used a picture of a smiling farmer proudly holding up a cob of hybrid maize that he had learned to grow, thanks to a development project. The picture continued to appear even after war had engulfed the region where the photograph was taken. The watchword was: 'Don't mention the war'. The intention was to show trust in poor people, but it implied less trust in the Western public. Instead of presenting information in a neutral way, there was often an attempt to compensate for an opposite racist view. This produced an inverted form of racism. Positive images meant positive discrimination.

At that time conflict was widely seen as inherently evil. The threat of nuclear war hung over the world, and development was seen as an expression of people's pacifism as opposed to governments' willingness to wage war. Poorer states, especially in Africa, were coopted into these Western concerns and portrayed as essentially peace loving. Conflict was seen as coming from outside – an external aberration of the rural idyll, caused by psychotic villains and greedy arms dealers. The possibility that farmers in Ethiopia might go to war because they were oppressed was not so popular. Fundamentally, the developmentalist mode existed in opposition to the revolutionary mode of the 1960s. As I had found in my work in India, development sometimes undermined more revolutionary movements.

In 1979 a new statement of Oxfam's fundamental beliefs ('Oxfam – an interpretation') for the first (and last) time included a commitment to 'non-violent means'. It was drafted by one of the last highly influential Quakers in Oxfam. The theory was that conflict was generally a senseless activity, and should be stopped and replaced by development. Where this left farmers who were taxed into starvation by regimes backed by the East or West was not addressed – not in Africa, at least. And so, as famine developed in Ethiopia after the disastrous rain failure of 1983, Oxfam was committed to developmentalism and strongly influenced by pacifism.

Developmentalism had also grown out of the technological approaches that characterized the last phase of colonialism. It had been the age of the expert, who was nearly always white. 'Experts' were not used to looking critically at political issues because, just a few years earlier, they had been employees of the colonial power. Like most aid agencies Oxfam had its share of ex-colonials, as well as student radicals like myself. Their non-political approach prevailed because, with the superpowers now locked into icy conflict, opportunities for political change appeared to be very limited. Western governments were unwilling to antagonize the Eastern bloc and therefore political influence was directed at maintaining client relationships and undermining the influence of the other superpower. This gave African leaders the chance to use that power for their own purposes, regardless of the opinion of their own people. Developmentalism could improve the yield of land by new ploughing techniques, but it could not stop the ruler from taking away the profit in tax, or leaving the farmer with a crushing debt for items which she (most farming in Africa is done by women) did not really want but was persuaded to accept by extension workers. Very likely the loan was accepted by the man of the house anyway, and he did not know enough to decide whether it was useful. Since Western strategy was dictated by the Cold War, there was little to be achieved by advocating political action. The room for manoeuvre was very small, and so aid agencies focused on apolitical local development.

* * *

My report on the reasons why aid agencies were so slow to respond to the Ethiopian famine of 1984 concludes:

Firstly, following the famine of 1973 a system of 'nutrition monitoring' had been put in place by the aid agencies, with regular weighing and measuring of children, according to the best expert advice at that time. But the system had become so slow and cumbersome that nutrition figures were taking three months to be processed, and therefore reflected a food situation which was already long gone. Unfortunately, due to the absence of key staff in mid-1984, the processing of accurate information was worse than usual. Added to this, the nutrition monitoring system did not cover the areas of conflict, where famine conditions were most acute. Instead of alerting aid agencies and providing early warning, the system provided a false sense of security.

Secondly, all travel in Ethiopia was tightly controlled and journalists were repeatedly refused permission to travel into the crucial famine areas. The government excluded most aid agency representatives and made the process of obtaining permission extremely tedious and uncertain. Those that managed to obtain permission had to keep to the main road and government-held towns. Permits were more readily given to those with good standing, and that meant people who were unlikely to raise difficult questions. Those who were sympathetic to the regime were given a better chance to get on with their jobs. Individuals perceived as a threat found that life was made difficult for them. Consequently, the people who had worked there for long periods were generally those who overlooked the government's faults or acted as apologists. They often provided the briefing for new arrivals. In the early 1980s, Oxfam itself became alarmed that its own representative was acting as an apologist for the government. External suspicion of the Russian-backed regime meant that even when ambassadors drew attention to the famine and the need for aid, their views were discounted. Local representatives developed a culture of support for the regime, which they may have seen as a corrective to external hostility, which they perceived as ideologically driven. This meant that they were not necessarily trusted by their own organizations and the overall process hid both the famine and the oppression.

Thirdly, the attempt to reach an objective analysis of the food supply was confused by the UN. Although the government's analysis of the food supply consistently indicated a serious shortfall from 1983 into the crucial early months of 1984, the UN's World Food Programme (WFP) issued figures of food arrivals that gave an overoptimistic picture. It muddled commercial imports, food for specific projects and food for emergency relief. Donors became confused and therefore refused to respond. In the summer of 1984 when food was most desperately needed, WFP advised the donors that the ports would be unable to cope with more imports. The clogging of the ports was largely due to commercial food imports to feed the cities and also to the huge influx of military hardware for the war. When, after the Michael Buerk documentary, food aid was sent in massive quantities, ports did not prove to be a problem at all. They handled three times the capacity that WFP had predicted.

Fourthly, the aid community in Addis Ababa, represented by its coordinating body the Christian Relief and Development Association, virtually ignored the famine until October 1984, shortly before the Michael Buerk documentary, when a statement of concern was issued. Instead, the minutes of those meetings through the summer of 1984 while people starved reveal *the aid agencies to be preoccupied with relatively trivial development issues and the collection of agency 'round-ups' on internal events as if nothing catastrophic was happening. The government's relief commission had stopped sending representatives to the meetings because there was so little discussion about the famine.*

None of these reasons would have been enough on their own to leave the famine hidden for so long. But taken together, and with careful manipulation by government – which was deeply ambivalent about the possibility of food reaching the conflict areas – news of the famine was effectively suppressed. Conditions were certainly disastrous from May 1984 onwards, and many thousands of people died before October when the world was suddenly and fortuitously made aware of the scale of the famine.

*   *   *

The war did not fit within the developmentalist analysis. If people could escape from poverty by learning to fish, or learning a new system of ox-cultivation, why on earth should they go to war? What aid agencies persistently underestimated or even ignored was the effect of heavy taxation, compulsory food procurement to feed the cities and the conscription of young men into the military forces. All of this operated through a rigid system of party cadres who had no choice but to follow orders to the letter. In effect, wealth and assets were sucked away from the rural areas of the north as fast as they were created. The soil conservation and forestry projects supported by aid agencies were only of very limited value to farmers because they had no ownership of the land and feared that if their land was improved it would be taken away. Better harvests through improved agriculture might simply lead to heavier government taxation or draw attention to young men who could be conscripted. Behind the scenes there was deliberate oppression of certain ethnic groups that were seen as a particular threat to the regime. The government responded to rebellion in the north by using starvation as a method of war.

During the early 1980s, rebel groups made the northern areas of Eritrea and Tigray almost inaccessible to government and set up their own administrations. The famine was a chance for the government to hit back and undermine their base of support. The military offensives of 1984 had deliberately targeted food-producing areas, while aerial bombing of markets and roads made it impossible for people to move food from one area to another. In Ethiopia's mountainous terrain, there were always great variations in rainfall, even between one village and the next. By trading, inequalities in food availability could be balanced out. Because the underlying problems of taxation, conscription and food procurement were successfully kept secret, the aid agencies in Addis Ababa came to caricature the war as a mindless attack on the development process that government and aid agencies were cooperating in for the good of the people.

* * *

It is worth pointing out how fortuitous it was that the famine was 'discovered' at all. During the early months of 1984, as the famine raged unnoticed in the north, Oxfam pestered Michael Buerk to go to Ethiopia. This was a lucky chance facilitated by a single individual, Oxfam's communications officer, Paddy Coulter. Coulter had worked in Ethiopia during the previous major famine, in 1973, and now instinctively felt that something was wrong. Relying on what he heard from various contacts, and based on his knowledge of the dangerous secretiveness of Ethiopia, from the spring of 1984 onwards he urged Buerk to visit. Because of the travel restrictions he suggested that Buerk should visit Wolayita in the south where there was also a serious famine, but where the atmosphere was not so politically charged. Buerk obtained permission relatively easily, but his documentary about the green vegetation in Wolaita had less impact than the stark empty plain of Korem. It coincided with a joint agency appeal for 'famine in Africa' which had been launched in mid-1984 because so many countries in Africa were suffering simultaneously from food shortages. The appeal was surprisingly successful, and in order to develop relief projects on which the funds could be spent, two Oxfam emergency staff (unable to get permission to go north) visited Wolaita again in August 1984. Like Coulter, they picked up warnings that the situation in the north was now extremely serious. They were so struck by the lethargy of the international response that they called for Oxfam to send a shipful of grain as a gesture to shame the international donors into action. It was an unusual step for a private organization, and only possible because the 'famine in Africa' appeal had given Oxfam the ability to consider it.

Coulter continued to press Buerk to find a way of going north, and by chance Buerk found that the cameraman, Mohammed Amin, had also been trying to visit northern Ethiopia. By another lucky chance, official attention was diverted to the celebrations of the tenth anniversary of the revolution, and permission for the visit was finally granted. Amin and Buerk teamed up to make the most famous and influential humanitarian recording in history. Simultaneously, by another extraordinary chance, the shipful of grain which Oxfam had mobilized after the visit to Wolaita was sailing down the Red Sea to the port of Assab, and arrived there just in time to capture the attention of another documentary film crew from British Independent Television (ITV). In yet another coincidence, the transmission of the ITV documentary was delayed by an industrial dispute until Buerk's programme had already been shown. As a result, the sequence became Buerk telling of the famine and then, by an apparent miracle, Oxfam food arriving a couple of days later. This provided firm grounds for the public response which quickly overwhelmed the world in a way never seen before or since. In fact Oxfam had been deeply divided about whether to respond at all.

That politics were kept out was certainly a factor in this response. This made it possible for the response to take on overtones of the world's people defying the superpowers that had dithered and sent weapons when people needed food. The 'biblical famine' of Buerk's TV presentation was described in some of the most moving language ever used by a reporter, and Buerk's footage of a dying child was seen by an estimated 470 million people around the world, raising perhaps a billion US dollars for famine relief. But it was not really a 'biblical' famine in the sense of being a simple lack of food. Buerk scarcely mentioned the war. The plains of Korem were quiet and peaceful. Buerk did not record the scream of Ethiopian jet fighters that often broke the silence as they flew northwards to bomb the rebels. He did not swing the camera sideways to show the multiple rocket launchers that also occupied the plains of Korem. Even today, most journalists and aid managers continue to take the view that it was in the greater interests of humanity to keep the issues simple and elicit the largest possible response. But was it really so?

The best argument in favour of this sequence of events, in my opinion, is that nothing otherwise would have been achieved. Cold War politics still prevented any real pressure from being put on Ethiopia to end its oppressive practices and to seek a settlement to the war. The government could turn to Russia for support, and Russia would give arms to Mengistu purely in order to prevent him from going over to the Americans. It seemed unlikely that a serious challenge by the West would do more than reinforce Russia's grip, and the Western interest was to weaken it. As a result, the West was ready to offer food aid to win public support, but not to impose sanctions to enforce a change of policy. The subject was left to a new and unusual emissary of the West: Saint Bob.

* * *

Early in 1985 I went to London with a colleague to meet Bob Geldof and find out what he was going to do with the money he had raised through Bandaid. The aid agencies were naturally interested in a man who knew nothing about relief work and had millions to spend. Like a lottery winner, he had a stream of aid agency callers. To him we were vultures and he told us, in his characteristic manner, where to get off.

Geldof was wary of us as if we were pickpockets and he was the fat man with the wallet. It was a game he knew he had to play. He kept evading making a decision, fundamentally uncertain because he had to get rid of the money but did not trust bureaucracy. He wanted to play against the system and make a protest, but found himself being engulfed and becoming part of the system himself, as others of us had done. When it became obvious that there was no option but to work with and through established organizations, he left it to others to do the talking. Like many of us, he seemed to find the gap between humanitarian ideals and humanitarian practice rather distressing, and he was lucky – we sometimes felt – not to have to make a living out of it.

He filled a London warehouse, intended for buses, full of clothes and then asked us to get rid of them. What happened to the London buses that were parked in the rain, or us, deluged with unwanted clothes, did not concern him. When I went to his house, I saw him as a mirror of how I must appear to others (to Africans in camps, for example): an arbitrary 'arrival' with unlimited power and an uncertain temper, to be assuaged with promises of honesty and endless reports. With Geldof it was an obsession with cost. Nothing was to be wasted. Every penny was to reach the poor even if others had to pay to make that happen. His offices were equipped with donated furniture, and a benefactor paid the phone bill. The trick with Geldof was to appear invisible, not to remind him about money and get out of his house quickly.

Overall, Bandaid was a breath of fresh air, challenging old ways and reminding slothful developmentalists to get off their backsides. Nothing was assumed. Bandaid expected people to do something for nothing, whereas aid agencies paid and operated by rules and procedures. Bandaid's appeal went straight to the heart: the small person against the big bad world. BandAid pulled the lever on business, and business knew that BandAid was a very good brand with which to be associated. BandAid negotiated a low-cost contract for ships to ferry supplies to Ethiopia cheaply, but the ships were filled with a lot of junk, and it cost others money to distribute it. BandAid's throb of human goodness did not come cheap.

Geldof thrust morality into the faces of politicians. He travelled across Africa, demanding engagement, honesty and common sense. Perhaps his greatest legacy is that he opened the way for others, especially the quietly persistent Comic Relief, secretively nurtured by Richard Curtis and made into a reality by Jane Tewson. Like BandAid, this was essentially a very personal kind of humanity, where the real heart is better left hidden.

Geldof attacked the miserliness of Western governments but avoided issues to do with the war in Ethiopia. He saw only suffering bodies, not people aspiring to freedom.

* * *

As famine conditions began to develop in the war areas of northern Ethiopia, the Tigrayan rebels shocked the aid agencies by claiming that there was food available for purchase. How could there be food available in the midst of famine? And if it was there, how could it be possible that hungry people did not eat it?

These questions troubled the aid agencies, and most managers simply refused to believe that it was anything but a trick. However, if a beggar dies on the steps of the Bank of England no one asks why he did not help himself to the money, or how such money could be left idle while people were starving. We have strangely different standards for judging societies other then our own. The situation in Tigray was that some areas had not been affected badly by rain failure and had escaped the predatory actions of the government. There were (relatively) rich merchants in Tigray with food stacked in their back rooms, which I had witnessed myself.

The groundbreaking study on famine by Amartya Sen, published in 1981, included a study of the previous major famine in 1973. On the basis of unpublished information provided by John Seaman of Save the Children, it showed that food was available for sale during the worst of the famine at prices that were not much higher than usual. Famine was not caused by lack of availability but because people did not have the money, or other 'entitlement', that would enable them to obtain it. This analysis gave a clear theoretical framework for the food purchases in Tigray, and in Oxfam's case helped tilt the balance.

The direct implication of Sen's analysis is that the most logical response to famine is to find a way of increasing the entitlement of the needy, most obviously by giving them cash. Strangely enough, the developmentalist bias has never tolerated such a notion. While groups of people are envisaged as having the capacity to transform the state, the individual is regarded with suspicion. The fear is that 'he' will waste the money on something else. Our perceptions are optimistic about the group and pessimistic about the individual.

The idea of giving cash to poor people is clearly indicated by theoretical analysis, but is very rarely considered acceptable. Even people who give to beggars are anxious that their gift should be used according to the wishes of the donor, not of the recipient. This is a strange form of giving!

In the case of the rebels, there was the fear that cash distributions would somehow end up being used for guns. This fear rests on the assumption that the donor is able to say that a gun is not the best use of money. In other words, it implies a totally pacifist ideology. Still deeper is the idea that poor people are only bodies and need only food. They do not need guns with which to defend their rights.

Because of such public prejudices, Oxfam went to extraordinary lengths to ensure that food was given to poor people rather than cash. Delegates travelled, illegally and at night, into Ethiopia from Sudan carrying huge quantities of money (tied in huge bundles around their waists so that they looked like balloons) to make purchases from farmers and merchants. The stocks were then transferred to the rebel humanitarian organizations and selective spot checks were made on distributions. Sceptics still asked: 'Why do the rebels not commandeer the food and give it to the hungry?' Detailed inquiry revealed that far from being in favour of undermining trade and commerce, the rebel leadership in Tigray (many of whom were city people) recognized that trade was an essential part of rural survival. To commandeer food would undermine the economic system and rural support on which they depended.

The sceptics were still not convinced. 'Then the rebels must be secretly in league with the merchants and receive secret taxes.' Again, close analysis by talking to merchants and farmers, including cross-checking by interviewing those who had fled from the region and had little sympathy for the rebels (which I did myself), confirmed that the rebels did not operate that way because they did not need to. Because people realized that an Ethiopian government victory would have extremely serious consequences, they made a careful assessment of their own food and security needs. Certainly no outsider could do it better. Social pressure may have been considerable, but this was rather different from the forced procurement, taxation and conscription programmes that they had experienced in the past. On my travels in Tigray I found the level of public motivation something palpable. People were deeply interested in political issues. Wherever I stopped people would quiz me on British and American politics. Although it was impossible to be sure of any information (who tells the truth to an outsider during war?) the facts, as I observed them travelling in the region, fitted well together.

Indeed, the lesson for me in all this was to relentlessly seek out facts, and seek them from people whose interests and biases I had already had a chance to analyse. Instead of interviewing fearful peasants inside Ethiopia, I switched to talking to those who had fled. Instead of believing rebel leaders, I walked about and observed people, conducted interviews and cross-checked. Oxfam alone mounted over a dozen major assessments of the rebel areas. Gradually, the evidence wore down the resistance even of such sceptics as Chris Patten, then minister for overseas development in the UK government, who eventually put his weight behind the idea of internal food purchase and the validity of relief work with the rebels. Quietly, the European Union (EU) was also persuaded to send food and to conduct food purchases. But many private agencies remained aloof. They had already made up their mind and remained obstinately impervious to facts. I have little doubt that in such cases their own interests were a key factor.

If the rebels had shown less interest in communism, and portrayed their relationship with the merchants as an example of encouraging free enterprise, the US might have been persuaded to offer support. Then the US might have questioned the UN's unilateral support of the Ethiopian government and demanded that aid should flow on both sides. But unfortunately, at the height of the famine, with US officials watching carefully and interviewing every traveller (including me) who went into the rebel areas, the Tigrayan rebels declared their support for the views of Enver Hoxhe, communist dictator of Albania, and the chance for change collapsed. The Eritreans decided that Russia remained a strategic ally, and fell out with the Tigrayans over this ideological dispute. The two rebel groups actually fought battles during the famine, over that question. Their sympathizers stepped back, aghast. The US gave up on the rebels and the spies pulled out, until by 1991 it became evident that the rebels were going to win. The famine remained apolitical.

Now that the Cold War has ended we find Western governments saying, as Britain does in the case of Sierra Leone, that training soldiers to fight is the best response to the causes of famine. This is a solution that sounds natural for a government, but has always been considered unnatural for an aid agency. Thus, it was not simply the situation that limited political responses but an ideological framework within which aid agencies operated. To provide arms might have been going too far in the defence of personal freedom, but to allow people to buy their own food does not seem excessive. Instead, the aid agencies decided, literally, to 'spoon feed'.

* * *

Many of the staff who came to work during the Ethiopian famine had gained their experience in the 'classic' refugee camps of Somalia and brought their ideas with them. Just as developmentalist ideas had prevented the aid agencies from addressing relief needs as they arose, so now (after they had been propelled into action by Geldof and others) the response was characterized by an inappropriate 'refugee camp' ideology. In Ethiopia about seven million people were affected by the famine and they were scattered all over the country. Most of them remained in their homes. In Somalia, in the early 1980s, about 100,000 nomadic people gathered together from the Ogaden Desert, where fighting and drought had wiped out their animals, lived in camps where they received a general ration of basic foods through the UN system. The role of the voluntary agencies was to provide supplementary feeding to the weakest children. Each child would be weighed and measured at various stages to determine their progress. Different levels of malnutrition were categorized and the whole system became highly technical, managed by a cadre of doctors, nurses and nutritionists.

In the Somali camps, the basic food supply and the supplement could be regulated by the same group of aid agencies in a controlled environment. But in Ethiopia the problem was famine on a national scale with varying problems of access and politics. Most donated food aid was distributed through the government, and the government had interests other than simply feeding those most in need. Following the Somali model, many aid agencies, including Oxfam, set up supplementary feeding centres where the more vulnerable children could be cared for. While in a refugee camp such centres were not far from the *tukuls* where their families lived, in Ethiopia the families often lived many kilometres away. In practice, mothers had to stay with their children at the centre and were therefore unable to work or to look after her other children.

Meanwhile, the general ration failed to arrive, and so the only person in a family to receive any food might be the child in the 'supplementary' feeding centre. Aid managers began to argue for concentrating all efforts on getting the general ration out to where people lived, but ran up against defensive reactions from the specialists in the selective feeding centres. After a visit in mid-1985, I wrote: 'Supplementary food intended for the child is diverted to the rest of the family. Indeed, since children come off the programme if they gain weight, there is an obvious incentive to divert food to other members of the family and keep the child within the category that qualifies for help.' In other words, mothers had an incentive to starve their own children.

Oxfam prided itself on its expertise in the evolving science of selective feeding. It had pioneered many of the established techniques and had produced the standard manual used by all other aid agencies at that time. Its professional advisers were especially reluctant to abandon their expertise and status. Simply moving sacks of food to families was not, at that time, seen as the appropriate role for aid agencies. That was for governments and truckers. A certain professional elitism had crept into the issue.

A more cynical view is suggested in Oxfam's internal evaluation:

It must be noted also that from a public relations point of view a supplementary feeding programme was an attractive proposition. The media tends to take less interest in water projects and plastic sheeting during a famine than in pictures and descriptions of starving people. The recommendation to undertake supplementary feeding, though not made for public relations reasons, did have the effect of putting Oxfam nurses in the front line and thereby satisfied a public relations need.

In my own view as the manager trying to bring about a change in strategy but without the authority to impose such a change, the problem was mainly to do with 'professionalism'. Oxfam worked on a very consensual basis, and every effort was made to reach a common conclusion. The experts had gained considerable organizational influence from their successes in Somalia.

Analysis of food distribution figures showed clearly that the problem of basic rations was chronic. It was not just a case of missed deliveries but of months passing without food reaching those in need. Yet Oxfam's senior medical adviser continued to oppose proposals to focus on basic rations. He argued that it was the government's job, and it should not be let off the hook. After much debate the only compromise was that Oxfam began distributing small amounts of non-cereal foods to families, as well as feeding the most badly affected children. But the numbers of people affected were tiny, perhaps 20,000, compared with the enormity of the famine and the starvation caused by failure to deliver basic food grain.

Very gradually aid agencies began to realize that government was manipulating the food supply for its own purposes. Local officials in Wollo began to state explicitly that food was only to be available to those who agreed to be resettled. Challenged on this issue, senior representatives in Addis Ababa denied any such intention. When asked about the lack of food deliveries for the non-settlers, they said there was a lack of trucks available for transport. However, as an Oxfam nurse bitterly noted in her diary after three weeks in which no supplies had been delivered to the village where she worked: 'Eventually only two empty trucks came to Bora and took away 100 people.'

Under pressure from highly influential medical staff, Oxfam continued with 'supplementary' feeding while, as its internal evaluation recorded, 'hunger was escalating and malnutrition was worsening'. The representative in Wollo noted:

We have expressed our anxieties on this decline to the RRC [the Relief and Rehabilitation Commission of the government]. The problem, we understand, is lack of transport. Virtually all trucks in Wollo are currently on first call for the transhipment of resettlers.

By this time staff responsible for the 'supplementary' feeding were experiencing what the Oxfam evaluation calls 'a high degree of personal anguish and distress', and two nurses based in a remote village in Wollo decided not to renew their contracts. Oxfam became engaged in intense internal debate about whether to end the supplementary feeding programme. The evaluation records that the senior medical adviser was influential in this decision, advising that little would be achieved by closing the programme, and saying: 'I feel we have little choice – even knowing that the feeding programme is quite unacceptable in its present form.'

It took me a while to gather the courage to challenge this position. When I visited northern Ethiopia in July 1985, I examined records kept by the UN and found that in the first four months of the year nearly all relief grain had gone to resettlers, who were a tiny proportion of the total population and unlikely to be the worst affected by famine. It was clear that the government was directly using famine as a tool of the resettlement policy, and this policy was a way of winning the war by depopulating the north and starving those who remained. By this time I was visiting Ethiopia regularly, and in one shocking event I came across a crowd of about 2000 people who had walked over 20 kilometres in search of food but were turned away by local militiamen armed with rifles. There was no food available locally, but plenty available in the country. I wrote: 'In spite of huge stocks in Nazareth [the main government depot], Wollo continues to starve. In the above context, Oxfam's programme in nutrition continues to be a nonsense and the staff here are not disguising the fact. As already reported, they were on the point of issuing a joint resignation.'

But Oxfam's medical adviser continued to argue for continuing the programme. Finally he suggested a compromise which became the course taken. Oxfam would continue with supplementary feeding but also get involved in the distribution of basic rations. It would use its own trucks to take basic rations into the area and would lobby donor governments extensively to ensure that food was earmarked specifically for Wollo.

Accordingly, I met with and wrote to a number of UN and European officials. Matters improved considerably for a while but in October 1985 the government again stepped up the resettlement programme, regardless of international opinion. Clearly they had just been waiting for the fuss to die down.

The lesson from all this, the misuse of both the 'developmentalist' ideology and the 'professional' one, is that human bias affects the purity of our altruism. We do not take humanitarian objectives seriously enough. Neither the public nor journalists seriously questioned the selective feeding centres. On the contrary, they were routinely portrayed as shining examples of best practice in aid. The white nurse feeding the black child became the icon of the famine. But it was the wrong approach and should have been challenged; Oxfam's senior directors should have been more critical of the programme.

Above all, this experience shows that there is a fault in the theory that everyone involved in aid has a duty to be positive. Journalists may have felt that it was best to be silent about the war and about the way in which food was being misused. Probably they argued to themselves that speaking the truth would have diminished the response. But was it really in the best interests of the people in need?

* * *

In 1985, Oxfam and Save the Children Fund (SCF) staff working around Korem witnessed the use of force in the resettlement process and recorded the details. Such events became common and there was much debate among the aid agencies about what they should do. Oxfam's internal policies gave priority to humanitarian relief but instructed staff that they must not ignore violations of human rights; instead, they should record them and take appropriate action. For a long time Oxfam had been under pressure to support the resettlement programme by providing financial assistance. The government's argument, based on a World Bank report, was that the highland areas of the north were overcrowded and there was plenty of room in the south-west.

There were several problems with this argument. First, there were various political reasons why farmers in the north could not make the most of their land, including the fact that they had no right of ownership. The government's argument was that 'as things stood' the area was fundamentally overcrowded; but what if taxation, conscription and land rights were changed? Second, it seemed that the people concerned did not actually want to move. Third, there was a suspicious correlation between the policy of resettlement and the war; the aid agencies could not help but ask themselves if the government was using this policy as a strategy to depopulate the areas where the rebels were operating. Worse still, the government was using the centres run by aid agencies as magnets with which to draw unsuspecting people who were then whisked off to the resettlement camps, hundreds of kilometres from their homes.

One immediate outcome of witnessing the use of force was that Oxfam hardened its position on actually helping the resettlement programme. Some items of Oxfam water equipment had already found their way into resettlement centres, but the policy now hardened into an active ban on any collaboration. Should Oxfam go further?

The French organization MSF had witnessed similar events and decided to make a public protest. They encouraged other aid agencies to join them but none did. The government stopped MSF's permission to travel and they were forced to leave.

The problem for Oxfam was exacerbated by the fact that it was the only aid agency active in the provision of water. Nearly all the feeding centres relied on Oxfam to maintain their water supplies. Without Oxfam the outcome would be serious. Second, Oxfam was now delivering food by its own trucks into the remote areas of northern Wollo that were being targeted primarily for resettlement. Having learned the lesson about what government was trying to do, Oxfam was now playing a vital role in reducing the pressure for people to accept resettlement simply because they were starving.

Ideally, Oxfam should have consulted the people affected directly; but it would be impossible to get truthful answers. Visits would be monitored by local officials who would deal severely with anyone expressing any view contrary to the government's position. The only way of throwing light on the question seemed to be to consult the rebel organizations. Another factor was that the rebel organizations had issued a statement that any aid organization colluding with the resttlement programme would be viewed as an enemy. A former Oxfam staff member had already been abducted by rebels. But did the rebels expect aid agencies to join MSF in leaving Ethiopia?

The main rebel group in Tigray, the Tigray People's Liberation Front (TPLF), acknowledged that the issue was not so simple. They objected to aid agencies that did not even consider the dilemma and simply went on blindly doing whatever was easiest. They bitterly criticized organizations that had directly supported resettlement. The particular difficulty for the Tigrayan rebels was that the resettlement programme was most active in northern Wollo, which was not within their own scope, and the relationship between themselves and rebel groups in Wollo was sensitive. They would have liked to argue that Oxfam's food distributions from the government side were not essential because food could be brought from Sudan through the main rebel humanitarian organization in Wollo (the Ethiopian Relief Organization). But they knew very well that this was an ineffective and incompetent organization. Oxfam had already sent an exploratory mission to find ways of working with it and found the organization's abilities so limited that despite the acute needs, it was impossible to use it as a channel for assistance.

The Tigrayan rebels were cautious about giving formal advice and used their words carefully; but personal contacts indicated that if Oxfam could actually deliver food to people, this would be the best outcome since it would relieve the pressure for resettlement. The real issue, according to the rebels' view, was not the physical violence itself but the effects of starvation that made huge numbers of people vulnerable to low levels of coercion. They ended with the warning that if food simply acted as a trap to attract people who would then be taken for resettlement, Oxfam itself might become a target for rebel action.

It is perfectly possible that the government monitored these exchanges and the ensuing correspondence. Governmental practice was to allude to the cross-border operation in their conversations (such as mentioning the names of staff). They advised Oxfam to keep reasonably quiet about it or they would be forced to react. It was never clear to what extent officials were trying to use their own positions for the benefit of suffering people. I often suspected that they were, and were tacitly allowing aid agencies scope; but the bottom line was that they were themselves under surveillance and could take no significant risks. It remains just the same today.

Commentators on the resettlement debate like to talk about principles. However, if we accept that our objective is humanity – concern for the person in need – principles can be a hindrance rather than a help. Can a principle of speaking the truth in public take precedence over the use of discretion for a humanitarian purpose? MSF has adopted twin objectives of 'witness' as well as humanity. But for Oxfam there was just the one objective – the humanitarian one – and therefore it behaved (quite properly, I think) rather differently. Nevertheless, in viewing the aid response as a whole it is sad that no other agency supported MSF. Its stand raised the question of whether human rights and humanitarian functions can coexist in the same organization.

There are also some historical factors to be taken into account before returning to the story of how Oxfam sought to balance human rights and humanitarian objectives. During the Cold War, the issue of human rights had been coopted into Cold War politics, particularly in support of the West's criticisms of the former Soviet Union. The West's sincerity about human rights was in question, particularly because of the United States' ambivalent stance on human rights in Central America. US aid agencies could not help being involved. A separate branch of humanitarian discourse emerged that was essentially in opposition to the US position. Elsewhere, aid agencies were not prepared to adopt such a position and were wary of human rights issues. During the 'golden age', in short, humanitarian work was not political and therefore the issue of human rights had an uneasy relationship with the main political agenda. Many aid agencies ignored them altogether as irrelevant. The report on forced resettlement by the human rights group Survival International was widely dismissed as biased and politically motivated. There were grounds for scepticism about some of the human rights reports. One major report based on testimonies collected from the Somali border was presented to its audience of humanitarian workers from the US embassy in London. As the Cold War thawed, organizations such as Human Rights Watch gained credibility and widened their global reach, writing important reports that linked human rights issues with humanitarian ones.

At the beginning of 1988, the government relaunched the resettlement programme with unprecedented ferocity. Oxfam staff witnessed events in which local people were rounded up at gunpoint and forced onto lorries for resettlement. Some of the men were beaten with guns in the process. By this time Oxfam had a new representative in Addis Ababa, Nick Winer, who was determined that something should be done.

During the deliberations at that time, the question was: what can be realistically achieved for the people in need? The use of force was recognized as an infringement of personal freedom that could not be separated from physical needs. Our assessment was that making a public protest might have looked good but would achieve very little. I will give the story directly as I wrote it at the time in my report to Oxfam after discussing the issues with Winer in Addis Ababa:

The forced resettlement incidents on 3 January and 8–12 February are significant as human rights issues, but more particularly because they will scare people from the government feeding centres and could lead to uncontrollable migration (into Sudan).

The most alarming aspect of the problem is that Priestley [the UN representative] will not be an effective channel for representations. He told Nick [Nick Winer: the Oxfam representative] and me that the UN could not work in any way against the government, that he was constantly stressing the importance of the issue (he had met both president and prime minister last week), but he would not criticize government on behalf of NGOs. It is difficult to interpret this emphatic outburst. Nick took it as a clear statement of Priestley's actual position, and feels that we will need to galvanize him into a more active position by discreet pressure through New York, and in Addis through ambassadors.

Here, too, the line up is by no means united. The Swedish ambassador did not attend a meeting called by the British ambassador (at Nick's suggestion) to discuss the issue. The European Economic Community (EEC) delegate clearly takes a strong view on the human rights issue. So does the German ambassador who chairs the EEC group in Addis. Through the foreign ministry in Bonn, the EEC political committee has asked Ethiopia to restate its policies on resettlement following the Korem incident in which Oxfam was involved.

The British ambassador is personally very favourable, but faces some opposition from London where the destruction of Patten's 'work only on one side and all will be well' policy has left some sensitive wounds. The Korem incident is the opposite of what they want to hear.

The European ambassadors' group had intended to meet to discuss representation to government, but this had not taken place due to lack of time. But when they did ask for a meeting they were turned down by the foreign minister, and it now seems that the best they will achieve is a meeting with the RRC commissioner.

Nick stressed that the facts of the February incident were beyond dispute and that the forced resettlement programme had gone on for three days after the incident was first reported.

The change of policy by Chris Patten referred to above was Patten's decision – after much persuasion and evidence from Oxfam – to provide humanitarian aid through the rebels. Both on this issue and on the issue of resettlement, Oxfam had clearly been able to change the positions of donor governments, although it had not been able to influence the UN. The decision to pursue those issues had been taken not by Oxfam's trustees or directors, but by Nick Winer and me. This sense of individual personalities at the middle level of management making up their own minds was very characteristic of aid agencies during the later part of the Cold War period when aid agencies began to test their role on seriously political issues.

But to return to the resettlement issue, the main risk we perceived in making our protest, however discreetly, was that Oxfam had made an enemy of lower officials, especially the commissioner in Wollo. These individuals were likely to receive a reprimand (for the sake of formality) from Addis. We anticipated that the commissioner would retaliate by having aid agency staff expelled as a warning, restricting travel or harassing us in some other way. I noted in my report that: 'Our staff in Wollo will need to be very careful not to infringe the smallest regulation, as this would offer an excuse for reaction.' Winer made a contingency plan to go back to the ambassadors' group in case of further incidents, observing that:

> It may equally be true that the different messages we are getting (some officials hinting their support) reflect profound differences of view within the government itself. We also do not know what pressures are being put on the international community to distance themselves from the issue. In the end we will just have to wait and see what happens.

In a recent personal communication Winer observes:

> Both Ambassador Hooky Walker and I are stubborn people. It was a lucky coincidence. Our [Oxfam's] policy was to bear effective witness and share information. When I went to Hooky with the news he sent the news to his counterpart in Khartoum. He forgot to classify the message and so the TPLF were immediately informed of Oxfam's role. Knowing what we had uncovered and that we were sharing the information was well received by them. We were worried that this might damage us in the eyes of the government. Indeed, I had various headlines for two weeks calling me (but not by name) 'an enemy of the revolution', or 'a subversive fanatic'. We removed all staff involved in the north to holiday status. Will Day dealt with the local governor and I with Addis. Worse than Priestly, whose position was at least consistent with his mandate, even if taken to rather an extreme point, was that of the US ambassador. As I sat down to lunch with him to explain what had happened in Korem, he said: 'I really don't want to hear this.'

One of those involved in the discussions was Hugo Slim, who was then working for the UN in Wollo and was impatient with the UN's unwillingness to collect information on the abuses of the resettlement programme. In an article written many years later he asked whether, in philosophical terms, MSF's decision to make a protest could be squared with SCF's and Oxfam's decision to stay on. He questions the view that MSF was acting on principle and the others were not. Instead, this was a case of two conflicting principles – a genuine dilemma. One was the defence of human rights and the other was the imperative of offering humanitarian relief. Following one principle would result in negative consequences for the other. He makes the point that, having made the decision about which principle takes precedence in the circumstances, there is a responsibility to consider and mitigate the negative consequences of the other. He applauds the fact that in this case MSF had arranged for its work to be covered by another agency (actually SCF) so that suffering as a result of their withdrawal was minimized. Similarly, he says that SCF made attempts to protest discreetly about what had happened. Each agency had reacted in relation to its fundamental mandate (MSF placed emphasis on 'witness', which SCF did not) and in the broader interest of the people concerned. Hugo Slim's analytical method offers aid managers a useful way of approaching dilemmas: Choose between the principles and then compensate for the side effects. But dilemmas only occur when the value of different principles is exactly equal. One of the objectives of this book is to look at the problem in a different way. It seeks to clarify the values and then order them according to precedence. Explanations involving different mandates are not entirely satisfactory.

If we focus on humanity, including both physical needs and personal freedoms, and view each case separately, the distinction between humanitarian aid and human rights becomes meaningless. This leads us to the need for an understanding of the people concerned.

Developmentalism and professionalism caused particular problems and failures in the response to the Ethiopian famine. These were ideological faults – of minds being shaped too firmly by experiences and perceptions that had their origins outside of the immediate situation and did not relate to the person in need. Underlying all this was an exaggerated Western respect for the notion of the nation state. The aid response was dominated by the UN, which, in turn, was dominated by its members. The UN Charter put sovereignty above all other issues including humanitarian need and human rights. It also made many agencies believe what the government of Ethiopia told them and that its intentions were, as they expected from a nation state, benevolent. But the concept of the nation state is relatively new in human history, and the preconceptions of Western minds may be very different from the realities of Africa. For example, in the Western model, leadership brings responsibilities. This is not necessarily the way it is perceived elsewhere. Leadership might be construed to imply a freedom from responsibility – or an ability to do what you like. This is not necessarily a bad construction, but it leads to very different situations.

Where the concept of leadership is different, the behaviour of governments is unlikely to follow Western expectations. I do not want to caricature African governance or generalize too wildly, but it is important to recognize that the notions of leadership in Africa are very different from in the West. The broader issues is that our perceptions, and therefore the way in which we apply principles, are culturally subjective. The golden age was really the age of the individual. Oxfam's medical adviser was able to sway the organization in favour of selective feeding. Nick Winer's political intelligence enabled him to tackle the extremely sensitive political issue of resettlement. A different representative might have been less adept. Oxfam's style, more than most other agencies, was to encourage and develop individuals, and at best that gave them the confidence to listen to other people. I feel proud of my own involvement with the cross-border operation. I believe that I made Oxfam understand something about internal food purchase that it might not have otherwise done. I believe that Winer and I took the right course on resettlement. I have to say that these successes were essentially our own and not Oxfam's. In fact, Oxfam was scarcely an entity at all but a group of free-moving individuals.

Today there is much more emphasis on accountability and corporate behaviour, but it is worth reflecting on the successes of the past and the limitations of the new concept. The past did produce remarkably creative ways of operating during an oppressively rigid political environment. We found cracks in the system and used them. The disadvantage of accountability is that it usually means accountability to those outside, not to the person in need. Journalists and academics should question aid agencies as hard as they can – but whose needs are they going to be talking about: those of the donor or the recipient?

There is a danger that we will reinforce our own misconceptions if we do not relentlessly pursue the process of understanding the person in need, in their full practical environment.

Chapter 3
Sudan: Impartiality and Self-respect

On a wintry day in November 1989 a group of mourners assembled at the Oxford crematorium for the funeral of Melvyn Almond, an Oxfam field worker who died tragically at the age of 38. The ceremony, with piped music and artificial flowers, could not do justice to the event. It needed the massive clamour of an African funeral. Talk of achievement and character made the loss seem greater. The death of a man so valued, and so clearly in his prime, could not be passed over as a smooth and routine case of 'dust to dust and ashes to ashes'.

The grey mist in the Oxford air contrasted in my mind with memories of the dazzling light that fell on the cattle as he explained to me the mysteries of pastoralism. The dark, respectful suits of the mourners seemed unnecessarily formal compared with the naked, ashen-black bodies of the tribesmen. And the priest, standing at the lectern for a few minutes, doing his best but wondering about the clock, seemed to give short and trivial attention compared with Melvyn's long hours of travel to remote cattle camps, or to the long meditation of the herdsman who stands motionless for hours, leaning on his spear, guarding the dusky animals that are his livelihood and source of pride.

A synthetic imitation of 'The Lark Ascending' trembled thinly above the stark silence as I remembered the cattle camp where I had last seen Melvyn. Then, the sound of cattle munching filled my ears as he explained the nomad economy. His death had been untimely and unexpected. After a routine visit to review Oxfam's work with the Beja nomads in the Red Sea mountains, he suddenly developed a stomach pain and within two weeks was dead from pancreatic cancer. Before that he had lived and worked in Sudan for eight years as a livestock specialist and had become Oxfam's principal adviser on pastoralism, travelling all over the country and working with all sides and all peoples in Sudan's complex conflict. His work had mingled with the war, but the war never seemed to shake his confidence in himself or in the people around him. He had seen some of the worst of the war in the south, living with pastoralists who were devastated by attacks promoted by the government. But when he went to live in Khartoum he got on well with individual government officials, treating them as people of goodwill rather than symbols of an enemy he had come to hate.

Reflecting on Melvyn's life, I decided that most aid workers are not like that. Aid work is essentially emotional. In the profession, we may be more prone than others to the influence of emotions – why else would we take up such work? And if we are deeply committed to one set of people we will tend to develop a dislike for another. During disputes we, more than most people, quickly take sides, and in cases of conflict we find it hard to be impartial. But the key, my thoughts told me as I watched Melvyn's funeral, is not whether people have strong emotions, but whether they have self-respect.

This chapter is about the issue of impartiality in war and the danger that humanitarian aid will fuel conflict. The main example I use is the para-veterinary project in southern Sudan that Melvyn Almond ran for Oxfam during the 1980s. The chapter is also about another kind of conflict: between aid workers who favour relief and those that favour development. I ask how this came about and what it represents. I also look at the conflict between the idealist and the pragmatist. The underlying theme is the danger that the powerful emotions that drive humanitarians can blind them to humanity. The inner voice shouts so loudly that we cannot listen.

At the heart of humanity are not only conflicts of selfishness and altruism, but the paradox of being emotional enough to feel concern while not being so emotional that we limit that concern unfairly. We need both attachment and detachment. And it is particularly tempting to feel 'concern for the person in need' rather more strongly in the case of those whom we like, and to attack those whom we do not like even if their ideas and objectives are similar to our own. I touch upon a theme that will be developed in later chapters: that our nature is not necessarily 'good'. People tend to identify with power, and vulnerability has a tendency to evoke disgust. We identify with what we like rather than with the real needs of humanity.

* * *

Working in remote parts of the world, it is easy to become attached to groups of people or societies with interesting cultures and ways of life.

In Sudan it was easy to admire the pastoralism. An Oxfam visitor who travelled to one of the cattle camps with Melvyn Almond at around the same time as I did in 1985 described the scene:

> *On arrival we were met by the headman of this camp... a powerful man called Bulan who was the only male clothed. The scene at the camp is unforgettable as 500 or 600 head of cattle, with some sheep and goats are individually pegged out in a comparatively small area. Several dung fires were burning in the sun with drifting smoke to keep the flies and mosquitoes away and all the men and children have ash smeared on their naked bodies to help keep off the flies.*
>
> *Many of the men are well over six feet tall, in contrast to the many small children running about peering inquisitively through their smeared masks, the girls wearing a short skirt round their loins.*
>
> *The children in the cattle camps are generally healthy as they are fed on a milk diet, but the ones left behind in the home areas are the most undernourished as they have little or no milk and a shortage of grain. Bulan was obviously a fairly wealthy man as he had five wives and was complaining that he had to buy half a bag of grain for each! His family appears to own about 300 head of cattle.*
>
> *The available water away from the river was drying up and the grazing likewise, so they would shortly be moving north to spend about three months on the large islands in the Nile which they used as their dry-weather grazing reserve. They will first be holding a meeting with other camp leaders in Terekeka to make decisions, because a lot will depend on the security situation. If, for any reason, they are not able to go to these islands then they will be in serious trouble.*

Or, to paraphrase, the herdsmen protect their cattle behind wooden palisades against their enemy and then make a dash for their secret island hideouts. Men and boys, dressed in war paint and with little more than a spear or rifle, wander far and wide with their animals, defending them against attackers. The women, girls and younger children have to stay in 'home areas' where they do the cooking and cultivate small patches of land cleared from the bush. Could it be a fantasy from an old-fashioned children's story, written for boys?

Prized animals have the status among Sudanese men that fast red cars have in the West. Indeed, the colour of an animal may similarly add to its value as a status symbol. A man, as described in the extract above, will be measured by the number of cattle he owns, and a young man cannot marry until he has acquired sufficient animals as the 'price' of a bride. Having cattle is definitely sexy. The men eat blood-soaked grain and drink milk. They have to endure terrifying initiation ceremonies. The women and children often go hungry, but they are out of the way. For aid workers, especially for males, the combination of an exotic pastoral society and the excitement of war can be an intoxicating mixture. We may forget that we are to help those in need, not to admire those who seem to fulfil our fantasies. It is not easy to be impartial without knowing how and why we react. But if we do not know these things, we may find ourselves advocating aid programmes for people whom we say are in need, but really we simply like. Self-knowledge is the prerequisite of humanity.

There is a lot of 'masculinity' in emergency work, and some 'femininity' in development. The business of 'saving lives', especially in a war zone, has a great deal of attraction for a man, and relief workers often talk of an adrenalin surge when the action gets tough, especially when they are living in danger. Some become addicted to it and are listless without the excitement. An African woman recently told me how appalled she was, after the Rwanda genocide, to find Western aid workers yearning for more and more dire events so that they could prove their prowess.

If the objective is to prove oneself, it follows that other people's advice and support is an admission of weakness. Such an attitude separates the aid worker from the need to listen or to extend the circle of knowledge, especially to women. Male aid workers can be fiercely competitive and seem to gain greater pleasure from proving themselves (including the ability to devise theories and analysis) than helping those in need. Competitive behaviour evokes similar reactions from other aid workers, especially expatriate men in other aid agencies who may see it as a challenge. There can be futile competition between those with power and those with knowledge. To local people it may appear extraordinarily arrogant that a person so newly arrived and so ignorant should assume such a sense of superiority. In return, they withhold explanations, teasing the testosterone-tippling expatriate with an appearance of stupidity and laziness. Groups of expatriates with similar negative views then confine themselves to small networks and develop a culture of self-reinforcement by indulging in endless complaint against those they regard as 'slackers', 'wimps' and 'fools'. As relief staff members lose confidence in local people, they lose perspective on the longer-term issues. They see only a series of day-to-day problems that they glamorize by referring to the situation as 'saving lives'. Relief work is defended against other cultures of aid, especially development aid. The origin of the 'relief versus development' debate is found in the arena of competitive, mainly male, aid workers and commentators, and their lack of self-respect.

* * *

Alex de Waal's book *Famine That Kills* (1989) told the aid agencies that it was local people, rather than themselves, who did most to alleviate the famine in western Sudan in the mid-1980s. When I read some early drafts of the book and discussed them with de Waal my efforts to organize relief in western Sudan were still fresh in my mind so I reacted negatively. It struck me that there was an element of deliberate 'challenge' in his position, but was this because I could not cope with this analysis or because he really liked to attack?

In 1998 I commissioned de Waal to make a short study of survival strategies in the rebel-held areas of northern Ethiopia. Here (as I rather suspected), de Waal come to rather different conclusions:

> *Provision of food relief assists many survival strategies, as well as providing direct nourishment to rural people... survival strategies should not be regarded as a magical ability that rural people have, which enables them to withstand famine in the absence of food aid.*

De Waal's well-known sympathy with the rebels in Ethiopia seemed to be colouring his view. This suspicion enabled me to dismiss de Waal's other contentions and so I did not learn as much from him as I could have done.

I turned to a less politically committed analyst, David Keen, to make a more comprehensive review of famine survival strategies in Africa. Keen was already working on the famine in Sudan (making extensive use of Oxfam reports), which would result in his book *The Benefits of Famine* (1994) This describes the political economy of the Sudan conflict and especially the role of merchants who were making a great deal of money out of the famine. Keen points out that many actors in a conflict play out self-interested roles and that conflict can best be understood by examining those interests. In a sense, de Waal was doing the same: examining the interests of the aid agencies. But in a situation where thousands of people had died, it was virtually impossible for him to remain detached. In the humanitarian field such debates are likely to go into emotional territory and thus become more difficult to resolve. Keen had carefully avoided value judgements about the activities of the merchants who had created famine. Nor did he ask the question of whether the merchants enjoyed a sense of power. But de Waal worried about these issues and went on to analyse them in his later book *Famine Crimes* (1997) where he accuses aid agencies of self-aggrandizement.

In turning the debate into a question of 'who does most – aid agency or the people?' we had created an argument based on competition; in reality the issue was very complex. Keen drew attention to the fact that survival strategies can be highly undesirable for the people using them. I appreciated his point. In western Sudan I had seen people boil poisonous roots that were still quite dangerous to eat even after long periods of cooking. Keen observed that:

There is a danger in assuming that the pursuit of a survival strategy somehow implies that it is successful... A cursory reference to survival strategies runs the risk of implying that relief is unnecessary. By contrast, a close examination of survival strategies is likely to reveal a number of ways in which people can be helped... More often than not, relief gives people an additional option, rather than crudely determining their behaviour.

In parts of Uganda prostitution and letting old people die have been reported as survival strategies. Clearly, leaving people to resort to such extremes was not a good policy. Keen, himself, pointed out that the debate about survival strategies and aid agency relief could be exploited by governments seeking to reduce the volume of aid. 'One researcher reports that during a visit to Khartoum many donors were talking in glowing terms about people's coping strategies and apparently using these strategies as a justification for the small quantities of relief delivered or planned.'

But by now the debate had polarized and focused on the aid agencies rather than the people. De Waal claimed that:

Despite the central role played by the foreign relief worker in media coverage of famine, and in most aid agency commercials, international relief is at best a marginal contribution to the survival of people living at the margin. In most recent famines in Africa, international food aid has been 10 per cent or less of the overall diet of famine-stricken people.

There was no comprehensive study of the contribution of food aid to the diet of Africans during famine, and de Waal's last sentence is an assertion that is impossible to prove or deny. But such figures and assertions can be misused by those who do not like aid, or perhaps have no concern about human suffering. The aid agencies backed off from public debate, hoping that if they did not argue, de Waal would be ignored. But this seems to have provoked de Waal into more direct confrontation. In his book *Famine Crimes*, published in 1997, he made his most direct challenge: 'Throughout Africa, aid agencies are surrounded by a mystique of power, wealth and opportunity.'

He writes further that aid agencies 'must not inflate the marginal contribution they make to saving lives and livelihoods. Any humanitarian agency that cannot survive on this basis should die, and famine-vulnerable Africans will not regret its passing'. He particularly targets the self-importance or self-confidence of the aid agencies and seems concerned about how they consider themselves: 'The humanitarians deceive themselves about their own importance.'

In attacking humanitarians, de Waal draws onto his side various categories of Africans:

The recipients of this tyranny of compassion tend to see things rather differently. Increasingly, Africans who are subjected to these new forms of philanthropic imperialism are bitter and resentful. They see organizations suffused with arrogance born of power without responsibility, and a new hegemony of humanitarianism that allows no criticism. The estrangement between motivated African professionals and international charities is deep and becoming deeper.

But by appointing himself champion for Africans, de Waal has steered the debate into an area where Westerners argue with each other about what Africans need and think. Each side becomes emotionally committed to winning the argument rather than debating the issues. Above all, such debate tends to exclude the person in need, because it is difficult for anyone else to add to the debate without taking sides, or seeming to take sides. Meanwhile, outsiders with other interests can take advantage of the stalled debate between academic commentator and aid agency. Aid workers can ignore de Waal's criticisms and simply rally to the support of their own cause; donors can reduce funding because de Waal has attacked the process of aid. Finally aid agencies can criticize de Waal for causing those results. Is such emotionally-driven debate effective?

* * *

There has been a similar debate among staff within aid organizations about 'relief' and 'development'. For much of the time, it is a friendly rivalry between those who focus on short-term needs and those who focus on long-term ones. Both are trying to understand and help the person in need, so there should be no problem. But there is. At several points in its history, Oxfam has identified this debate as the cause of major organizational rifts. The formal evaluation of Oxfam's response to the Ethiopian famine of 1984 concludes that developmentalist perspectives blocked the response. I will give another example of Somalia in 1992 in Chapter 6. Why is the debate so damaging?

Before analysing it further, it may be helpful to widen the perspective. What makes the difference between a war which is destructive and one which transforms society or reflects inevitable changes in global relationships? Oxfam's field director in Sudan during the mid-1980s, Mark Duffield, has argued that wars today are likely to contain important elements of global transformation. As countries adapt to new global circumstances, conflicts may ensue or be exacerbated. It follows that preventing conflict is not necessarily desirable, any more than it is desirable to prevent debate. Conflict, and even wars, may reflect profound and inevitable changes in the modern world, creating new relationships between the state, economic and social interests. Arguments and wars both seem to have the capacity to transform and destroy. Indeed, argument, conflict and war are simply words given to points on a continuous spectrum of human relations. Therefore debates about them are likely to suffer from endless problems of semantics.

Until the 1990s, at least, aid agencies tended to take the view that all conflict was harmful and therefore had to be prevented. Conflict mitigation and prevention became objectives in themselves and organizations were set up to deal with them. But with the end of the Cold War, and the loosening of the global political framework, it became more likely that conflicts would include processes of legitimate and necessary transformation. Theoretically, debate about the role of the aid agencies should have become easier. During the Cold War, the aid agencies represented the main capacity for intervention in humanitarian crises and there was a tendency for anyone concerned about humanitarian issues to defend them. But more recently there has been nothing to stop governments from intervening directly, or applying their full political weight to the issues causing conflict. Therefore, private aid agencies can no longer claim to be the sole up-holders of humanitarianism itself. Unfortunately, the debate about the changing role of aid agencies has been stalled by de Waal's initial attack. The aid sector needed to discuss its new role, but de Waal's charge of self-interest may have put it on the defensive, unable to come to terms with the increasing role of government. Today we may need to transform the aid machinery, but cannot find a middle ground on which all sides feel confident. Meanwhile, issues of resources and competition between aid agencies have made the situation increasingly difficult.

The debate now rests with de Waal asserting that the basic ideology of the aid agencies is to maximize their own resources, and the aid agencies suspecting that de Waal's views would minimize the funding available for the poor. Both sides argue from the 'African perspective' and use arguments that are also convenient for themselves.

There may be something to learn from the 1980s debate between relief and development. It became so deeply rooted that it created opposing cultures within humanitarianism. As Nicholas Stockton (Oxfam's representative in Juba in the mid-1980s) pointed out at the time:

> I have frequently heard the development lobby dismiss the relief people as a bunch of cowboys and boneheads. Likewise, I have heard the relief lobby dismissing the development people as a bunch of dithering pinkoes who couldn't fight their way out of a paper bag, etc. The conflict spills over into arguments about recruitment policies (developers for equal-opportunities, the relievers against), staff training and development (developers for, relievers against), workshops and conferences (relievers usually dismissive, 'it's just a lot of bloody talk'), technology (developers always suspicious and wanting to know where it came from and who made it; relievers simply interested to know whether or not it will work), social science (developers for, relievers highly suspicious), gender (relievers: 'what is it?')... and so on.

It could be added that Oxfam relief staff, especially engineers, tend to be men, and development staff tend to be women. In a conflict like Sudan's where all humanitarian aid is ultimately a failure (the war never stops), there is a constant underlying fear of personal responsibility. The thought that someone else has succeeded, or is perceived to have succeeded, can be hurtful. People begin to be defensive and resent the perceived successes of others. They envy those who appear on TV. There is very little thanks handed out among aid agencies, and it tends not to be given arbitrarily. The media sometimes brings accolades of public appreciation for a pretty nurse in a feeding centre and ignores an ugly engineer dealing with the (far more important) sanitation. Most of the time it is hard slog in forgotten places. If one aid worker is shown on TV, there can be an instant ripple of nervousness and resentment among the others. Why were they chosen? Is there something wrong with what we are doing?

Managers and other staff at headquarters often view those in the field as the lucky ones living with exotic people and in the forefront of the public eye. The reality is very different. Aid workers, and anyone passionately committed to bringing an end to human suffering, suffer feelings of failure that are easily projected onto others as envy and anger. The management systems of aid organizations tend to be unsupportive. This is partly due to a feeling in aid agencies that staff members are there to help others, not to expect attention for themselves. This culture of self-sufficiency becomes potentially damaging during emergencies when management time is preoccupied with other issues and the stresses on field staff are greater than ever.

Interestingly, the relief–development cultural division invariably disappears when field staff actually meet for any considerable length of time away from their work. Soon after Stockton wrote his caricature piece about 'boneheads and pinkoes', there was a conference for staff members from all over the region in Kampala. They spontaneously agreed a statement that 'Oxfam's work is both relief and development'. The 'bonehead and pinko' caricature became a friendly joke. It is a pity that the same has not happened with the de Waal argument, or the war in Sudan.

The polarization of relief and development has been perpetuated into the 1990s by being translated into more elevated academic terms and being conducted over greater geographical distance. Mary Anderson in the USA became the proponent of 'developmental relief' – meaning an approach to relief that draws on lessons from development, such as ways to ensure the participation of local people and to build local capacity. She has argued for the active involvement of aid workers in conflict resolution through methods bringing about better mutual understanding. Mark Duffield in the UK continued his attack on 'developmentalism' by arguing that conflict is typically an adjustment to new realities in the world and that interfering with conflicts and rebuilding old capacities was not necessarily helpful. He argued for a much wider analytical approach. An American and a British discourse emerged. A French discourse (the independence of aid agencies from governments) developed in parallel. In a recent exchange of views between them, there are more elements of a cultural difference than a disagreement about the fundamentals of humanitarianism. Anderson begins her 'defence' by checking that they are both following the same values: 'Mark Duffield is concerned, as am I, with the preservation of humanitarianism and its motivation, compassion.'

Duffield makes no reference to compassion but does not want to discuss the issue of motivation. He is interested in structures. He keeps his argument analytical and conceptual, and blames Anderson for failing to do likewise: 'I am concerned that an understanding of conflict as an historically determined political act finds little scope within the argument.'

Duffield emphasizes the need for analytical work on conflict and Anderson seems concerned that Duffield should acknowledge the importance of compassion. It appears to be a debate about 'what sort of person you are'. Instead of the usual 'short-term' versus 'long-term' distinction between relief and development, the argument is now between Anderson's local focus and Duffield's global one. Many aid workers facing local practical difficulties have found Anderson's advice helpful; others have turned to Duffield for the wider picture.

The debate overlooks what, in my experience at least, is a far more important cause of conflict between relief and development workers – the allocation of resources. For aid workers, control of budgets is one of the prime ways of defining personal power and responsibility. Aid budgets are sharply divided between relief and development, and this creates serious tension. In Oxfam the budgets for field offices were known until recently as 'development' budgets. They were controlled by local representative who therefore had a considerable stake in 'development' but had little control over 'relief'. When the Sudan situation took a turn for the worse, relatively large amounts of money could suddenly become available, but were usually earmarked for relief rather than development and might have to be spent within a limited time. This tilted the balance between those arguing for building local capacities and those saying that it was best to simply provide immediate relief.

Such sudden shifts in power caused resentment and distrust. The divisions were reflected in structures within aid organizations.

Oxfam's management structure was deeply divided between relief and development. To those in the field, the movement of funds between the categories would often appear arbitrary. In Oxfam training programmes, the theoretical question 'how does Oxfam define an emergency?' was often answered with 'when the emergency department budgets are involved'.

Underlying these shifts of resources were very human issues of power and status. A kind of class system operated within the relief and development debate, with the development staff occasionally claiming to deride money altogether. The ideology of the period generated a tendency to regard development as the norm, but the Sudan case made a nonsense of the theory. Although the majority of spending was for relief, there was always a feeling that developmental inputs would be superior. The most serious stress was perhaps that experienced by individuals who had to switch cultures suddenly. When a disaster occurred, the impact on managers in the field was a sudden influx of huge amounts of money and the obligation to spend it quickly. However, although it might seem that this would give the local representative greater power, it was often experienced as a sudden loss of control because more senior managers became involved in every decision and the approach was organizational rather than personal. Field staff would sometimes be told that shipments were being sent or visitors were about to arrive with little or no consultation. Perhaps the greatest of all cultural tensions was between expatriate workers, arriving suddenly to 'do relief', and the local staff who had been trying for years to manage with scant resources. Suddenly, all the norms were broken.

The separation of budgets arose because money from public appeals and from governmental donors had to be kept in specific accounts that were earmarked for the emergency. Humanitarian crises present varying mixtures of short-term (relief) and long-term (development) needs, and agencies use a similarly wide range of analysis according to their perspectives. The fundamental problem was that the donors, both public and governmental, were not seriously engaged in understanding the actual nature of humanitarianism. Aid agencies were more inclined to take the money than to explain that it was required for long-term and non-sensational purposes. Increased public scrutiny in recent years has made agencies panic and promise to spend money ever more rapidly, rather than argue that wars of transformation take time and that aid workers spend money better if they feel they are supported and trusted.

Even so, if problems of budget and management support can be resolved, is it possible to be impartial in a conflict that has become polarized? In the next section I will briefly describe the dynamics of the Sudanese war and then examine Oxfam's attempts to find a genuine impartiality.

* * *

The war in Sudan is often described as a conflict between north and south or between Muslims and Christians, but this, too, is a caricature. Competition for resources has always been a more important factor. To some extent, the issue is about oil reserves in the south, but to a much greater extent it is about cattle. The momentum of the war, and the inability to reach conclusions by discussion, stems from the ability of political leaders to make profit out of the war, and particularly out of cattle. Sudan is incredibly rich in cattle – rich enough to fuel a war that has already gone through three generations, with only a short gap, since 1956.

The roots of the conflict can be traced to the failure of 'decolonization' or to colonization itself. After independence, the northern-based government tried to impose its will on the south. People in the south armed themselves, Christians against Muslims, and in the polarizing world of the Cold War, were given arms by outsiders. This allowed the strong to oppress the weak, and tribes to steal cattle on a grander scale than ever before. The wonderful cattle camps described earlier are deceptive. The pastoralists are not poor people, but include exceedingly wealthy men who might have cattle worth US$50,000. Over time, raiding was legitimized as an ideological struggle. Many of the worst atrocities took place not in direct confrontations between north and south but in the many secondary conflicts in which small tribes were reduced to destitution by the ruthless extraction of wealth by more powerful forces ostensibly on their own side. Society became militarized, with heavy concentrations of wealth and power and consequences for the balance of relations by gender and age. The cattle wealth was plundered and became the the fuel of war.

By the 1980s, the Cold War had reached deep into the remotest parts of southern Sudan. The government in Khartoum, with support from Libya and links with the Soviet bloc, armed some of the northern tribes and encouraged them to raid southwards. The US moved to defend the Sudan People's Liberation Army (SPLA), whose leader, John Garang, had been trained in a US military academy. Arms now began to flow in from the south, through the United States' client, Kenya. The war became a tangle of international and local politics. Ethiopia, although a client of Russia, wanted to undermine Sudan, partly because Sudan was tacitly helping the rebels in Eritrea and Tigray. The SPLA acquired support from both East and West, fought the northern tribes for a while, and then turned back to enjoy rich pickings within the south itself. They turned on other southerners and used their external support to consolidate their power.

Lives depended as much on possessing a gun as on having food. Any kind of external assistance poured into this crucible of conflict could be converted into guns; it therefore became impossible to separate humanitarian aid from the war itself. Although aid agencies may not have been keen to admit it, providing a few sacks of food was virtually the same as providing a Kalashnikov rifle. They could be exchanged for each other within hours of delivery. The Kalashnikov was the symbol of the new power. Its arrival had dramatically changed the pattern of raiding, leading to massive concentrations of wealth and terrible massacres. It militarized society, marginalized the elders and broke down traditional systems of peace-making. A couple of young men with Kalashnikovs could steal cattle and suddenly become rich.

It is possible to be detached and impartial? Humanitarians sometimes felt obliged to take sides. Anthropologist David Turton reacted strongly to a particularly vicious attack by the Nyangatom, an SPLA client, against the Mursi, whom he was studying, in Ethiopia:

In February 1987, their south-western neighbours, the Nyangatom... who had recently obtained Kalashnikov automatic rifles [from the SPLA], launched a massive attack on the southern Mursi, killing several hundred people [possibly 500], mainly women and children, in one day. Immediately afterwards, the Mursi evacuated the entire southern part of their territory. When I visited them in December 1987, they were confidently expecting a second Nyangatom attack within the next three months. Unless they could arm themselves with automatics, they said, they would be driven from their lands entirely and have to find refuge where they could in the highlands, on either side of the Omo valley. Although they would survive there as individuals in scattered enclaves, and although their clan names would persist, the 'Mursi' would have disappeared.

Turton arranged for humanitarian help to be given to the survivors and persuaded the Ethiopian government to protect the Mursi and also to supply them with weapons. He had been associated with the Mursi for a very long time and lived among them. He felt that getting them weapons was the 'humane' thing to do. He was well aware of the possibility that arming the Mursi might lead to revenge attacks against the Nyangatom, but felt it was impossible to do nothing. The Nyangatom were not his problem. The Mursi were close to annihilation. Ultimately he could argue, with some support in international law, that this was a case of genocide.

He persuaded Oxfam to send food to the Mursi and no doubt both he and Oxfam were aware that if the Mursi chose to do so, they could exchange the food for weapons. Oxfam could ensure that the food reached the right people, but not what they did with it afterwards. The Mursi were desperate for food, but their cultural survival was the most important issue. They might even allow some people to starve in order to protect themselves as an entity. The question whether to eat the food or exchange it for weapons might turn on a calculation of strength in which outsiders would have no part. If the Mursi felt they could win against the Nyangatom, they would attack. The more food Oxfam gave, and the more weapons the Mursi could acquire, the greater the likelihood that they would try to kill the Nyangatom.

Talk of impartiality or neutrality appears irrelevant here. Oxfam's local representative in Juba at the time, Nicholas Stockton, grappled with the question, writing:

> In a society being destroyed by an internecine war, where the real agents of underdevelopment and oppression remain relatively unscathed, any intervention by Oxfam must avoid inadvertently providing fuel to the conflict… With starvation used as a principle weapon in this war, we have been extremely careful with food and mindful of the dangers of escalating the conflict… Food distribution has manifestly contributed to the instability and ultimately to greater hunger and destitution in the resulting conflict.

But what does being 'extremely careful' mean? All resources can be mobilized for the war and therefore the principles of neutrality (not taking sides) and impartiality (not distinguishing between people except on the basis of need) are very difficult to put into practice. The Geneva conventions and the International Red Cross make a clear distinction between combatants and non-combatants, but Africa's resource wars are not ones in which the combatants can be safely identified by their uniforms. The SPLA and government regular troops might wear uniforms (when it suited them), but much of the fighting was carried out by tribal militias acting on their behalf. If they wish to invoke the protection of international law, aid agencies are expected to be impartial, and the Red Cross interprets this in the strict sense of neutrality. But what if there are dozens of warring factions, and it is impossible to construct a reliable analysis of need. What, furthermore, if food can be traded for guns? The result is chaos.

Donors tried to adhere to a set of principle in their operations. Neutrality and impartiality were interpreted in Sudan as meaning the distribution of equal amounts of aid to both the government and SPLA. But Stockton pointed out that this did not amount to 'genuine neutrality' because it concentrated power in the hands of the two parties who were inflicting the most damage. They held onto most of the food aid for themselves, sometimes gave it to client populations as a reward, but most commonly exploited the power conferred by aid for purely selfish ends. Stockton wrote: 'We can only admit to have failed when the current relief programme in the south reaches only 20 per cent or less of those in need. The biggest disappointment must concern the recent polarization of the warring factions and the increased tendency of donors to capitulate to the awful dangers of an "even-handed" policy of food distribution at the expense of genuine neutrality.'

In a later paper, Stockton added: 'A new phenomenon exists. That is, the actual creation by international aid agencies of the necessary machinery to achieve through the food weapon, rural domination on behalf of the SPLA.'

Stockton wanted food to be pushed outwards beyond the clients of the government and the SPLA to those who were most needy. He emphasized the idea of a consortium of aid agencies to truck food from the government-held town of Juba into areas held by other tribes, some of them supporters of the SPLA. His concept of neutrality was to deliver food as far as possible to the end user. The consortium was successfully formed and a great deal was achieved, but if either of the main parties chose not to cooperate (and they often did not), the aid agencies were left helpless. The project needed the backing of more powerful political forces. Stockton and Mark Duffield, Oxfam's representative in Khartoum, lobbied the donors to provide support but got little response. Following the usual Cold War pattern, donors at that time scarcely linked their political influence to their humanitarian aid.

The United States' relationship with the SPLA was aimed simply at containing the influence of the Libyans and the former Soviet Union. Humanitarianism was not the prime goal. For many other donors in Khartoum, the issue was to wean Sudan away from Libyan influence by offering bilateral aid; as a result, they were reluctant to antagonize the government over issues to do with trucking far away in the south.

Without the possibility of external pressure, the only path to impartiality was to find a situation in which the political leadership on both sides would agree to put the interests of the 'person in need' first. This was the basis of the Operation Lifeline Sudan agreement brokered by the UN to bring food into the south by sharing the benefits equally between warring parties. The problem was that these parties had used the leverage of food to strengthen their positions relative to the people in need. Humanitarian aid had been neutral between the two parties but not impartial between the people in need. Those who were favoured by the Khartoum and SPLA leadership benefited disproportionately. Impartiality disappears in a climate of personal and political interest.

* * *

Finally, let us return to how these issues played-out within Oxfam's aid programme in Sudan, and to Melvyn Almond.

The Mundari people living around Juba were protected from SPLA or Dinka attacks by government forces, but their livelihood had been deeply undermined by the changing circumstances of the war. Disease in cattle had become an acute problem, and veterinary services had practically ceased. Melvyn Almond wrote:

The war had forced stock owners to move their herds into less suitable areas... often located within tsetse-fly infested woodlands. The higher stocking rates have facilitated the rapid spread of disease... In June this year an attack by the SPLA forced the evacuation of Terekeka district by the local inhabitants... It is my contention that the unusual concentrations of cattle around Juba, together with the inevitable mixing of cattle from Terekeka district, Juba district and cattle from the East bank, triggered off the East Coast fever epidemic that we are now witnessing... From investigations I have made so far it appears that this disease is unknown to the Mundari.

In proposing to help the Mundari protect their cattle from disease, Oxfam was aware of some political complexities. The Mundari did not rely wholly on government protection against the Dinka and the SPLA. There was constant talk of the SPLA capturing Juba or the government abandoning it. The Mundari knew that the government would ditch them if there was trouble, and the worst scenario for them would be revenge by the SPLA after Juba was taken by force. It was therefore in their interests to keep open a line of communication with the Dinka and the SPLA as a possible basis for reconciliation. They also needed to travel in areas where there might be SPLA or Dinka forces. Far away from government troops in Juba, they needed access to unprotected lands along the Nile and islands where they traditionally grazed their animals. They knew that they could not defeat the highly armed Dinka and needed a level of goodwill. For their part, the Dinka had also suffered serious losses of animals because of the breakdown of government veterinary services. Their attitude towards the Mundari was also ambivalent. They intended to capture Juba and wanted to keep open the possibility that the Mundari might change sides and support them. The political factors were complex, but there was one issue on which both sides agreed: cattle were the centre of life and there was an acute need for veterinary services. This cut across tribal divisions and also across divisions of wealth and status. To secure a bride a man had to have cattle. All men had an interest in cattle, and men were the political leaders.

In 1985 Oxfam launched a cattle vaccination programme based in the Mundari areas around Juba and extending outwards into Dinka territory. The project had been agreed by leaders on both sides and was run by a local Mundari organization with Oxfam's financial and technical support. The herdsmen were charged for each vaccination or veterinary treatment. Melvyn Almond acted as technical adviser and arranged for the purchase and supply of vaccines from Nairobi. His assessment of the reasons for cooperation was as follows:

Oxfam's para-vet programme ensured that even though government services had broken down in the rural areas, vaccinations against rinderpest and some drugs were available. It was made clear to all sides in the project area by local chiefs that fighting would prevent the vaccinations and other remedial work from going ahead. Since most of the tribes in the area depended on their livestock, they realized that it would be foolish to jeopardize their own survival. Traditional power structures reasserted themselves and hostilities in the project area have been greatly reduced compared to elsewhere.

Remarkably, the project has been in continuous operation since 1985 and the Mundari para-vets (local people given some veterinary training) still roam widely into Dinka territory. They have never been attacked. It is certain that, although no calculation has been made, the value of cattle saved has been enormous. In 1988 Stockton wrote:

> *Perhaps the most remarkable aspect of the para-vet project has been the extent of its coverage – unlimited, it would appear, by tribal–military boundaries. Large numbers of Dinka cattle in SPLA-held areas in western Terekeka have been vaccinated by the Mundari para-vets who have delivered cold boxes and kerosene by bicycle to Tali Post to keep the refrigerator operational. On a recent tour of some very remote Nile islands near Terekeka, where I saw several para-vets at work, I couldn't help but draw a comparison with the government veterinary and 'community' health officials who have all refused to return to Terekeka since the fighting began there over two years ago... It is quite impossible to calculate the value to the Mundari of the livestock deaths averted by this programme, but their continued willingness to pay for the vaccines must be indicative of their own convictions in this respect.*

And in conclusion: 'The incentive of participation in an emergency cattle vaccination programme has promoted a *modus vivendi* between two otherwise warring tribes. It is unlikely that a conspicuous food distribution programme would have achieved such an outcome.'

Instead of standing outside the conflict, Oxfam had entered into its flow and used the perspective of the people themselves. Rather than battling to deliver food across hostile lines, the project was run by local people with little more than outside technical advice and the air freight of vaccines.

There were some specific reasons for its success. The Mundari chief was himself a former veterinary assistant and gave his strong personal support to the project. If the Mundari leadership had not acknowledged a sincere interest in maintaining links with the Dinka, the Mundari para-vets might have been inclined to fail in their duty to vaccinate Dinka cattle. Similarly, the Dinka could easily have murdered the Mundari para-vets at times of tension between the tribes, but this never happened. It is a good case of what Paul Richards, in his book on the Sierra Leone war *Fighting for the Rainforest* (1996), has called 'smart relief', using the war economy to deliver humanitarian aid.

But despite Stockton and Almond's attempts to think through all the aspects of impartiality, a problem remained: the project overlooked the status and needs of women. This needs to be put into perspective. It is not an easy business to understand what women feel in a society dominated by men. Indeed, getting any sort of information from the pastoralists of southern Sudan is an art, as Jok Makut Jok has described:

> *It is a pointless and frustrating process to ask a Dinka person the number of cattle he owns. This is not only because of the possible bad luck of stating the number of one's cattle, but most Dinka people do not know the exact number of the herd. It is also rude... The needs assessment process has taken on a life of its own: for the intended beneficiaries it is often a wearying experience, but one which can yield benefits if the 'correct' answers are provided to sometimes ridiculous and often insensitive questions.*

Person-to-person surveys with direct questions cannot be guaranteed to produce accurate results. Jok describes a visit by aid workers to Luo people in southern Sudan. In the chief's own words:

> *They came here several months ago and called us together, asked us a lot of questions to which we did not know how to respond. Then, two months ago, one of these young girls came back with five other people and asked us the same questions for which we gave different responses each time. And now they are here again asking if Luo people have acquired cattle from the Dinka, since Luo people are good cultivators and the rains have not been as bad here as in in Dinka areas. They wanted to know whether Luo people purchase cows from the Dinka. We do not know what to tell them other than yes, some people have bought cows, some have not, and yes our people are hungry, and you ought to help them. Bring food, more food.*

It seems from this account that the questioners were being obtuse. But is that so, or was the problem the deliberate obstruction of the Luo chief? Is the real problem that he is being questioned by 'young girls' rather than an old *mzee*, or a man with many cattle? And how can society transform itself if young women cannot ask questions?

Oxfam basically ignored the role of women in the para-vet project, but the evidence of a problem was near at hand and existed in Oxfam files at the time. The people who suffered most in the famines of the Sudan were not the men and boys out with the cattle and able to drink milk and blood every day, but the women and girls who were left in 'home areas' and who were expected to rely on crops that were prone to the vagaries of the weather and the predations of raiders. Improvements in the health of cattle might have an indirect impact on the health of women when supplies would be sent back to the 'home areas', but otherwise there would be many months when the women and children got little benefit from the animals. The main impact of the para-vet project was undoubtedly on men.

There were several of these 'home areas' around Juba and they were basically places of starvation. Oxfam was deeply involved in the attempt to bring food across the border and deliver it to the camps; but the supply depended on political factors and the political leadership had little interest in the plight of women and girls. As a last resort for women who were starving, Oxfam devised a project offering work at a tree nursery on the edge of Juba, run by Dr Linda Small, Melvyn Almond's partner.

It was situated across the river from Oxfam's base in Juba, over a rusty iron bailey-bridge that looked like a survival from colonial days. Under the shade of leafy trees, women hoed and planted, and filled little plastic pots with soil. The project had two main objectives. One was to provide 'a wide range of fruit, nut, forage, shade and fuel wood trees' and the other was to provide food (as food for work) for the women who worked in the nursery. It was not exactly relief nor exactly development but offered elements of both in a context that took into account human dignity in contrast to the demeaning handouts of relief distributions. The project was operated on a 'food-for-work' basis, and it was flexible so that women could come and go as they pleased. This allowed time for the care of children.

The problem was that there was never enough food to pay the workers. Even if food arrived in Juba, there were many demands for it, and the tree nursery held a low place on the list. Among the group of aid managers who decided allocation it was given low priority. Because it had a developmental dimension it was somehow assumed to be not quite so urgent as 'relief'.

For two years Linda Small had trained a local woman, Sunday Makelele, to take over from her as the person in charge of the nursery. In 1988, when Small was about to leave Juba and move with Melvyn Almond to Khartoum, the local committee refused to accept a woman as the head of the project. Small explained in a 1988 report for Oxfam:

They proposed a man to take over Sunday's job, even though she had been extremely well trained and had successfully run the project for 18 months. The proposed man had no experience of the programme... They commented that they had no objection to women doing the day-to-day manual labour, but they could not accept a woman in a salaried position, involving decision-making, responsibility and being head of the project. In Mundari society, traditionally only men are educated and they find it very difficult to accept that women are also capable of fulfilling such posts. No self-respecting Mundari man will take orders from a woman... Through depriving women of education, the men can maintain their elite position over the women.

The project management that refused to accept a woman to run the project was, Small writes, 'made up totally of men'. Should the Mundari be challenged? Small tried hard, calling on men in the Oxfam office to give support; but the issue of women earning money in a forest nursery never acquired the status, even within Oxfam, of a serious project. After months of work, Small achieved some success; the possibility of women managing their own project was recognized. She wrote:

After endless meetings between the committee and Oxfam, it was finally put to the vote. It was emphasized that local people working with, and enlightening, their own community are more likely to succeed. These local women who had gained valuable experience while involved in the Juba nursery can help build the strong foundation of community involvement. The vote went in favour of the women's project, with the statement: 'the nursery remains as a woman's project, with the decision-making and administrative posts to be held by women'. Women nursery assistants were then appointed. Sunday Makelele has continued to run the nursery as project manager very successfully to date, but has continuing problems with the committee, who do not give her the support and understanding they would for a man.

Later Small began to doubt whether the real reason for this concession was that Sunday Makelele was the chief's daughter. This made the affront to male supremacy bearable. It was not that Oxfam was unaware of the marginalization of women, but that despite all their analysis and self-criticism, Oxfam felt uncertain about challenging pastoralist society. The following year Oxfam brought in a gender adviser to work on the issues, but evacuated her almost immediately on the grounds that there were security threats and she was non-essential.

* * *

There is so much to learn and understand. After eight years of work on pastoralism in Sudan, Melvyn Almond wrote, as if he had only just arrived: 'The characteristics of pastoral communities – that is, their mobile nature and their suspicion and even contempt for outsiders – makes it difficult for an agency to develop a partnership with them. However, Oxfam has begun to tackle this problem.' The problems of being impartial assail us both from outside and from inside. To reach impartiality is to reach total self-knowledge, and perhaps that is unattainable. The fact that aid workers can never reach perfection does not mean that their work is a failure. On the contrary, Stockton's penetrating analysis and Almond's balanced wisdom are about as good as it gets. Perfection may come closer through partnerships and working together than it does through conflict and argument. Peace in Sudan is an issue for Sudanese people, but peace among aid workers is an issue for all who aspire to humanitarianism.

Chapter 4

Mozambique: Vulnerability and Power

M y left eardrum burst as we nose-dived in the little Cessna aeroplane to reach a small town in northern Mozambique. It was surrounded by RENAMO rebels, backed by the power of mighty South Africa, and we were coming to help the poor. I was sitting next to the pilot and, despite the pain, felt a responsibility not to distract him. I kept telling myself that a professional was in charge and I must abandon my fears to his superior skill and knowledge. The plane dropped downwards as if pressed by an invisible hand and the roofs of the houses lurched upwards. My eardrum seeped blood but I gave a faint smile in case the pilot was watching. Nothing mattered except his life-saving concentration. We flew above the track to the airstrip, with the dust spraying from the whirl of our propellers and children waving wildly, then rushing to hide as we passed them. Irritated with my own weakness I thrust the red-stained tissue into a sick bag and decided not to say anything. How could my small pain compare with the pain of Africa?

We shot suddenly into a gap between stands of elephant grass. I lifted my eyes from the pilot's controls in front of me to peer over the rim of the glass as our wheels lunged forward onto a bare, bumpy field. As the engines slowed, figures stepped out from the gigantic, reed-like stems. One man in ragged clothing was quietly sharpening a machete. At the end of the 'runway' the engine whined, and then its noise dropped lower, slowly ticking to stillness like dripping sweat. I could hear nothing in my left ear and felt disoriented by my earlier sense of fear. I glanced at the pilot gratefully. Strangely enough, there had been a pleasure in abandoning myself to his power and skill, knowing that I had no role in the issue of my own life and death, nothing to do, no responsibility. I had discovered the pleasure of vulnerability.

* * *

This was Mozambique at war and most people had nothing at all. They lived and died among the ever-circling machetes of the rebels, who crept up at night looking for victims off their guard. The life expectancy for young men was maybe a couple of years and for everyone the next night's attack might be the last. What did it matter if there was a little more blood? I felt a kind of solidarity with their suffering and told myself not to worry. As an aid manager it was a familiar process – adapting to a new place, absorbing its customs and values.

But this way of looking at things was also about to change. As the officials stepped forward deferentially to shake my hand, I felt pleasure in the reassuring sense of control over their lives, especially since I had been scared about my own. Slowly I reminded myself of who I was – a person with power, more power here in war-torn Mozambique than I could dream of in my own life in a village in England. I was here to decide whether people received life-saving aid, and whatever I chose they had to accept. Now, while the pilot saw to the straps that held the plane to the ground in case of high wind, the plane became a symbol of my wealth and power. The pilot who had seemed so powerful before would now have to wait for me, bored and inconsequential, while I rose to the peak of glory. Saving lives can be intoxicating, especially when people are weak and vulnerable.

All around there were signs of terrible poverty: ragged clothes on dirty skin, people with a sense of purposelessness and fear, tattered shops with nothing in them that had seen better days. Young men stood around with nothing to do but wonder at my appearance. A few women shuffled to get water and food, but for most of them there was no purpose in life except standing and watching. I felt a pang of fear as we walked away from the reassurance of the modern machine and the well-engineered gleam of the plane's propellers.

'Wait for me', I wanted to say.

I longed for the time when I would get back into the plane and it would all seem like a dream. Mozambicans at war had no permanence, no security. In contrast, I would soon fly back to concrete and brick, to offices and files. It was a pleasurable feeling. I was like the person who watches TV and reassures himself with images of starving people, before reaching for a pizza from the fridge.

I had to justify my imminent escape from Mozambique. I heard a voice inside me saying that if the Mozambicans were so poor and weak, perhaps they deserved what they got. What the bullies did was natural. Weak people needed to be treated roughly in order to bring them back to strength. And when I thought of my own power, I found deep in myself a desire to tease and ill-treat the victims of disaster, a pleasure in not giving rather than giving.

Is there something inherent in human nature that makes us react to weakness with feelings very different from human concern? We are supposed to feel concern and pity but sometimes the reaction to poverty is more like contempt. We have learned not to recognize these feelings; but that does not mean that they do not exist nor have an insidious effect, especially when we suddenly find ourselves in positions of power. Perhaps we see our own weakness in other people and want to vicariously punish ourselves. It is a reminder of days at school, when the values of civilization were suspended and we saw children cleverly identify and attack weaknesses in each other. Is this some collective instinct in our genes, derived from our history as hunters and gatherers? Is it part of ourselves?

The problem for humanitarians is that the motive of pity so easily interacts with the motive for cruelty, and the desire to help so easily becomes the desire for power. Outer values often mean that we overcome or hide such feelings, but this does not mean that they have no effect.

The aid relationship is generally described in moral terms such as 'helping' and 'concern', but the underlying imbalance between Western resources and the vulnerability of poor people, especially in times of disaster, creates the possibility of abuse of power. We work in circumstances where both bully and victim can emerge. Alex de Waal has depicted a 'disaster relief industry' that revels in such power, but I doubt if he has identified anything other than a natural human tendency and therefore has not depicted the tragedy of the humanitarians who find themselves to be cruel. Managers in the 'disaster relief industry', like those in charge of homes for children or the elderly, have the opportunity to abuse power because they are dealing with vulnerable people. To assume that humanitarians always succumb to this temptation is insulting, but to bring it into the open as a problem of human nature may help. We live in a post-optimistic age in which the assumptions of a past generation are no longer valid. We used to believe that aid workers and those who care for children are above human temptation. But in recent years there have been serious scandals, not only relating to the abuse of children by those running children's homes in the UK, but also by aid workers abroad.

But what can be done about the imbalance between the powerful and the weak and the abuse of power by those who give aid? They may not force children into sex, but they might design a refugee camp in their own way rather than in the way that the people want. And they might do so not because they are ignorant, but because they enjoy their own sense of power.

Charles Dickens wrote a great deal about the abuse of power. His descriptions of Mr Bumble's self-importance in *Oliver Twist* are particularly well known. Bumble revels in his power over the children in the workhouse. Dickens contrasts this with his abject weakness in relation to his wife. After being humiliated by her, he reacts by shouting at paupers, and his life falls apart when he can no longer do this. It is easy to understand, in Dickens's fictional world, that being horrible to someone weak makes us feel better. Dickens points out that power in the hands of the weak is dangerous. His heroes are often men of immense physical and psychological power, such as Joe Gargery in *Great Expectations*, who deliberately allow themselves to be dominated by others. In Joe's case he allows his wife to bully him because his own father was violent towards his mother and he does not want to repeat that mistake. But this is not to say he is never tempted.

Of all humanitarian temptations, the abuse of power is the most persistent and the most undermining. It occurs not only in the relationship of aid giver to recipient but also within the internal functions of aid organizations. It is all too possible for the person who puts self first, exploits power for its own sake and then conceals it, to rise to prominence in aid work because so many others are struggling to put self second. This abuse may be unrecognized by the person concerned and the issue only becomes apparent when personal power is challenged. I have noticed that the benevolent white-haired patriarchs who present a kindly image of aid agencies to the public can be surprisingly ruthless when it comes to their own power and dignity. This is not an individual fault but a problem likely to arise where the issue of power is swept under the carpet.

The abuse of power in relation to those in need contrasts starkly with the principle of humanity. Instead of 'concern for the person in need', the motive is concern for the self, a kind of self-pity that manifests itself in the desire for power over others. It can become institutionalized as an identification of personal power with the power of the organization, and the power of the organization with the needs of the poor. Such people often argue that any criticism of the agency will undermine the interests of the poor, when what they really mean is that it will undermine their own sense of security.

* * *

During my visit to Mozambique, I was travelling with two other aid representatives. After our plane landed, we were led quickly to see the administrator, a tall man in a shabby blue-grey suit who somehow reminded me of my uncle. This altered the way I thought about him, making me more sympathetic but also bringing in other attitudes which I might have been less able to identify. We greeted each other, and having exhausted my Portuguese very quickly, continued speaking through an interpreter. I was about to commence my usual series of questions (how many men, women and children; what are their main needs; what other help have you received?) when he suddenly motioned us outside onto the dusty street. We walked quickly behind him, trying to keep up as he strode ahead past the remnants of shops where people bowed their heads as he passed. There was nothing to buy and people were just idling away the time. Nothing ever reached Nipepe, 800 kilometres from Maputo and surrounded by rebels. At the end of the 'street' (or rather an oblong of dust which became unrecognizable at the edge of the village) a crowd of people stood with their backs to us. As we approached, they turned one by one and, seeing the administrator, fell back to leave an opening through the crowd. We emerged into a circle of people, and an arena of bare earth.

For a few moments I wondered what was happening, expecting that perhaps the administrator intended to make a speech to the people. I was preparing myself for a long and boring occasion, and wondering how I might be able stop it, when I saw two naked men tied together with thick ropes which wound over their shoulders and fastened their hands and feet together. They were big heavy men, smeared in ash. Because of the tight ropes their limbs were all muddled up as if they were wrestling, and it was difficult to tell which belonged to each man – a heap of man and muscle. They were smeared with ash and blood. As I looked more closely I saw that on their bare skin there were cut marks, and the flesh inside was sprinkled with dust. It was beginning to peel away, as if someone had pulled it back to see what was underneath. One of the men looked up at me quickly with a sullen, apologetic kind of expression. The whites of his eyes flashed, but there was no recognition in his eyes, only (as I thought to myself) a quick, frightened return into the blank comfort of his heart. The other one did not look up, but kept his head turned to one side as if he resented our arrival and was angry with the delay. As we waited and tried to make sense of what we saw, his finger touched the ground and moved in a circle like a little boy playing with sand.

For many years I 'forgot' the scene and I never talked about it at the time. Then gradually I made myself peel back the skin of memory. Now I can admire the image of those huge magnificent limbs like classical statues. The muscles of the men seemed heavy and strong compared with the emaciated figures in rags who stood around watching. The administrator in his old suit still reminded me of my uncle going to Sunday chapel. Around them I can see machetes in the hands of those who were waiting to resume the killing. It is strange that the men on the ground appeared to be the strong ones with massive muscles. The killers were thin and weak. But they were getting their revenge. There were cuts on the men's faces, over their eyes and on their cheeks. Flies had began to gather on the open wounds.

As we turned away, following the administrator, I wanted to ask and speak, but there was no question, and I realized that the event needed no spoken explanation. The men on the ground were from the 'armed bands', the fearful phrase for RENAMO guerrillas. The administrator was showing them to us. They were probably local lads who had broken away from the town and joined the rebels to escape from a life that seemed boring and pointless. I finally realized that they had been captured during the previous night's attack before we arrived.

I felt keen to go back to the administrator's residence, or 'bungalow'. There we were given long speeches about the way in which the men had been captured and how the officials had managed the fight. We were given descriptions of RENAMO forces and what they were doing, told about plans and fears, and asked to tell Maputo to send guns because they were nearly out of ammunition and without it the town would be overrun and everybody killed. The roles were suddenly reversed. The administrator had the power, and now he gave us a long lecture on the district's aid problems. But we had lost the desire to pursue the conversation. We had lost interest even in our own subject; we could not recall the confidence of power. He was no longer the man we had met earlier – a person in need. Instead, he was a man revelling in victory.

We checked what time we were leaving, calculating and exaggerating the minimum hours to reach Maputo safely before dark. Already I was beginning to imagine the comfort of the plane, the pilot's reassuring stripes on the epaulettes of his crisp pale-blue shirt, his baseball cap and friendly greeting. I said that we must leave, and rather hoped that I would get a seat at the back this time, where I could huddle against the luggage in silence.

The yellowish wall of the administrator's room had stains on it like a map. As I listened to the drone of voices, I formed the impression that it represented an ancient vellum chart that Portuguese navigators might have used to show their ever-increasing colonies. The administrator sat in a grotesquely carved chair behind a massive table, all remnants of Portuguese rule, too heavy for them to take away. The Portuguese had abandoned the country when FRELIMO made it too expensive to stay, and they destroyed almost everything when they left as an expression of hatred towards those they had ruled. I reflected on the history of oppression and power – the Portuguese farmers, treated as dirt in their own country, now lording it over the Mozambicans and finding excuses in religion and culture to whip, rape and enslave those who were weaker and poorer than themselves. Historians said that the Portuguese made the worst colonists because they sent the poorest people, who had been bullied themselves and were unused to exercising power, whereas the British sent the richest, who might be arrogant but were used to handling power.

FRELIMO began as a rebel movement, ejecting the Portuguese by force, and leading the people towards a socialist utopia. Russians, Cubans and Chinese were sent to help, while in the West, even during my university days, Mozambique was a favoured destination for idealists. Christians pushed bibles into Mozambique in opposition to FRELIMO's atheism, and right-wing whites in surrounding countries set up RENAMO as a way of defeating socialism. Mozambique was the place where everyone tried out their ideals and fought out their emotional battles.

The result of war was terrible destruction and human suffering. I interviewed a woman who had just fled from Mozambique and was in a refugee camp in Malawi, just across the border, and wrote afterwards:

Her name was Martha Zeka, about 30 years old from the Chale area of Mutarara district. We saw her in a group of 10 women, 2 men and 19 children who had arrived just a few days before and were sitting under a tree to protect themselves from the burning heat. Most of the children were naked. Martha wore only a sack wrapped round her waist, and was trying to get her two sons, aged maybe eight and ten, to eat some of the pumpkin that she had found growing wild in the nearby swamps.

The children were in a dreadful state – emaciated, listless. One of them coughed continuously as he lay under a covering of sackcloth, while his mother waved her hand across his face to drive away the flies. She had given birth to eight children of whom three had died before she left Mozambique. For three years she had lived in an area controlled by RENAMO, much of the time hiding in the bush and living off what they could steal from the fields that they used to own. Finally her husband was captured and taken away, and she decided to flee to Malawi. First of all, she sent the four older children ahead with some relatives, for it was impossible for her to manage so many children. Then she set off with her baby, naked, running through the night in fear of the bandits and wild animals.

On the way she was captured by a RENAMO gang and forced to (walk with them). On the excuse of passing water she went behind a bush. A soldier followed her, but she went further, and eventually managed to slip away, holding the child, and run through the undergrowth, while the RENAMO soldiers tried to find her. In the end they moved on and she walked for six days, eating nothing, moving only under cover of darkness until she reached Malawi.

Finally, she arrived at Nsanje and was relieved to find that her other children had arrived there safely. But the day before we came, the baby died. She told us in a matter-of-fact, far-away voice, as she fingered the unwanted pumpkin on a rafia bowl that she had borrowed from her friends.

It would be hard to imagine greater suffering. And yet there were 170,000 people on the plains of Nsanje, each of whom could have told a similar story.

Examining the story now I can see that it has positive aspects. The woman was greatly helped by her relatives, and despite all of her suffering she retained the determination to look after her children and to escape. There is even a hint that the RENAMO soldier may have colluded in her escape.

But officials in Mozambique became used to the world's pity and would say: 'Just give us what you can. Plead with your governments to give us more. Help us run our country.' And by deliberately exaggerating their weakness they could attract the attention of aid donors who wanted to feel strong. In Mozambique it was easy to believe that we had the right answers because no one else had any at all. What I came to realize only very slowly was the sophistication of African abilities, or rather the ability of African leaders to exploit the white outsider's perception that only he is strong. I suspect that it derives from the way that they often handle their own leaders, puffing up their pride until it bursts.

By appearing weak, a person can attract the protection of someone stronger. Similarly, the strong person can be challenged by someone who is perceived to be even more powerful. Because the objective of aid agencies is to identify with the weak, they may oppose the strong. In the 1980s, while war and famine raged in Mozambique, the ideology of aid agencies was dominated by opposition to apartheid in South Africa. This was undoubtedly a very important cause, but it blinded aid agencies to problems within Mozambique itself. Opposition to apartheid fitted the aid agencies' perception of themselves as fierce opponents of anything resembling racism. Practically all aid agencies in Mozambique operated on a policy of unquestioning support for or solidarity with FRELIMO. There was no semblance of neutrality. RENAMO was the enemy.

By extension, Mozambique became the friend – but not an equal. If South Africa was strong, Mozambique had to be characterized as weak. It could have no abilities or capacities of its own. It was the 'does he take sugar?' syndrome, in which the disabled person is assumed to be unable to say how she likes to drink her tea.

* * *

However keen we were to get back to the comfort of Maputo, before leaving Nipepe we had to go through the motions of being aid workers. We talked to people, determined categories of need, worked out requirements for stocks, food and clothes and recorded the findings in our notebooks. We then made our exit, hurrying onto the plane, checking that the sick bags were available in case we hit a thundercloud. I already imagined the airport in Maputo and the little fork-lift trucks (a fantasy) that would rush out reassuringly when we arrived. I was rather pleased with myself because I had identified a need for women's clothing and I was fairly sure that we would be able to send a large amount soon. This seemed to put a satisfactory end to the visit. Something could be done. Papers could be written, forms filled out. And so it became possible to convert the image of suffering into a schedule of activity – activity directed by ourselves.

The issue of women's clothing had been overlooked by most other aid agencies, perhaps on the basis that people could stay alive without clothing. This relief operation was about saving lives. But a particular advantage of the clothing was that it gave women the confidence to work in the fields or take their children to clinics. Dressed only in bits of bark they would not. Also, it enhanced dignity, and I was beginning to realize that this had value in itself, although it was difficult to articulate it within the language of aid agencies. I had become disillusioned with the interminable programmes of food aid which seemed so undignified and kept people from their homes and from taking control of their own lives.

As we took off I again had to sit next to the pilot (in order to balance the distribution of weight) and watched the shifting lights of the control panel. The sky rose up like a great fish shooting out of the sea. Internationally, we would become Mozambican advocates and prise funds out of unwilling donors. We had 'right' on our side. We could walk into rooms and demand donations. On the basis of a couple of days of visits in Maputo and London we could quickly become experts on Mozambican poverty. The clouds floated over the ocean as we sped down the coast far away from the rebels.

At some point on that flight, I remembered a boy at school who was being beaten up and humiliated by older boys. He was huddled up naked on the floor in the showers, crying. He looked up at me and I felt no pity but only disgust, and fear for myself, and almost a sense of rejoicing because it was not me. I felt a sudden and deep sense of shame about those men's deaths in Nipepe, but there was nothing I could do. A few clothes would clear us of the deed. To do nothing at all would be worse. And so I worked and pushed to get those clothes to Nipepe, and succeeded. And I forgot about the incident until many years later when I began to unravel the reasons for what I had done.

So many aid workers played out their past and their own problems over the lives of the poor. Here is a description of a visit, akin to my own but described by a follower of an evangelist missionary, Ellie Hein, whose father had been killed by black activists in Zimbabwe (formerly Rhodesia). She arrived in a remote part of Mozambique that was controlled by RENAMO.

The next morning we discovered that thousands of people had gathered not far from the village centre, in anticipation of a religious service and the distribution of goods. All around us we saw people affected by the war: a man with no arm, a woman with no foot, small malnourished children sitting for lack of energy in the dust, ill-clad women holding naked infants crying with hunger in the folds of their arms. Few people were properly clothed. Some were fortunate to have secured burlap sacks or parachute material to wrap around them. The look of poverty, depredation and starvation was evident.

Ellie had planned to preach but when we arrived she was horrified to discover that the gathered worshippers belonged to a Zionist sect whom she regarded as heathens. Although she gave a short sermon, translated by a RENAMO leader, the crowd was anxious for its own leaders to resume. Ellie quickly escorted us away to find another service, but that one turned out to be Catholic. The South African Broadcasting Company (SABC) camera crew, impatient for good footage, had RENAMO stage a scene of 'happy' villagers harvesting the fields. A few villagers with implements were taken out into the field and told to sing and chant.

So fierce was Hein's commitment to religion that she seemed to exploit human suffering. Like other aid agencies, Oxfam was constantly publishing articles and books that used examples of suffering in Mozambique as arguments against apartheid. Lists of damage to the Mozambican economy were not being used as indicators of suffering but as charges against white South Africans. This seemed to be more a power struggle between whites than a humanitarian attempt to understand the needs of blacks. And in pursuing it, aid agencies ignored what was actually happening in Mozambique. In order to blame South Africa for everything, Mozambique could not take any blame, and therefore no one looked for faults.

Oxfam collected and published stories such as this one from Senhora Paulina Chauque, who was midwife at the health centre in Chicualacuala on the railway line leading into Zimbabwe. Describing the RENAMO guerrillas, she says:

They used to come into the villages to steal food. They would take the food and make people carry it to their camps. They would say they had come to liberate the people, and when they were in power no one would have to queue for food or clothes. Some people believed them, others didn't. In 1984 they began killing people.

On 2 October 1985 I was in my village of Mpuzi when they came. They began shooting and everyone ran into the bush. They killed four villagers; I knew them all, they were relatives. The bandits burned the school and seven houses... the bandits are the enemy of the state and of the people.

They only want to kill people. When they catch children they kill them. How could they govern if ever they get power? What will they be like if they kill children? If a bandit is caught they should do to him what the bandits have done to the people.

Chauque's statement that 'the bandits are the enemy of the state and of the people' reads like a political slogan and probably is. It was what she was meant to say, and so she said it. This is not very surprising since she worked for the government and would lose her job if she said anything else. Furthermore, interviews by aid workers invariably took place in public. Chauque's story is typical of hundreds that aid agencies quoted as examples of popular opposition to South African apartheid. The problem was portrayed as if women like Chauque were constantly bothering themselves with the situation in Soweto, or pondering the relative merits of socialism and capitalism – just as Ellie Hein behaved as if the issue was which church people belonged to. In Mozambique, aid agencies were perceived by the people as being part of the government – and this was a fair assumption, because most agencies, including Oxfam, adopted a position of solidarity. As a result, aid workers were unlikely to hear anything other than what they expected to hear and what the government wanted them to hear. The effect was that we drastically underestimated the level of popular support for RENAMO, and failed to see crucial weaknesses in FRELIMO that had a bearing on the aid programme. Wanting people to appear weak, we were not conscious enough of the power of propaganda and self-deception. Or put another way, we exploited Mozambique for its potential to offer material that would support strategic public campaigns.

On my first visit to Mozambique in 1986 the issues had seemed very clear. I visited Chicualacuala, a little ghost town near the border with Zimbabwe.

The railway station, at the border itself, still bears the scars of vicious attacks by Ian Smith's forces pursuing guerrillas into Mozambique during the Rhodesian war. The blue-tiled station and most of the houses are riddled with bullet-holes... We travelled with an escort of eight soldiers, including one with a bazooka who was in the habit of perching precariously at the back of the army lorry that took us on our journeys out of town. When some villagers took a ride with us the weapons were passed around to those sitting in the most convenient places. One young man ended up with a steel-band record in one hand and a Kalashnikov in the other. A woman sat on the floor cradling the famous bazooka.

The attitude of FRELIMO soldiers was always friendly and courteous, not only to us but also to the village people. There was no suggestion of any lack of trust. The last major incident in the district was in April when a truck similar to ours was ambushed. One person was killed and several injured including the same director of agriculture who came with us on our journey – his hand still bandaged.

I admired the bravery of the director of agriculture and the lightly armed young men who were trying to help people in the remote villages. They risked their lives on every journey. Because we were on the same side I did not question what they were doing, nor what I was doing myself. During the 1980s in Mozambique, it had become normal practice for aid personnel to travel with military protection and, because FRELIMO's army was considered 'weak', for aid agencies to pay for military escorts. The military was given at least enough money to cover the fuel. Sometimes it was not clear whose pocket this money was going into, but 'solidarity' mode meant that few questions were asked. Agencies chose not to ask whether these escorts might gather intelligence while acting under the cover of aid, or use the opportunity to move troops around while defended by emblems of aid. As time went on the army began to demand more money and better protection. It claimed not to have appropriate vehicles for escort duty and donors should not expect soldiers to sit on the sides of open trucks and drive along roads where guerrillas could easily be hidden in the long grass. Nor, they said, was it reasonable to expect soldiers to travel in vehicles that had no protection against land mines, which were the most serious threat to life. Land mines accounted for 50 per cent of all casualties during the war, even though, to be accurate, most of them had been laid by the government. The army needed to fix steel plates under the chassis. Would donors pay?

Oxfam's director, on a visit to Mozambique, was horrified to see a large gun mounted on an Oxfam truck. He took up the matter with the British ambassador, who persuaded him that this was nothing special and that all aid agencies did the same. 'Unless such things happen, the relief goods will not arrive', he pointed out. There was nothing to be gained, he said, from expressions of principle when people were starving.

After some debate, Oxfam continued to allow troops on its vehicles and gave fuel for military escorts. Iron sheeting was provided to build shields on the sides of trucks. Furthermore, Oxfam urged the UK government, which was already training officers of FRELIMO's army in special camps in Zimbabwe, to supply further military equipment that would enable FRELIMO to carry out escort duty for humanitarian purposes. All this seemed justifiable at the time because it was aimed at equalling the odds with the massive power of apartheid.

However, over the years, I began to see the issue in a different light. On my next visit, in 1988, I visited the town of Mocuba, which had been attacked recently by RENAMO, and held long discussions with the administrator. The night before I arrived, his nine-year-old daughter had been captured, repeatedly raped and sent back to him. I felt unable to ask more than a few cursory questions about the supply of food and clothing and left quickly. We persuaded the government's emergency department in Maputo (DPCCN) to despatch food immediately, and Oxfam supplied women's *capulanas*, which by now had become an essential part of our response. I recorded complaints about:

> ... *chronic breakdowns in the economy and transport system, leading to a collapse of the market economy. Since nothing is available in the shops, rural people have no incentive to produce or market surpluses. As a result, there is no food available in the towns, nor any consumer goods available in the rural areas.*

But I excused FRELIMO from blame, because of incidents like the rape of the administrator's daughter in Mocuba. We assumed that because people were suffering, they must be good and they must be helpless. When I travelled in Chacualcuala with the director of the agricultural marketing organization, I had not asked questions about his work but just assumed that he was advising farmers. I assumed he had little power to do more. But gradually a very different picture of agricultural marketing began to emerge. By a series of chances I learned that food grown on collective farms or procured at low prices from farmers was hoarded in warehouses even when there was famine. Huge amounts of money were involved in these transactions and the directors of agricultural marketing were very powerful people. In fact, official food policy was partly responsible for the famine.

One of these chance encounters occurred when I returned to Mocuba, the town where the administrator's daughter had been raped. While doing the usual tour of the town, I haphazardly asked what was in a warehouse. I was astonished to find, after four years of sending food aid halfway around the world, that it contained several tonnes of locally grown maize that a local official said was rotting because no one had the money to buy it. When I asked what was in other warehouses, which I had assumed to be empty because Mozambique was 'devastated', it turned out that there was more food. Large stocks were available inside Mozambique and were actually stored inside the 'famine' areas, just as I had found in Tigray in Ethiopia:

At Mocuba in Zambezia we found that DPCCN [government emergency department] had virtually no food and was predicting starvation and death for the deslocados [displaced people] in Lugela. The problem was said to be a lack of convoys from Quelimane. These, in turn, were said to be stopped due to fuel shortages and the absence of armed escorts. But only a few yards from the DPCCN office there were hundreds of tonnes of food stored by a private trader. DPCCN had no funds to make a purchase; or if they had the funds there was no procedure to buy it locally. Instead, a shipment of food was being organized from Pemba, using 175,000 ECUs. Even more ironically, it was known that food from Mocuba was being smuggled down to Quelimane to be sold to the urban middle classes for double the official market price.

Like the disabled person who is assumed to be unable to say whether she wants sugar in her tea, Mozambique was assumed by outsiders to be incapable of feeding itself. The South African-backed attacks were supposed to have destroyed everything. In a sense, we wanted Mozambique to be weak in order to caricature the nature of apartheid. We constantly published figures showing how many roads, houses, schools and hospitals had been destroyed. Because Mozambique was too weak to defend itself, it followed in our argument that it was too weak to feed itself. Time after time during the 1980s we had defended the Mozambican government against criticism. Yet it was now apparent that it could have done much more.

In this case, Oxfam quickly arranged to buy the food in Mocuba and sent it to the famine area. But how had such a possibility been overlooked for so long? Having realized that there was food available inside Mozambique, I came across case after case of unnecessary and senseless starvation:

Two days later we flew into Maua, Niassa and found that DPCCN had nothing to give to the 12,000 displaced. There was food in the AGRICOM (state agricultural marketing company) warehouse but people had not found a way of buying it. Moreover, the AGRICOM representative said that much more food was available with the farmers. It would rot unless collected. The representative had the money to buy it – the problem was lack of sacks in which to collect it. Where were the sacks? In Cuamba waiting to be airlifted. We spoke to the provincial delegate in Lichinga. His problem was lack of foreign exchange to move the sacks.

The lack of sacks and foreign exchange was a problem that the government could have addressed easily if it had the will to do so. Numerous aid agencies were trying to strengthen their capacity, and the government was being paid large amounts in foreign exchange for internal transport of food. Once I knew what questions to ask, the answers became clear. The problem was not lack of knowledge or even lack of will by the local officials. The problem lay in the functioning of government. I noted that the head of AGRICOM in the province of Niassa:

... was extremely keen to market the surpluses in Niassa to DPCCN. He estimated that in the province as a whole 11,000 tonnes was the marketable surplus in 1989 and it could increase dramatically if there were more buyers. He pointed out that money paid out to the farmers for food then stimulates the economy. It attracts small traders to bring in goods such as salt, sugar and soap. It is the key to economic recovery.

Government had created a problem through the rigid application of socialist ideology. It discouraged and ignored private enterprise, yet left its own structures so badly run that the famine relief operation was a shambles.

Amartya Sen's entitlement theory was proving itself true yet again. It was not that there was no food in the areas where people were starving but that they had no power to buy it; as a result, it was being channelled to the cities, where people were better off. Conceivably, this suited the government rather well. At the same time, food aid was being brought in from abroad and channelled through the cities to the rural areas. Rich people were profiting by both transactions. Government restrictions had simply created a thriving parallel system, a black economy that diverted resources to people with influence and money. Merchants had been able to find ways to transport food despite all of the FRELIMO restrictions and RENAMO threats. In spite of the war and apartheid, the economy was functioning, although not in a way that outsiders could easily recognize. One could not help but suspect that government officials had a stake in these illicit deals, and closer links with the merchants than they cared to acknowledge in public. Were we beginning to see why so many people supported RENAMO, which hitherto had remained a mystery, explained only by the 'cunning' of the South Africans and the 'ignorance' of the Mozambicans.

Other aid organizations also began to notice the phenomenon of food availability in the famine areas and, joining together, we persuaded the UN's World Food Programme to start a nationwide programme of food swaps. But the UN responded lethargically. Their staff took a very long time to arrive and then received little cooperation from the higher authorities. Senior UN officials gave little backing. Before the problem was solved, the war had ended and the situation changed.

It may appear surprising that the donors who were sending food aid from abroad did not make more fuss. But there were powerful political interests surrounding food aid. The US bought food surpluses from American farmers as part of a long-standing government policy of appeasing this largest and best organized of all the political lobbies. No US government dared risk stopping the flow. In Europe there was also a strong link between the disposal of food surpluses, the Common Agricultural Policy (CAP) and humanitarian aid, although this is much less the case today. Aid departments were concerned with getting rid of fixed tonnages of surplus food. The availability of food 'in-country' was not their concern. Similarly, the UN's food agency, the World Food Programme, had been set up to handle Western food aid and charged an overhead of around 7 per cent over and above actual costs on food aid transactions undertaken on behalf of donors.

Aid managers like myself might be disappointed to find that where the interests of Western donors conflicted with those of Mozambique, their own interests prevailed. But it was not difficult to understand or come to terms with ideologically. At that time, aid agencies tended to be critical of international institutions. In the early 1980s, Oxfam had launched a critique of food aid in a book called *Against the Grain*. What was new in the Mozambique experience was the evidence that private enterprise might offer better solutions than socialism. Most aid agencies were deeply imbued with a principle that companies, and indeed any forms of organized power, were wrong. This also led to a tendency to favour the weak along with an exaggeration of their weakness. As time went on the record of the government became worse and worse.

Inefficiency and corruption were too widespread to be overlooked. At the end of 1990 I wrote: 'USAID said that its food losses are unacceptable [12 per cent at port of entry and up to 50 per cent after that] and so have decided to direct all their assistance to NGOs such as World Vision.'

I had noticed that as the Cold War ended, Mozambique was losing its traditional support from socialist countries and the US was becoming extremely powerful: 'It is widely expected that the changes in Eastern Europe and the USSR will result in a dramatic decrease in the currently high numbers of Eastern-bloc advisers. This will leave huge gaps.'

But we did not think that this meant the end of socialism. Indeed, we saw the change as a threat to developmental objectives. My report refers optimistically to various Scandinavian donors stepping forward, and they may indeed have had some influence in the universities. However, the US not only had the weight of its own massive aid programme but could also use the International Monetary Fund (IMF) to impose its will in relation to fundamental economic and political issues.

For the aid agencies, these changes directly affected the issue of trucking, with agencies like Oxfam and Save the Children trying to support the government's fleet, and the US trying to privatize it. When I first visited Mozambique in 1986, the government was in charge of a large fleet of trucks that was used to deliver all humanitarian aid. This had a political effect that we tacitly approved of as an aspect of our fight against apartheid; all such aid was seen as coming from FRELIMO. Oxfam supported the government's trucking operation, adding 28 trucks paid for by BandAid. But by 1988, the US was pressing the government to give up its central role in transport and to encourage privatization. They used their influence over food aid shipments to give CARE, a business-minded US NGO, the role of advising government on the management of the fleet. With US support, CARE gradually became more and more dominant. Their idea was to introduce business methods and eventually privatize the fleet. To Oxfam, which was still running a major campaign against apartheid, there was deep suspicion that such weakening of FRELIMO indicated support for rich South African businessmen and therefore for apartheid. There was also a perception that the 'enemy' RENAMO was the party of privatization. Oxfam and Save the Children–UK (SCF–UK) both actively continued to support government-run workshops where the trucks were serviced.

Wary of the philosophy behind the CARE operation, I was quick to pick up on any failure. When CARE was slow in clearing the BandAid trucks I met its director to express Oxfam's concern. Seeing the large numbers of staff, I questioned whether CARE was undermining the government, and was told outright: 'Large government-run operations do not work... by establishing these workshops we are doing the country a disservice by not allowing the private sector to develop.' I recorded my astonishment: 'There is a serious problem if the man supposed to provide the government's main logistic support for its fleet and workshops can express views directly hostile to his main purpose.'

But there were different purposes here. Oxfam saw the purpose as being support for government, but the US/CARE position was support for the private sector. This became one of the crucial issues for aid agencies at the end of the Cold War. Most agencies, like Oxfam, had begun as popular movements around ideals, but had gradually come to resemble businesses, although remaining critical of business methods. As the ideological struggle between state and private sector increased, fuelled by donors and especially by the US, aid agencies were caught in a problem of identity. What were they? Some, such as SCF–UK, continued to focus on the role of support to government. Others like CARE acted as the vanguard of privatization. Oxfam sought to continue the older 'popular movement' type of work through its global advocacy on debt and trade, but with an increasingly business-like operation, raising funds in a very commercial manner and taking contracts from donors to run humanitarian relief.

The trucking issue in Mozambique also illustrates how the donors were now stepping forward to dominate political decision-making – from being dormant during the Cold War – even in times of humanitarian disaster. The donors promoted private enterprise and tended to be less inhibited by the ideological positions of the past. By 1990, there was clear opposition between aid agencies supporting FRELIMO as a proponent of socialism, and donors advocating private enterprise. The aid agencies reacted particularly strongly because private enterprise was associated with RENAMO. But gradually the certainties of the 1980s began to weaken. There were indications that RENAMO was not quite so bad or as unpopular as the aid agencies had imagined. The argument that RENAMO was purely a creation of apartheid was already wearing thin. Its increasing strength and widening field of activity did not seem to relate to the gradual weakening of hard-line politics in South Africa. A study of one district by K B Wilson concluded: 'Until the army counter-offensive in late 1990, RENAMO operated an administrative regime that was neither particularly intrusive nor violent, and that provided very basic health and educational services and allowed for some market activity.'

Gradually aid agencies realized that the people of Mozambique did not see things in simple black-and-white terms. However hard Oxfam tried to support the government, it found itself stumbling into private enterprise roles almost by accident. In 1986, when Oxfam started a programme of distributing women's *capulanas* by contacting private companies in Malawi and Zimbabawe, I assumed that there was nothing available in Mozambique. In 1988 I was astonished to learn that a government factory near Maputo was making them and I made plans to switch our purchases there, assuming that it would be a much cheaper option. But when Oxfam's purchasing specialists finished their investigations it turned out that the clothes from Maputo would be much more expensive. The government-run factory was hopelessly inefficient. Luckily we discovered that there was a practically defunct textile factory called FAVEZAL in Quelimane, Zambezia, close to the area where the clothes were needed. It was privately run by a Pakistani family, who had made themselves known to Oxfam's local representative. The price was competitive and Oxfam's contracts soon revived it as a thriving enterprise. Other aid agencies also gave FAVEZAL contracts, and once it became clear that goods could be purchased within Mozambique, other factories were discovered. To a large extent the problem was that no one had looked, because they did not expect to find such factories. We thought Mozambique was too weak and too devastated, and too much a victim of external aggression. There was also, perhaps, a lack of interest in supporting private enterprise.

Similarly, Oxfam had bought seeds from government agencies but found them unreliable. Purchases could be made through commercial suppliers more cheaply and efficiently. However, Oxfam was uneasy about this and attempted to buy them directly from local farmers, forming them into cooperatives. Nevertheless, the farmers lacked the essential skills to run such an organization and what Oxfam called a cooperative was really a type of private enterprise in which Oxfam was the entrepreneur, using its local staff to keep the operation going. This reflected the national situation. State farms and people's cooperatives often operated as the private companies of powerful FRELIMO leaders. Finding neither system ideal, aid agencies set up their own small workshops and factories that combined employment for local people and supply of materials for the relief programmes. But with their high expatriate management costs, these were inefficient and could be accused by the US embassy and others of undermining private enterprise. Gradually aid agencies became aware that their activities were not separate and detached from arguments about economic systems, which were as much a cause of war as South African apartheid. Their intervention amounted to a political statement about the benefits of old FRELIMO socialism. It was telling the people of Mozambique what to do and how to think: whether to take sugar.

At the time I felt deeply uneasy about all this, because it seemed to involve a shift in our fundamental values. I wrote: 'The whole issue of emergency relief in Mozambique is pervaded by the pressure to privatize from donors and the consequent weakening of government services.' But I had to admit that the state-run response was not working in relation to our fundamental mandate: 'The relief programme is an utter failure. Despite increasingly good pledges and food deliveries at the ports, deliveries to provincial level and beyond are totally inadequate. In most cases only a tenth or less of estimated needs are being met by food aid.'

In the end I put my concern for the needs of the people first and 'moved' my ideology aside to be worked on at a later date. The joint-agency famine assessment in which I participated in 1990 concluded that the only way forward was for the donors to give the responsibility for trucking entirely to the private sector and to abandon FRELIMO as a source of military escort. We were even prepared to privatize security: 'Informal military services [security companies] seem to be much more reliable than use of the army.'

For many aid workers there was a gradual and painful process of disillusionment with FRELIMO. It was hard to escape the conclusion that the purposeful socialism we had supported in the mid-1980s had sunk through lethargy and a sense of purposelessness into outright mental and financial corruption. But the evidence was overwhelming. I wrote:

When we arrived in Cuamba we heard that the district DPCCN director, who had stolen thousands of pounds worth of Oxfam relief goods, had been released from prison; the charges were lifted and he had been reinstated in his post. Even the most ardent Mozambique-lovers are becoming alarmed at the spread of corruption – all the more noticeable in a country that (even when I first came in 1986) was remarkable for its naive honesty.

Whose 'naive honesty' was the problem, I began to wonder?

* * *

Outsiders had decided that FRELIMO was overwhelmingly better for the people of Mozambique than RENAMO. But when elections finally took place in October 1994, and for the first time there was an indication of what the people themselves thought, the outcome was not what outsiders had expected. Public opinion was almost equally divided. RENAMO took 112 seats against 129 for FRELIMO. It was also a surprise that despite terrible transport problems in reaching the polling stations, over 80 per cent of those registered actually voted. In most of the remote districts where Oxfam had worked during the war, including the one where the two RENAMO rebels were killed, the vote was massively in favour of RENAMO. The victim had decided to speak.

For aid workers, the weakness of others is a terrible temptation. Solidarity, or identification with the person in need, is different from concern. It assumes that we know what the other person is thinking and that we have a similarity of views that enables us to act on their behalf. The person caring for the disabled person speaks for them about their choice of sugar. Aid agencies ignore local capacities such as stocks of food and views about RENAMO, but make public statements on behalf of the poor without always checking that they have the right to do so.

We enjoy our power, and by implication the other person's weakness. This is not altruism at all, only a hidden and profound selfishness.

Chapter 5
Afghanistan: Pride and Principle

O ur default position, I suspect, is the enjoyment of power rather than the application of altruism. Therefore we have to strive against ourselves. Otherwise, ideology and principle can be manipulated by our personalities. Some ideologies, such as socialism, appeal to us on a more intellectual level. The issues are 'outside'. But principles come from within our emotional being – the value system that drives our own lives. These can be much more difficult to adapt to the needs of altruism.

* * *

I was smuggled across the Afghanistan border in 1989, disguised as a Pushtun tribesman, wearing *salwar-kamiz* and turban, and having to take off my glasses whenever I might be spotted by the Pakistani security forces. Luckily, I already had a beard, so did not need to cover my face in sheep's wool, as my colleague on this journey had done. It was my first and only participation in 'the great game' – the age-old rivalry between the West and Russia, fought out through shifting allegiances among the tribesmen of the Asian frontier. I entered Afghanistan as a Western emissary of the Cold War, escorted by heavily armed Mujahadin guerrillas. The Mujahadin were financed by the US to fight against the communist government in Kabul, which was similarly propped up by the Russians. It was the one place where the Cold War was distinctly warm. The Russian army itself was involved, and US military support to the Mujahadin extended to sophisticated equipment such as ground-to-air missiles. The result, in the arid semi-desert of the Afghan mountains, was the Cold War's most destructive battlefield, with a third of the people displaced from their homes and six million refugees. Despite the appalling human suffering, the war was often portrayed in Western reports and films as a glamorous battle by the quick-witted frontiers-man against the stolid conformity of communism. It was the individual against the world. James Bond and Sylvester Stallone were the emotive representatives of Western perceptions.

The Afghans were not generally a poor people. Nor were they rootless nomads for whom a change of location was normal. The shock to their culture and way of life was devastating. The refugees fled from huge fortress-like buildings. These houses stood the height of tall trees; inside, a cool courtyard was home to an extended family – like a small hamlet that managed its own business of agriculture and trade. The crops were grown not only for subsistence but to sell, and the men were used to travelling widely and to defending their property against attackers. The division between male and female society was rigid. Outside the courtyard there was a guest room where male visitors could be entertained in the accustomed lavish style, but they could not enter the house, see any women or even talk about them. This blatant 'man's world' gave secret force to Western projections, and perhaps annoyed the few Western women who engaged with its problem.

Looking straight ahead as I travelled through Maroof, I saw barren mountains, scored with *karezes* – water channels that brought streams from far away to the clefts where vines grew, as well as peaches, apricots and nectarines. It was a land of milk and honey that was continually devastated by war. Even the *karezes* had been bombed and the men who repaired them risked their lives as the jets screamed along the valleys and dropped their explosives on the bare rock. Centuries of labour and skill in building these channels were being destroyed – skill in measuring the line on the hill so precisely that the channel fell to exactly the right place after 11 or 12 kilometres of wandering along the contours. The *karezes* were made of stone and carried water from the remotest ravines. The management of water required a sophisticated, disciplined society in which order and trust were all important. The water supply could be lost if a stray animal broke the edge of the channel. Each vineyard, furthermore, was a temptation to plunder, as were the houses and animals. Everything was guarded and the women were kept hidden.

It was a society built around the regulation of riches and conflict. But this war, with its massive external forces, had overwhelmed its delicate feudal architecture. Men had time for nothing but fighting and made a game of it, tossing bombs to each other to test their strength or rivalling each other in feats of bravery. The herdsman rested on a rifle, not a stick, and the boy goatherd no longer feared snakes, but mines. Because survival lay in fighting, and women were not allowed to fight, the value of women became less. Their protective incarceration lost its compensation of status.

For the men, each day might be the last and Islam offered a socialized form of fatalism, in which each shared out their risks in front of the glory of God. There was no way of knowing if a jet was coming until it was too late, or whether a mine lay under the bush that the shepherd needed to shake to yield fodder for the flocks. According to Western perception, the Russians had invaded a country of doughty nationalists who were rightfully defending their homes. They were heroic defenders of traditional life and culture – individualists who contrasted with the faceless stereotype of the communists. The communists looked back at the Mujahadin and saw an unjust society in which the rich exploited the poor and women were oppressed. Behind these statements of principle lay geopolitical interests. This was the meeting point of East and West – the outpost where the West defended the Indian subcontinent, and the leading edge of communism advancing from Central Asia to the sea. The West defended individualism and the East championed collective rights.

The communist government in Kabul, with Russian support, controlled most of the larger towns and made forays into the countryside, which was generally held by the Mujahadin. The 'Muj' were fragmented into innumerable groupings around charismatic 'commanders'. To be a commander required panache and the ability to attract foreign support. It was a colourful and exciting country, especially (and perhaps only) for men. Like the cattle camps of Sudan, it had all the essential elements of adventure and war. A good many expatriates fell in love with Afghanistan. During the 1980s, Oxfam had supported clinics and other projects inside the Mujahadin areas and my visit was intended as a review of our overall policy in Afghanistan. I enjoyed the hours during daytime when we rested from the heat in cool orchards, under trees that plopped apricots almost directly into our mouths. I became used to the rustle of grass and leaves as the overripe fruit fell all around while dozing in the late afternoon and waiting for the call to travel.

But I did not fall in love with Afghanistan. In my case, the prejudice worked the other way. I disliked the macho camaraderie of the Mujahadin because it was something I thought I would never have to face again after leaving boarding school. Eventually I argued for Oxfam to stop the programme that supported them. Subjective or objective?

I also disliked Afghanistan because I could not cope with the travel. The roads were guarded by Russian forces, so we travelled mainly along river gulleys in the back of four-wheel drive pick-ups that bumped and swayed until everyone was in agony. The trick among the 'Muj' was not to show pain, and I felt humiliated when I became so uncomfortable that I accepted an offer to ride in the cab. The 'Muj' laughed. They revelled (as I saw it) in their macho culture, and even played it up to attract the admiration of outsiders – especially the Americans, who seemed to love it and made the 'Muj' the stars of many thriller films.

At one point the vehicle suddenly stopped and the fighters rushed out, shooting wildly at what looked like a barren hillside. The 'Muj' had spotted a rabbit, and rushed off over the hills chasing it. With their powerful weapons they made the whole hillside crack and roar, all in hope of catching the rabbit. A little later a fighter tossed a small mine in his hands, showing off to a group of boys. He offered to throw it to me. Did I have the nerve? No, not even in front of the boys.

I may not have seen the Mujahadin at their best. When the Russians invaded Afghanistan in 1979 there had been a spontaneous resistance that could reasonably be called a *jihad* or holy war. At one time, according to all reports, there had been a deep sense of the religious. Even now, my escorts stopped five times a day, jumped out of the vehicle and spread their embroidered mats by the roadside to pray. Suddenly, from crude talk of violence they changed to postures of deep meditation and reflection. But now, after ten years and much interference by outsiders, the commanders were very clearly enjoying the luxuries of Western life and talked openly about money as their main driving force. They were not so much fighters as mafia bosses, engaged in endless talk of trade-offs between different backers and the constant shift of allegiance. One of the commanders told us proudly that he had just switched sides to the Saudi faction because they gave more money, and proudly displayed a black four-wheel drive vehicle, sparkling with polished chrome and featuring darkened windows behind which he could shelter from the sun. He said it was better than anything yet offered by the Russians, but then confided that he was seriously thinking of switching sides yet again if the offer was good enough. The rank and file 'Muj' demanded a share in this wealth and were losing the confidence of the people:

We heard many people grumbling that the 'Muj' themselves had become an elite. No longer the broken shoes and harsh asceticism of route marches in the mountains (as graphically described by Sandy Gall, et al) – instead the Muj we met were all well dressed, very well Kalashnikoved, and, since the government was not coming out to fight, rather short on battle experience.

Hence the attack on the rabbit. But what about the incarceration of women? Was it power, machismo, or what? I wrote:

Pushtun women in the Maroof area, at least, are virtual prisoners in their own homes. They may be allowed to scuttle, fully covered, to a nearby well and back but they are not encouraged to hang around and chat. They can tend the animals in the fields near the house but cannot go far in search of firewood (they have to get the men to fetch it if the distance is more than about 100 yards). And they are not normally permitted to enter any other house, except for the occasional organized visit to their parents. During our visit we spoke to no women, averted our gaze, and were warned not even to ask about their existence.

There were many reasons, no doubt, why I took the issue so seriously, but a particular one was that Oxfam was then going through the trauma of developing a policy on the issue of gender. The multicultural emphasis of the 1960s and 1970s was giving way to a similar discrimination in favour of women, to compensate for their widespread lack of equality. Throughout the 1980s, study after study had revealed that the needs of women were neglected in aid work. Male staff, in particular, had repeatedly failed to identify needs according to gender, and foolishly accepted the analysis of all-male leadership when planning their projects. This was not simply an objective debate in which men simply had to understand that they had overlooked an important issue. The gender issue challenged their relationships with women at work and at home, and it made women wonder why they had allowed themselves to be dominated for so long by men. The issue was intensely personal as well as public and organizational, and it reflected a deep shift in the cultural norms of Western society.

By 1989, when I entered Afghanistan, the issue was already very emotive within Oxfam and was to become even more so in the following years. It was widely agreed that women had not been treated equally with men either in Oxfam, in Western society or anywhere else. But whose fault was it? Should men feel guilty? Was the problem to do with the culture of a previous generation or something inherent within maleness? Was it essential that women should hold senior jobs, or could men take on board gender concerns and continue in their pre-dominant positions of power?

There were such uncertainties and sensitivities surrounding the debate that there was not much debate at all – rather, a sense of mutual suspicion about hidden thoughts and hidden motives. Some women were passionately committed to the new perception of women's rights but might not always acknowledge that their own interests were bound up with an abstract principle. Men feared that there was an unfair and personally motivated element of discrimination against them, and how-ever hard they tried to respect the equality of women they never succeeded. Some were afraid of reverse discrimination in their jobs but said that they could not argue their case because the 'gender thought police' might accuse them of opposing women's rights in principle. They felt affronted by a powerful and well-organized lobby inside the organization, particularly by those who went beyond women's equal-ity with men and argued the case for affirmative action in order to correct a bias that had been so deeply entrenched.

In Afghanistan (among leading men, at least) the trend was moving the opposite way. There was an increasing reaction against US influ-ences, which were seen to have corrupted the Mujahadin. Western views about the status of women were perceived as primarily US-led. Ironically, both in Oxford and in Afghanistan there was a perception that the wrongs of the past should be corrected, but they were moving in opposite directions. Afghanistan was moving towards even stron-ger entrenchment of male domination.

* * *

After my visit in 1989 I commented sardonically:

> *The oppression of women in Maroof eliminated much of the pleasure that I might otherwise have felt in the attentive hospitality and genial conver-sation of all-male company. It amounts virtually to slavery – a view shared by at least one of the Afghan staff. I do wonder whether Oxfam can accept such extraordinary violations of human rights.*

I was aware that it was not an issue of opposing cultures but of cul-tures that shifted to produce particular attitudes at particular times. In historical records I found evidence that Pashtun attitudes towards women had changed and the freedoms of women had been much greater in earlier periods:

In the 17th century, Pushtunwali seems to have included some elements of medieval chivalry; fighting for adored ladies became immortalized in famous songs and poems (those of Kushal Khan Khattak being the most famous). There were stories of heroic Bodiceas leading the attack with their veils in their hands. Not so today.

The problem for Oxfam, as I saw it, was essentially that women's lack of freedom to appear in public places affected our ability to help those in need:

Although some women do come to the clinics, and this is regarded as a major breakthrough, it seems unlikely that any substantial improvement in health can be made without deeper analysis of the causes of illness followed by close community participation in the solution. Since women look after all children up to the age of ten or so, the key to health improvement must lie in training women workers to visit the homes and talk intimately with the women about their problems, discussing realistic improvements.

For the previous three years we had received assurances on these points from the men running the project, but there had been very little progress. It was time for the crunch. I recorded that the male doctor in charge of the health programme 'agrees that such developments, beginning with midwife training, are necessary but feels that it is too early to do so now'.

We decided that enough was enough. We would stop working in the Pashtun areas. We had tried persuasion and it had not worked. As we reached this conclusion I remember feeling a sense of relief that I would not have to travel on those awful roads again and a rather vicious satisfaction in leaving the Mujahadin to sort out their own problems. Looking at the alternatives, Oxfam could still work in the huge refugee camps in Pakistan, but here the seclusion of women was also a severe restriction. It had been reinforced by a different set of factors – exile rather than war. Society was affected by the extremely cramped living conditions, the fear of losing traditional culture and the increased power of traditionalist leaders. In exile an exaggerated 'Pashtun' ethnicity had been created as a way of keeping up people's identification with their homeland and support to traditional leaders. This culture further emphasized the seclusion of women.

Instead, Oxfam switched the focus of the programme to a different cultural group, the Hazaras, who were (according to our reports) prepared to be much less rigid on the issue of women's rights. But it did not solve all of the problems, as Oxfam's most recent representative, Chris Johnson, records:

> While it is true that there was, and still is, much more freedom for women [in Hozara areas] than in Pashtun areas, Oxfam's programme was (certainly when I arrived there in 1996) overwhelmingly by men, for men. There were attempts to make it otherwise but progress was slow. We still struggle on this today, faced with incredibly low levels of education for women in the area.

The issue of women's seclusion was not simply a matter of rights, but of status – and status was closely linked to education. All of these factors were linked to the war. It was not that Pashtun Afghan culture favoured seclusion of women from male company and that the West favoured their inclusion. The issue was that the war had militarized Pashtun society in a certain way at a certain time. As the circumstances changed, the factors affecting the status of women would also have changed. The assertion of a fixed principle might point towards the direction that would benefit women but it might not be realistic in those circumstances.

Should Oxfam have directly challenged the Mujahadin on the status of women during that time? Could there have been a campaign of international advocacy to influence the Mujahadin, especially as they still depended on the US for arms and finance? Probably not, I suspect. Firstly, this was because Cold War attitudes in the West made the Mujahadin simply an ally in the fight against communism. There was no serious political interest in the status of women. Secondly, the Mujahadin were already facing criticism from the more conservative elements that were eventually to comprise the Taliban. Thirdly, the issue of women's status was closely related to the fear of rape as an aspect of war. This was not a war of fixed positions. There was little to stop Russian-backed raiding parties from going almost anywhere in the Mujahadin territory. In retrospect, it seems likely that rape was practised extensively. Instead, outsiders tended to assume that Pashtun men were acting out of a desire for power over women. Because rape was not spoken about by men, and women could not speak at all, the extent of this threat was not properly understood by outsiders. Without understanding it, attempts to persuade the Pushtuns to change their cultural norms might have seemed insensitive.

None of this justifies the restrictions on women, and I write this now with the benefit of hindsight, drawing on studies of the issue of rape in war as referred to in Chapter 1. But this historical perspective does raise some questions about the way in which women's rights later became the main focus of Western attention, and a means of attacking the Taliban. The whole issue was put down to Muslim fundamentalism, which by that time had replaced communism as the enemy in US foreign policy. Chris Johnson confirms that: 'People still talk and write as if violation of women's rights in Afghanistan began with the Taliban, whereas the freedoms of women in Afghanistan have been drastically curtailed for a very long time, during most of which the West was silent and even supported and idealized the men responsible, making them into the heroes of Western films. Indeed, it is arguable that the whole issue of women's rights has come to the fore in Western circles because it can be used as a way to criticize the Taliban, or because it feeds Western, politically motivated stereotypes of Muslim fundamentalism.'

* * *

In the years after the decision to withdraw from the Pashtun areas of Afghanistan, Oxfam gradually strengthened its norms about women's equality and, in 1993, adopted a formal gender and development policy which, among other things, committed the organization to 'develop positive action to promote the full participation and empowerment of women' and to 'confront the social and ideological barriers to women's participation'.

The language of this document is unusual among Oxfam policy papers. The phrase 'positive action' implies a divergence from the principle of impartiality, and the word 'confront' implies an uncompromising approach, regardless of the other person's situation. This was different from Oxfam's normal 'listening to and understanding the person on the ground' approach. Nevertheless, it was endorsed by the directors and trustees, and therefore had all the authority possible. But in approving this new policy, the directors and trustees had not considered perhaps what would happen if its categorical requirements conflicted with Oxfam's legal mandate for 'the relief of poverty, distress and suffering'.

The new policy was regarded as a great victory by those who had championed the cause of women's rights. However, a new emotive atmosphere began to develop when the gender unit, which had devised the draft policy, found itself being dismantled. There began to be a suspicion that the policy was just paying lip service to the idea of women's rights while actually undermining them. The fact that by this time there was no woman director was taken as an indication of lack of sincerity at the highest levels. Consequently, the atmosphere became charged with suspicion and emotion. Some felt that they had been tricked, and resolved to fight individual cases as a matter of principle.

Meanwhile, in Afghanistan, Oxfam had shifted its centre of operations to Kabul. When the Taliban forces occupied Kabul in 1996 and forced women into the same kind of seclusion that was the norm in Pushtan areas, Oxfam reacted strongly. The representative at the time, Nancy Smith, took immediate action, as described by her successor, Sue Emmott, who took over early in 1997:

It was clear that we could not ignore the Taliban's edict that women were not allowed to work and girls not permitted to attend school. Within a few days we had suspended the programme, pending negotiations with the Taliban, on the grounds that we could not achieve our aims without female staff. In addition, after full discussion with all-male staff, we requested them to stay at home until such time as their female colleagues were permitted to return to work. In Kabul such an action was possible, because women have long been active in the workforce at all different levels and all our male staff had wives who worked and daughters who attended school. A capital city is very different from the rural areas, and one of the main problems of the Taliban's edicts was the imposition of rural, tribal norms on an urban and often liberal-minded population.

Emmott explicitly referred to Oxfam's gender policy:

The fact that Oxfam–UK had a gender policy placed it in a unique position among international aid agencies in Kabul when Taliban forces took over the city. Although the effects of an extreme form of Islam were felt by all agencies, it was only Oxfam that had both a desire and an obligation to address the issue of gender directly. Within Oxfam, this was the first time that the gender policy would be tested in such a public way.

The stakes were much higher in every respect than they had been in 1989. The affront to women caused by the Taliban's restrictions could be considered even greater in respect of women who had enjoyed

Western-style freedoms under the Russian-backed regime in Kabul. Secondly, Oxfam's own culture was being reshaped around the issue of women's status. Thirdly, the consequences of withholding aid were very much greater. Oxfam was no longer simply supporting small health clinics as in the days of the Mujahadin, but had recently taken responsibility for renovating a major sector of Kabul's water supply. This massive project would provide 400,000 people with water. It was an almost unprecedented technological undertaking – so great that it had already begun to stretch Oxfam's organizational capacity. In addition, Oxfam had just been awarded a large EU contract to distribute winter clothing. In the extremes of the Afghan climate, this could be regarded as a life-saving project.

The decision to suspend programmes meant that work on the new water system stopped immediately and people had to revert to collecting water from the riverbed where the water was polluted. It is a measure of the strength of feeling in Oxfam, perhaps, that although both projects could have been handed over to another agency, Emmott, like her predecessor Nancy Smith, argued against on the grounds that:

> *Essential community-level surveys, communication and education work with and through women would be impossible under the Taliban regime, and as water had not flowed through the mains for four years and the programme was proceeding very slowly anyway, a suspension of a few months was felt to be relatively harmless. In line with the gender policy, and on the basis of sound experience, Oxfam believed that a water programme could not succeed without the participation of women. Furthermore, Oxfam was likely to be the only agency to speak out, and it seemed to be important that someone did.*

Accordingly, Oxfam argued that it would be inconsistent to allow another agency to take over the work. Indeed, Oxfam took active steps to persuade the EU, UK government and others to suspend all aid in Taliban areas, in support of Oxfam's view. The objective of the programme was to stop international aid in order to force the Taliban to change its position on women. Yet Emmott was aware that this would be very difficult to achieve: 'From the outset it was known that, although we wished to negotiate with the Taliban for the return of women to work, the cultural and religious distance between such a fundamentalist movement and a liberal Western aid agency was likely to render negotiations impossible.'

Reflecting on this situation later on, one of the senior managers in the region, Marcus Thompson, observed:

Politically we misjudged it, thinking we could bargain, that surely the Taliban must so want a renovated water supply in Kabul that they will allow us to employ women, etc, and thinking there is such general international agreement on the human–women's rights issue that the solidarity would hold, and the Taliban would have to back down. Actually, the Taliban could not have cared less; they had a war to fight, and the solidarity collapsed.

Was there ever a realistic possibility of success or was Oxfam taking a stand on principle simply because the issue was topical? One problem was that to back down would have been seen as a compromise on a principle that was especially important to the individuals concerned and to sections of the organization at that time. Smith and Emmott were aware that they were holding the fears and wishes of many others in their hands as they struggled with these issues.

In Oxford the debate showed some signs of polarizing between those who focused on the need for practical responses (generally men rather than women and emergencies rather than development). The issue was so sensitive that it was impossible to debate the issues objectively. The outcome was that the relief programmes were stopped and there followed a long period of inaction. It was not so much a question of what was appropriate policy for Afghanistan as whether Oxfam's gender policy would be applied or undermined. In 1997, Emmott wrote:

The Oxfam programme in Kabul remains suspended, more than a year later. During that time the gender policy has been subject to continuous challenge; but in defining a set of core principles for Oxfam, it has helped to focus the debate on those principles. The suspension has been both admired and criticized. The main criticism is usually that suspension helps no one and may worsen the situation of those who most need help... In the end, much of the focus on gender is about strategic rather than practical gender needs, and women's rights have been so severely eroded in Kabul and other parts of Afghanistan that at least one agency has acknowledged the need to look beyond the short term and to face the challenge of the future.

A couple of years later, Johnson concluded:

> *For me the biggest mistake Oxfam made in relation to the situation of women in Afghanistan under the Taliban was to confuse strategy (or even sometimes tactics) with principle. The principle is women's rights; our aim is to achieve an improvement in these... I'd say the initial suspension of the programme was a useful tactic because it drew attention to the problem. But our great mistake was not to see that it was a damaging long-term strategy that would achieve nothing, be incomprehensible to most people, leave us without contact with women, etc. We should from the very beginning have worked out how we were going to move on.*

But was the suspension of life-saving aid programmes consistent with Oxfam's legal mandate to 'relieve poverty, distress and suffering'? A later evaluation of the water programme sharply criticized Oxfam's decision to suspend it and estimated that this caused a risk of death to 1800 people because they were likely to contract diarrhoea as a result of drinking polluted water. No calculation has been made of the actual number of lives lost, but it would be a very emotive figure if it existed. There is also the issue of not distributing winter clothing to destitute people in Kabul, and preventing others from doing so. When Oxfam refused to undertake it, the EU did not have time to appoint another partner and the budget was cancelled.

Oxfam continued to grapple with its two conflicting principles – 'saving lives' and 'gender equity' – and there seemed to be no way of deciding between them. In fact, Oxfam became less capable of making a decision because it now had less information. Having suspended its programmes, Oxfam lost contact with the people affected. Tensions began to develop within Oxfam in Kabul. Staff in other aid agencies made jokes at the expense of Oxfam, especially its local male staff, accusing them of letting down the people in need. Although female staff members were not allowed by Oxfam to work on aid programmes, Oxfam did allow its female cleaner to continue working in the staff houses. Johnson asked: 'Is it OK for Afghan women to come to work to clean for expats but not OK for Oxfam to run programmes with women?'

But the most serious problem was that having made a firm stand on principle, Oxfam could not participate in the debates taking place among other agencies, which were trying to understand what was possible within the Taliban's edict, and how to bring about change through compromise. Because the issue was viewed as a matter of principle, Oxfam was not interested in compromise. As Oxfam withdrew from those debates, its perceptions became further separated from reality and common sense. Johnson emphasized: 'We got our-selves up a cul de sac. We talked about advocacy but what had we to say when we were no longer in contact with women?'

It is impossible, I suspect, to write about these issues without using emotive language. The evaluation of the water programme (by a man) gives little doubt as to his own strong views:

> Oxfam faced an ethical dilemma after the coming to power of the Taliban. Should Oxfam close its programme in Afghanistan in protest against the Taliban's gender apartheid and its denial of work or schooling to women; or should it continue to serve those in need, regardless of the policy of their rulers? Oxfam decided that it was more important to have a bargaining chip on women's rights than to prevent 1800 severe cases of diarrhoea a year in Kabul.

The 'bargaining chip' rather betrays the writer's views. By contrast, a female Oxfam staff member commented:

> Women's rights were and are central to all the work we were doing in Kabul and Afghanistan. I wonder how Oxfam would evaluate the success-ful completion of a technical programme managed, planned and executed exclusively by men, consulting only with men and boys, maintained by men, including little if any health education, and producing water for collection by men?

The word 'technical' seems to imply a limited and unsatisfactory approach. What seems remarkable now is the failure of senior man-agement to get involved more strongly in the debate. But they too were caught up in a conflict of policy in which they had endorsed both positions. 'Saving lives' and 'the rights of women' were top organiza-tional priorities. But which was was most important? No one wanted to say. For a long time, management ducked its responsibilites, leaving the debate to simmer.

* * *

Oxfam was by no means alone in facing this dilemma. The 'Save the Children Alliance' and UNICEF had also suspended their programmes when the Taliban captured Kabul, but gradually found ways of work-ing around the Taliban's edicts. Some women staff members were willing to continue working even though they faced a risk of being confronted by Taliban militia and might be humiliated in public. Others found relatives willing to accompany them when they travelled. The UN brought the aid agencies together and proposed a 'principle-centred approach to gender' that made a division between relief needs, where compromise on principle was necessary, and rehabilitation where it was not. In all cases, the 'UN agencies will be sensitive to cultural practices', but, more strictly, 'the rehabilitation of Afghanistan's socio-economic infrastructure must benefit males and females equally in participation and results'.

It was not entirely clear where the distinction was to be drawn between relief and 'the rehabilitation of Afghanistan's socio-economic infrastructure'. The 'principle-centred approach' was a fudge. Ultimately, the UN policy left the decision to the staff who defined the nature of the project and could weigh up the various factors objectively (and subjectively). But by this time others were becoming involved in the issue of the Taliban and its edicts about women. Powerful outsiders began to use the debate about principle for their own purposes. The US began to use the issue as a means to attack Muslim fundamentalism. The Taliban became a clear public enemy when they gave shelter to the suspected terrorist Osama bin Laden. Whereas in 1989 the US had backed the Mujahadin and ignored their treatment of women in Mujahadin territory, now the US turned on them (in their new guise as the Taliban) and emphasized the issue of women's rights. In other countries the US position was seen as an attack on Islam. There was a reaction in the UN General Assembly, which passed a resolution opposing 'cultural imperialism'. The UN 'principled-centred approach' was rejected as being based on a similar set of cultural judgements. The outcome, as a UN report describes, was that: 'General Assembly and Security Council resolutions explicitly prevent the use of conditionality in assistance to Afghanistan'.

UN analysts with a more Western orientation were sent to examine the issue. They restated the case as a dilemma:

In practice, conditionality has been imposed in an effort to restore human rights and fulfil basic human needs... The dilemma, in fact, is the importance of fulfilling the desperate need for assistance in Afghanistan, on the one hand, and, on the other, the equal importance of keeping the country – including its girls and women – within the ambit of the international community and the standards it has set for respecting fundamental human rights in all countries.

Afghanistan became central to the debate between the US and certain East Asian states over the issue of human rights: Was there an absolute standard for women's rights or was it a case of the US asserting its culture over that of other countries? Oxfam's managers in Kabul now found their position being caught up in a conflict between the United States' stand against Islamic fundamentalism, the UN General Assembly's stand against cultural imperialism, the increasingly powerful voice of those in Oxfam demanding that Oxfam must make some practical contribution to saving lives, and the Oxfam lobby still asserting the primacy of the rights of women.

As time went on, the situation proved to be very different from what was expected when the Taliban issued its edict. The Taliban leadership behaved like the UN (and Oxfam), making statements of principle, but leaving the real decisions to local representatives. This produced an unpredictable climate, but one in which it was possible for everyone, including women, to work, although with many limitations and risks. Because the other aid agencies gradually fell away from giving support, Oxfam found itself alone, and in a position that looked like direct opposition to the Taliban. Oxfam still hoped to make the Taliban recall its edict. In an advocacy strategy document of 1997, the tactic was to, 'lobby all major donors to engage directly with Taliban on the gender question, ensure that all visiting delegations include women, and to state in writing how they will ensure that the programmes and policies which they fund in Afghanistan are consistent with their own gender policies and continue to benefit both men and women'.

But it gradually became apparent that the Taliban lacked any process by which it could engage with these delegations. There was little point in conversing with commanders on the ground because they simply received orders and could not pass views 'upwards'. This was a military-style organization in which orders were not questioned. But the supreme commander, Mullah Mohammed Omar, the 'Commander of the Believers', was far away in Kandahar and he was a cleric who did not meet delegations. The system was impenetrable to Western processes of lobbying. The importance of the Mullah was to provide religious certainty as a unifying force. The edicts themselves could be quietly ignored, but the authority could not. Unfortunately, Oxfam headed straight for what was not negotiable, the edicts themselves. As the UN gender study explained:

The Taliban prefer ignoring, or pretending to ignore, necessary arrange-
ments that deviate from their policies, such as community-based schools
for girls, rather than engaging in a process that will force the movement to
engage in a policy-making process. Since such a process includes necessar-
ily the ability of members to have different opinions and competitive
interests, that will have to be balanced by the leadership. It would bring
into question the distinctiveness of the Taliban movement compared to
other factions, and the religious character of the endeavour.

Taliban officials sometimes struck back with accusations of double
standards. They pointed out that they were being asked to observe international agreements, such as the Universal Declaration on Human
Rights. But at the same time they had been denied a seat in the UN to
represent the Afghanistan government, which was still occupied by
their enemy – Rabbani's party in the north. 'Are we the state or not',
they asked.

Oxfam was also on weak ground because it lacked any clear mandate from Afghan women. The position was derived, instead, from a
global policy. At the International Forum on Assistance to Afghanistan in January 1997, which met soon after the Taliban had captured
Kabul to decide what the response of humanitarian agencies should
be, 230 delegates from international organizations and local NGOs
debated the issue of the Taliban's edict on women. Afghan women at
the meeting put out a joint statement that: 'Denial of female opportunities should not be used as a justification to stop aid.'

By 1998, the UN's gender report reflected a sense of frustration with
Oxfam, and substitutes the word 'intransigent' for the word 'principled':

Some of the NGOs, SCF–US and Oxfam, for example, played a significant
role in feeding this debate and arguing for an intransigent stand with the
Taliban authorities... An inflammatory discourse seems to embrace the
gender issue, with the use of antagonistic language in the media. One
might consider the extent to which such a discourse is propitious to the
elaboration of a common operational approach.

Oxfam's assertion of principle had now become an 'inflammatory discourse'. But messages of support were received from other Oxfam offices
around the world and Afghanistan had become a test case for something that was extremely important for many staff. The managers in

Kabul were now boxed in – any compromise would be seen as a betrayal. Their position was becoming more and more untenable. Although Oxfam's firm position made it impossible to negotiate with the Taliban, others had been able to do so, and as a result they knew more about its nature as an organization. The outlook for any change in the edict appeared increasingly hopeless. The UN's gender report explained that the Taliban was not so much a reflection of militant Islam. Instead, Islam was the one factor that could unite the country after the war. Many commanders had become corrupt during the Mujahadin era, but they still acknowledged Islam as a superior force to their own interests. They would still say prayers and attend the mosque. Throughout the country, the Afghan military forces all acknowledged the same God. The Taliban had emerged as a religious movement that, by uniting everyone behind Islam, presented an opportunity for peace.

In the Taliban view, Western opposition to their edict about women threatened the stability of Islam and hence the possibility of peace. If there were debate and disagreement between different commanders, the movement could be pulled apart. Since war was the worst possible outcome, women's rights had to take lower priority. In a rare glimpse into what had happened in Afghanistan, the UN report states:

> *The rigidity in the application of the Islamic law was justified, in the Taliban's perspective, by the debauchery that permeated the Kandahar society in the last days of the Mujahadin commanders, including open conduct of homosexuality and the sexual harassment of girls, particularly on their way to schools. The Taliban reacted strongly against these conducts. In the absence of sound and practical alternatives they decided to close the schools for girls until a proper civil order had been established. The Taliban admitted... that this particular decree was extra-Islamic but considered it justifiable under the circumstances.*

Right from the beginning the application of the Taliban edict had been applied unevenly, following the views of local militias. Sometimes in the rural areas women were allowed to work and girls were able to continue their schooling in apparent contravention of the edict. The application in the cities was more strict and caused particular trouble for Western aid agencies in Kabul. But some aid representatives may not have been aware that women in Kabul had reason to fear an invading force, such as the Taliban, and conceivably the Taliban had good grounds for fearing the use of rape as an instrument of war – as had happened after the previous fall of Kabul, in 1992, when the war-lord General Dostum encouraged widespread violence and rape. A later Oxfam report describes this:

> Remembering the past, a family in Kabul's Microrayan estate told a jour-nalist of how members of Dostum's forces entered their home and asked them to hand over their daughter. They refused. One of them lifted a gun and shot their daughter in front of their eyes. She was only 20 and had just finished high school.
>
> Another man tells of the woman who was kidnapped by the Mujahadin and used for four years. Then, he said, they contacted her husband and said he could have her back if he paid a ransom. He said he no longer wanted her, they could keep her now. So they contacted her father. He paid and brought his daughter back.

By comparison, the complaints about the Taliban made by Western aid agencies might seem rather insignificant:

> Forroz, a 28-year-old poet, lost her job as producer of a literacy programme on the state-run radio. One of her sisters lost her teaching position and the other had to give up her university studies. During the years of war, she said, Afghans lost almost everything. But this is worse; it's a war on our minds.

What exactly is 'a war on our minds'? It seems very different from what had been recorded two years earlier in a study of 40 poorer women in Kabul:

> Among the women interviewed, trauma was predominantly associated with the loss of relatives through death, disappearance and imprisonment. 'I've been losing close relatives one by one... You can stand hunger and thirst, but losing people, that you can't stand,' said Samaha.

In the same report a woman who had lost her whole family says: 'The kind of pain we have, you cannot really explain. We do not feel well. We ask God if life is so bad, then why have you crushed us?'

In the end, Oxfam found itself judged by its ability to support people in need. CARE was pumping water; Oxfam's pumps were idle. Chris Johnson wondered what 'right' Oxfam had to make such decisions. She wrote:

We seem to make an assumption that we are completely free to make our own decisions in other people's countries, that we can simply choose to do what we please, because we are paying the bill ... The Taliban are very angry at our spending a lot of money on a scheme and then pulling out with absolutely no benefit to show; they want the water. They do not understand our rationale, our technical reasons for pulling out now ... There is a real need for the organization to look more carefully at the long-term implications of its decisions and to be far less arrogant about thinking it can just stop and start as it chooses with no price to pay.

Oxfam may still have been right to make an initial protest, but it was not close enough to the people in need, not listening to them intently enough, to pursue the issue when it meant a choice between providing water and keeping up the principled stand. And there are questions now about whether Oxfam had another reason for dropping the water project. It was just too complex, and there were already concerns as to whether Oxfam should have been involved in the first place. Pulling out of it as a matter of principle was rather too convenient a solution. As a key Oxfam staff member in Oxford recalls:

The gender issue was not the only reason for many people wanting to pull out of Logar [the water project]. There were other reasons, including: the lack of funding for completion; running costs; Oxfam's lack of appropriate expertise for a project of this size and complexity; the extreme unlikelihood of persuading a commercial company to undertake the technical work; the vulnerability of the system to further destruction by the ongoing conflict; and, most of all, the total lack of capacity of the government to take this project on.

The hidden reason for backing 'women's rights' may have been a fear of technical failure. The same writer concludes: 'The gender issue became a side issue. This happened to be convenient for those who strongly felt Oxfam should pull out because of the women's rights issue – several agendas at work here – confusing.'

The motive for invoking a principle has a convenient habit of remaining hidden. To find out exactly what factors were in the minds of those who made Oxfam's crucial decisions would be impossible; they might not even know themselves. The objective and the subjective were ravelled together in a 'judgement call'. It is, however, a sobering reflection that what Oxfam viewed as one of its most principled stands in the last decade came to be widely regarded as unprincipled. Ultimately, it probably undermined rather than strengthened Oxfam's commitment to gender equity.

* * *

Finally, in 1999 Oxfam's senior management stepped in. Oxfam's good name was in question. The public stand was quietly dropped, new projects were started and compromises were made. New managers were able to intervene because they had been outside of the debate and did not need to defend or attack the past. No doubt there were some individuals who saw this as a betrayal of Oxfam's commitment to gender equity. Oxfam's management had initiated an organization-wide debate about the importance of saving lives. This process reaffirmed the precedence of 'saving lives' over all other issues. The gender policy was not rescinded but there was a clearer sense of order among the principles. As Oxfam's special representative in the region, Marcus Thompson, put it:

> *I think my overall conclusion from the Afghanistan experience is that we have, as an organization, to rank the humanitarian values. If meeting conventional humanitarian need as best we can (water, food, shelter, etc) is ranked higher (even if only just higher) than gender equity, we have to hang in there, do what we can on the humanitarian front, but continue to press the gender issue at every opportunity.*

Chris Johnson pointed out that a significant part of the problem lay in the word 'confront' which had been included in Oxfam's policy statement:

> *If you confront, in the sense of telling the Pashtuns (be they local leaders or Taliban authorities) that they are wrong, then for sure you will achieve nothing. If you seek out spaces on the ground and work with local people who are more progressive (and they are there) and let them push for changes they believe in, then things can change.*

But for Johnson the fundamental problem was not the clash of two opposing principles; instead, it was a confusion between principle and tactic: 'It isn't that the principle [women's rights] changes, but that the way to make progress differs... We need to analyse much more carefully how to bring about changes in a particular situation.'

There seems to be no easy answers. We have to analyse how to apply principles and also to identify which principles are more important than others. We need to recognize that there are temptations to follow our own interests rather than those of the people we are trying to help. It is not principles that are the problem but how we use them. In her novel *Pride and Prejudice*, Jane Austen explores a similar issue of two lovers who judge each other against rigid principles. At the end, when they are finally united, Darcy says: 'I was given good principles but left to follow them in pride and conceit.'

From the perspective of the lovers, much of *Pride and Prejudice* was about 'principle', but Jane Austen's title refers to 'prejudice'. The distinction between following a principle bravely and following a prejudice foolishly is a narrow one. A principle held regardless of the realities is a prejudice. The reason for holding such a prejudice may have more to do with our own lives than with the lives of other people.

Chapter 6
Somalia: Emotion and Order

Military intervention for humanitarian purposes has a long history. Approximately 3000 years ago, Greek forces set out to retrieve King Agamemnon's sister-in-law Helen, 'the face that launched a thousand ships', who had been abducted by the Trojans. This was supposedly a humanitarian mission to uphold the values of society and save Helen from suffering. But it gradually lost its sense of purpose. The war dragged on, and men began to die pointlessly as a result of fighting and disease. Helen seemed to be reasonably happy where she was, and there began to be a suspicion that the war was a cover for rivalry between the two great powers of the time, or that it was simply an expression of pride by the king and his aggrieved brother – a family problem for which others felt little sympathy. The Greek coalition began to break up. Some upheld the view that they were fighting for ideals – others, that ideals were just a front for a different purpose. The leaders themselves seemed to lose conviction and argue. Each went their own way, fighting without regard for any rules or not fighting at all, as they saw fit. In frustration against a society that had cheated them of their higher ideals, some individuals discarded the whole notion of social order, ideals and principles.

Such, at least, is Shakespeare's version of the story in his play *Troilus and Cressida*. There are parallels between the Greek expedition against Troy in the second millennium BC and the US-led expedition to Somalia in 1992. The Greek force was similarly a 'multilateral' force, including contingents from many places with only a very tenuous interest in retrieving Helen. They were there out of obligation or as a result of their own political strategies. In 1992, famine in Somalia was the image that 'launched a thousand ships'. However, there is a great difference between a distant, idealized prospect of relieving famine and actually being there. What the soldiers saw were not starving children and grateful mothers but young men looting aid convoys.

Many came to hate the image of what they had come to save. When they expressed their anger by attacking Somalis, they were treated with horror by the outside world. There is little that arouses more anger than the feeling that our ideals have been exploited.

Similarly, it is hard for the staff to maintain a sense of idealism in aid agencies. It is not necessarily that things are so very bad, but simply that they fall short of our ideals.

Shakespeare portrays the result in terms of a loss of social order, the 'failed state' of modern analysis, contrasting with unrestrained emotion. In his famous speech, Ulysses laments the loss of social order as an ideal in itself:

> O! When degree is shak'd,
> Which is the ladder to all high designs,
> The enterprise is sick. How could communities,
> Degrees in schools, and brotherhood in cities,
> Peaceful commerce from dividable shores,
> The primogeniture and due of birth,
> Prerogative of age, crowns, sceptres, laurels,
> But by degree, stand in authentic place?

As the Trojan and Somali expeditions both show, violence tends towards the absolute. It is difficult to sustain an ideal once people are killed. The original objective of the US-led Somalia expedition was to restore law and order and relieve a famine that was said to have killed over 200,000 people. When this was not instantly achieved, the soldiers became irritable. When they were shouted at they atttacked. Some Pakistani soldiers were shot and finally some US soldiers were captured and tortured. Sympathy turned to anger. The messages from political leaders shifted with changes in public reaction. The expedition leaders found themselves uncertain of their real objective (was it now to save US lives?) and at risk of humiliation. Their own emotions became part of the problem. Leaders blamed each other and the result was increasingly poor cooperation between the different elements, both within the military forces and between those forces and the UN. The soldiers, lacking ideals and leadership, turned individually on their enemies and committed atrocities that further undermined the high ideal of the original expedition and the possibility of carrying it out.

Military intervention for humanitarian purposes is more likely to occur today than during the Cold War when the threat of Russian opposition might prevent it. The level of public awareness of acute situations may be greater because of the globalization of the media, making human suffering immediately visible all over the world. But the media-driven intervention may give little time to really get to know the situation and its people. Instead of the rapid gunboat diplomacy of the past when objectives were achieved in a couple of hours, we now have long drawn-out conflicts with plenty of time to develop their own emotional dynamic.

Similarly, the aid agency that rushes into a new humanitarian crisis without proper local understanding and links, believing that its feelings of concern are enough, will find itself drawn into problems it had not expected. Quite likely, local people will exploit their goodwill. This makes aid workers angry. But do aid agencies have the right to expect that they should be treated specially because they represent the high ideals of the West? Should they be surprised when others point out that they are part of a Western humanitarianism which is often shallow, contains a good deal of self-interest and frequently gets hijacked for political purposes. Yet, if people do not respect our ideals we tend to feel cheated and angry. Our concern rapidly turns to detachment and even hatred. Sometimes our ideals are our enemy.

This chapter describes Oxfam's response to the famine in Somalia. A relief programme was launched but was too late and was based on ideals rather than information. There were wide disagreements, staff felt undermined and the outcome has been considered a failure. What lessons did Oxfam learn? What does the experience tell us about idealism and the principle of humanity?

* * *

What happened to Oxfam was similar to the experience of the whole US-led military operation, and both cases reflect different aspects of change in the global order following the end of the Cold War. The Berlin Wall had been torn down in 1989, but there was no firm basis of understanding for the Western intervention in Somalia. Indeed, it was founded on a misunderstanding. The US-led expedition had set out to restore 'law and order', but 'law and order' was not necessarily what Somalis most wanted at that time. They had reacted against the rigid Western-backed government of Siad Barre by driving him out of the country in an unusual tactical alliance of the clan militias. This did not necessarily mean that the alliance formed the basis for a Western-style state. Barre had exploited military power derived mainly from the US to pursue his own personal interests while claiming that he was acting in the name of government. Somalis did not necessarily want the reimposition of a new Western-backed regime, and at the time, perhaps, were not necessarily unhappy with being a 'failed state'. In the West the situation was viewed (initially at least) as an appalling breakdown of society and a threat to world peace. From another perspective, it was simply a country run by combinations of business and traditional structures rather than by a formal government of the type that the philosopher Hobbes had invented in the 17th century as a reaction to the English Civil War and the Thirty Years War in Europe. The related concept of the 'nation state' was formed during the colonial period and the Cold War and had a powerful protector in the shape of the UN. But arguably, Somalis had their eyes on a much more modern, or post-modern, concept of the state as a shifting interaction of business and clan relationships, modified by cultural norms, which maintained an overall balance of power. But at the time we reacted simply – 'famine bad; government good' – and sent soldiers to restore order.

The US-led forces found it difficult to work with concepts of governance that were so different from what they had expected. Perhaps they might have recognized in it a reflection of a US right-wing ideal: the stateless state. But they had come to save a helpless people, not to learn about futuristic modes of governance. Instead, they looked for a reliable figure to make into a supremo to be supported by state-run police, judiciary, elections and the rest. They tended to take Ulysses's view that anything that was not a continuation of the past was anarchy. However, it rapidly became obvious that there was no path towards this objective. The mission lost its sense of purpose. Men were risking their lives and the leaders did not seem to know what they were doing. This produced serious problems of morale, much as Ulysses described in the expedition 3000 years earlier:

The General's disdain'd
By him one step below, he by the next,
The next by him beneath; so every step,
Exampled by the first pace that is sick
Of his superior, grows to an envious fever
Of pale and bloodless emulation.

James Woods, who was US deputy assistant secretary of defence for African affairs in the Somalia crisis reflected some years later: 'The

UN failure in Somalia was not a failure of policy, of process, of personalities, or of tactics. It was, in part, a failure of strategy, in part a failure of capabilities, and mainly a failure of collective will and leadership.'

This view reflects the consensus of the book *Learning from Somalia* (1997), which offers retrospective essays by many of the leading protagonists. The overview analysis by US diplomat Walter C Clarke is revealingly entitled 'Failed Visions and Uncertain Mandates in Somalia'. In relation to the US-led military United Nations Task Force (UNITAF) which finally went into Somalia in December 1992 and dramatically filmed for CNN as they landed on the beaches, he says:

> *International intervention ultimately is sustainable only when there is an agreed political end result of the intervention... Lacking political purpose, UNITAF focused its tactics on force protection rather than the achievement of strategic goals. Much loss of time, money, and domestic US commitment to multilateral action resulted.*

But even in this retrospective book, no one is sure what the strategy actually should have been. Rather like the case of Helen, either you get her back or you do not. In Somalia it was: either you restore order or you do not. Once it became clear that Somalis themselves were not cooperating with the mission, the task became impossible and everyone was confused. Leaders on the ground in Somalia felt increasingly betrayed by uncertainties back at home. The US administration was transfixed by internal debates. According to the same book, the US president was unsure about Congress, and Congress was unsure about itself.

The underlying cause of all this was, first, that there had not been enough time, since the fall of the Berlin Wall in 1989, to reappraise global strategies. Second, no one had really studied what Somalis thought and what they wanted. There was no US presence in Somalia to guide the deliberations. The intervention was based on different assumptions acting in a policy vacuum. Different parts of the administration favoured different strategies. However, because whatever was proposed for Somalia would form the basis for the new world order, officials were not going to let go lightly. They feared that another department might achieve a better position for the future. Everyone wanted his or her say, but no one knew what to do.

US policy in Somalia had always been rather uncertain. In the 1970s, Somalia was backed by the Russians and Ethiopia was backed by the

Americans; then both changed sides. The region was sensitive because of proximity to the Gulf, but not in its own right. During the Cold War a military intervention would have had a clear objective at least in relation to the Russians. It would be a war of political interest without any talk of ideals and altruism. But humanitarian intervention, without a Russian factor and simply to restore law and order, had not been forseen. There was no easy way of measuring public opinion against political strategy. In short, as Clarke concludes: 'The debate in Congress did not suggest the evolution of a new foreign policy doctrine but reflected uncertainty among policy-makers about the US role in the post-Cold War world.'

The question could not be resolved in front of TV images of starving Somalis, which became more and more terrible during the summer of 1992. What was the balance between self-interest, altruism and global responsibility in the new world order? Despite rumours of massive oil interests and other hidden strategic interests, the case for intervention in Somalia was basically one of morality and international obligation. But the issues were complex. Was the US standing out to uphold a new global morality, or retreating into traditional (Republican) isolationism? No one knew.

With the US president unsure of what to do, different government departments sensed the need to push themselves forward to secure advantage in the new world order. Much of the debate was about position rather than humanitarian response. Andrew Natsios, then assistant administrator of the US government's aid department (USAID) recalls the debates in mid-1992:

> *A contentious debate within the Bush administration took place with USAID, the state department's refugee office and the African Bureau of State, on the one side, and the Bureau of International Organizations (IO) on the other. IO argued that Somalia was not a central strategic interest of the United States.*

In all of this confusion, the decision to launch a military intervention seems to have been based at least to some extent (although there is debate on this) on an emotive reaction by George Bush while watching TV images of the famine. According to the story, he got up and decided that enough was enough. He ordered the military into action on a gut feeling. Although this is perhaps a 'marketed' view of what happened, it does seem possible that in the absence of clear policy, emotion may have made a crucial difference. According to Natsios, a special reason for Bush's emotive reaction was that it reminded him of a visit he had made to a feeding centre in Sudan: 'Bush, clearly troubled by his memory of that feeding centre, drew a direct parallel between that famine and Somalia, a parallel that said much about his motivation for sending in US troops. In President Bush's address to the country announcing the Somalia intervention, he reasserted this motive for the effort.'

The problem with such decision-making, even if it is only supported by rumour, is that the people carrying out the orders doubt their validity. A soldier might ask, 'Would I die for George Bush's emotions?' People might easily divide into two camps: 'I genuinely believe it is a just cause' and 'weeping presidents don't make good policy'. The way was already open for people to undermine the expedition or simply to use it for their own ends. The UN's envoy to Somalia, Mohamed Sahnoun, concludes that the delay and hesitation itself was fatal: 'If the political and humanitarian intervention had been made earlier, then the military option would have presented itself in a different fashion. The banditry and chaos and warlordship had built up too far.'

The problem was compounded because the cadre of political officers who were supposed to accompany the US-led expedition was cut out of the budget during the debates in Congress. The mission now became purely military, without a capacity for dialogue and understanding. By now the two rival warlords, Aideed and Ali Mahdi, representing the main clan groupings, had built up huge followings of heavily armed young men. They did not fully control them, but kept them in check by manipulation, concession and persuasion. They had been allowed pickings from the process of aid and now realized that this was to be stopped by the international force. Inevitably, they saw the US-led force as their enemy. Perhaps some of these cocky young men relished the chance to tease the world's greatest military force. Within Somalia the traditional leaders, notably the elders, were losing influence because so much now depended upon possessing a gun; but arguably a Somali version of law and order was still achievable. However, this could only be achieved if there was an emphasis on political dialogue and understanding rather than the use of force.

Within days of the expeditionary force landing on the beaches in Somalia, it became apparent that there was no easy way of achieving the 'law-and-order' objective. Neither of the warlords seemed to offer an attractive proposition as potential government representatives, nor did they seem to want the responsibility of government in the sense of providing services to people. Unable to see a clear way forward, and increasingly frustrated at being attacked by the people they had come to save, the leaders of the military expedition in Somalia also found themselves suddenly overruled by staff in Washington or New York, as departmental wars raged in the corridors of power.

Like Achilles in the Trojan wars, the UN decided that it was not being given enough respect. Many of the UN staff retired to Nairobi, claiming that the situation was too dangerous, and sat it out in luxury hotels, undermining the idealism of the UN by being criticized in the media for drawing large personal payments while doing nothing. An exception was the UN envoy Mohammed Sahnoun, who risked his life travelling around Somalia, trying to engage in debate with the Somali elders and consulting with them and other local leaders about what the UN should do to create sufficient law and order to allow them to withdraw. But Sahnoun found himself acting alone and in his personal capacity rather than with the full authority of the UN. One of the sensitive issues was the UN's decision to send yet more troops. Sahnoun was negotiating an appropriate figure with the Somali elders. In the midst of these discussions he was astonished to hear, over the BBC radio, that his boss Boutros Boutros-Ghali, the UN secretary general, had announced a figure of 3000 troops: 'The Somalis turned to me and said, "What is this nonsense? How can you send 3000 troops here without telling us about it?"'

Perhaps Boutros-Ghali was keen to assert a sense of strong leadership but the result was the opposite. He undermined both himself and his envoy and reflected the overall lack of strategy. Like other leaders, he appeared to be acting in an arbitrary and dictatorial manner. This further undermined the morale of those on the ground. As Ulysses in *Troilus and Cressida* put it: 'The General's disdain'd by him one step below'.

The various different operations in Somalia – military and humanitarian – were characterized by lack of cooperation. Relationships between the military and the NGOs deteriorated over the question of security. Natsios recalls that military protection was offered to the NGOs:

... on the condition that they would consolidate over 500 NGO facilities in Mogadiscio alone into a much more manageable number and live in compact facilities with more rigorous security procedures. NGO autonomy

made this difficult – NGOs refused to agree to the consolidation and the military, in turn, refused to provide the protection.

The NGOs themselves were engaged in fierce competition. There was no government or UN system to coordinate their activities. From my own experience, from visiting Somalia in the summer of 1992, I know that agencies kept their plans for feeding centres secret in case another aid agency got there first. Within the military contingent there was competition between units from different countries. In the US government there was competition between the various departments concerned with aid. The result was that Somali capacities and interests were almost entirely overlooked. Natsios could not get support for proposals to engage with Somalia's most powerful resource, its business sector: 'Convincing all of the actors at the field and central headquarters level that the proposition should be transformed into a programmatic initiative proved frustrating and time consuming', he wrote.

The outcome was one of the worst failures of humanitarianism. The initial hesitancy reflected a lack of policy about humanitarian intervention in the new world order. Consequently, the military intervention was too late and, as it began to fail, leaders sought to distance themselves from it and blame each other for the failure. Recriminations and uncertainties undermined the morale of troops on the ground, who had perhaps arrived with high ideals. The Somali youth gangs took every opportunity to make a profit out of the intervention, and in the end the military turned on them in anger. The upholders of ideals simply became a further party to a messy conflict. UN troops became embroiled in local conflicts and killed people without justification. In turn, they became the direct targets of the gangs, and the conflict escalated until the prime motive on both sides became revenge. All of this culminated in an attack by US helicopters on a house where the warlord Aideed was supposed to be staying. But, in fact, the clan elders were meeting there instead – the same people with whom Sahnoun was trying to work. Many of them were killed. Ironically, the expedition to restore law and order ended up destroying the remaining mechanism by which it could have been achieved.

These events need to be put in historical perspective. The Somalia failure was not a failure of any particular part of the system, or of the system itself, but of the system in transition. Ideals became, briefly perhaps, divorced from analysis. The outcome was particularly distressing because the emotional reasons for the intervention contrasted so strongly with their disastrous outcome, leaving all involved wondering if it was their particular fault. To make matters worse, a few soldiers have been tried for violations of human rights as if their crimes were somehow separate from the overall failure. To an extent, they have become scapegoats for international guilt. Similarly, in aid agencies, it is easier to put the blame on individual failure than to grasp the totality of a universal tragedy.

Sahnoun writes: 'Eventually, the UN, which is supposed to make peace, found itself killing people, hunting people and bombing a meeting of elders under the mistaken impression that General Aideed was among them. In terms of human ethics, this was not a happy page of history.'

But is the proper conclusion to turn on the UN and blame it for all the world's problems? The UN was simply the figurehead of a military mission essentially run by the US. Its core decisions were all dictated by the UN security council with the US taking the dominant role. Instead, the Somalia experience reveals the conflict between human emotion and rationality.

* * *

It would be unwise to conclude that all military interventions and all ideals are out of place in the modern world. Although individuals and individual units have been blamed, it is important to see Somalia in its unique historical context at the very end of the Cold War. The world order was ready for punitive missions against rogue states, such as Iraq, but not clear about humanitarian principle or whether the notion of the nation state was going to give way to something new. In the case of Somalia, the question 'what is the US strategic interest?' was never answered clearly, and could not be addressed without first asking: 'are we saying that national interests should now be globalized like everything else?' To put it another way, the unanswered question was whether the US was going to play a global or purely national role.

Officials could not function on the basis of 'ideals' alone and needed some sort of answer. Underneath all the talk they feared that the intervention was really just an electoral ploy by the president. Unfortunately, the main outcome was that idealism itself was devalued. The opportunity to incorporate humanitarian principle into the new world order was lost, at least for the time being. The US retreated from binding itself to global obligations, refusing to sign up to most of the 'humanitarian' treaties of the following years, including those on land mines and the rights of the child (ironically, the only other nation to refuse to sign was Somalia). The lesson seemed to be to have no ideals, nor to help other people or risk American lives for law and order in far-off countries. The price of failure in Somalia was paid by the people of Rwanda who were left unprotected against genocide in 1994. When ideals were needed, the West exhibited only self-interest and distrust.

* * *

There are a number of parallels between the American experience and Oxfam's experience in Somalia. Oxfam was similarly unprepared for the event. It had closed its office in Somalia at the end of 1990, and although some projects were still supported, this was done by periodic staff visits from outside. The crucial difference was that there were no longer local staff members based in Somalia who could provide Oxfam with the insights necessary to gain an understanding of what was happening. The process of closing the office had been difficult because it meant getting rid of staff who had proved their loyalty to Oxfam over many years. Loyalty and trustworthiness tend to be rated more highly in poorer countries than in richer ones, and by vulnerable people rather than those with power. This creates a different value system between rich and poor that underpins the humanitarian relationship and creates many problems. Staff in Somalia might be told Oxfam's reasons but still felt betrayed. By leaving Somalia, Oxfam not only lost credibility in Somalia and knowledge of what was happening, but also lost its reputation for trustworthiness. The context for Oxfam's return was one of distrust, of betrayed idealism. While I did not see it then, I suspect that this was one of our main reasons for failure. We believed that we could simply go back and pick up the pieces, but it was not as simple as that.

Oxfam also made a mistake in relation to its own mandate by closing the office when disaster in Somalia was likely. The record of the previous 20 years had shown a series of disasters and there was no reason to believe that the situation had changed. The interior areas of Somalia are drought prone and inhabited mainly by pastoralists who have lost much of their dry-season grazing land to Ethiopia. Small political shocks, such as restrictions on movement, could often turn rain failures into famine. The politics of the region have been deeply affected by the Ethiopia–Somalia war in the 1970s. Oxfam had been repeatedly drawn back to Somalia because of famines, and had habitually tried to build up development programmes. But the issue of the Ethiopia border was not something that could be addressed through development, and the Somalis tended to favour a business approach to development, either expecting the private sector to be involved or treating development projects as businesses from which they could expect to make money. Oxfam was unable to come to terms with this apparent clash of self-interest and altruism. Basically, the decision reflected a developmentalist position – if development is not possible on the aid agencies own ferms then Oxfam should not be in Somalia at all. At the time there was a management policy of 'focus'. The funds would be better allocated elsewhere in Africa. The arguments might look like rationalization in Oxford, but in Somalia they looked like inconsistency and betrayal.

Even while Oxfam was closing its office there were rumours that there would be war to overthrow President Siad Barre. The different clans were vying for power within and outside government and were aware that with the end of the Cold War, the US would not do much to support Barre. War broke out and raged back and forth through 1991. The functions of government collapsed and famine conditions began to develop in Somalia in 1991. Dominant clans turned on smaller ones, especially the non-Somali groups that had supported Barre during the period of supposed democracy. They faced a terrible retribution for having colluded with a Western-imposed notion of the state.

Although conditions were serious, Oxfam was unwilling to reverse its decision. There continued to be a clash (as there had been in Ethiopia in 1984) between two opposing ideologies in the organization that could be characterized as 'relief' and 'development'. Although the evaluation of the Ethiopian response had urged Oxfam to make it clear that relief work was mandatory for all staff, nothing significant had changed and staff tended to regard themselves as exclusively devoted to one or the other. In the 1990s, positions had diverged following a senior management emphasis on 'focus on success'. The idea was to limit the programme to projects where the impact of development work would be greatest. This was good in itself but these projects might not occur in places where disasters were likely. Indeed, the trend would inevitably be away from such areas, as happened in the case of Somalia. One of the main lessons of the 1980s had been that Oxfam's best emergency work transpired when it acted in a developmental way, consulting local people and concentrating on the longer-term issue of rehabilitation. Oxfam characteristically came to the fore when other agencies were leaving. This process often led Oxfam into long-term development projects. Local staff, contacts and continuity were crucial. Senior management rarely intervened but the system worked reasonably well until the issue of 'focus' produced a sudden divergence. The Somalia office was closed basically without reference to the issue of disasters.

Underlying the debate was the question of whether Oxfam was 'global' or not. Was it enough to have scattered development projects as markers of excellence, or did Oxfam have a responsibility to gear itself for an emergency response anywhere in the world? Although we did not realize it at the time, the question was the same as the one facing the US government – whether to globalize or not. To put it another way, the question was whether to focus on what we knew, or take risks according to ideals.

As in the US, the uncertainty played out as competition between departments over the control of resources. The decision to close the Somalia office was taken by the regional staff in order to focus their limited budget on purely developmental activity. This left the emergencies department, of which I was coordinator, with a budget for emergency work but no office to implement it. The concept of focus had been approved by directors who also increasingly insisted that the emergencies department should work anywhere in the world. The leadership was confused, making it impossible for anyone to do the right thing. This set the stage for the confusion and demoralization which ensued.

As reports of famine reached Oxford during 1991 and 1992, managers staved off the crisis by compromise, making emergency grants to support other organizations, notably the ICRC. But as the scale of the emergency increased and the TV images of starvation became more and more alarming, staff began to question whether grants through other organizations were an adequate response. Did Oxfam have nothing to offer except funds? What about its understanding of Somalia built up over many years and its specialist skills in disaster response? Did the public expect the UK's largest international aid charity to respond directly to a disaster like Somalia, or did they accept a specialization in development? Was Oxfam behaving like Achilles, retiring to our tent because the situation was not what we had anticipated?

Normally Oxfam's local office would have made an immediate response, and local knowledge and contacts through development projects would have been put to good use in support of relief programmes. But the absence of these advantages now made Oxfam more hesitant than ever. Through the early months of 1992, Oxfam continued to debate the issue. Without a clear line from the overall leadership, the tension between the development and relief factions increased. The issue centred on conflict between those who thought it was right to reflect public opinion and those who suspected Oxfam of being led by media images, behind which might be fund-raising interests. Staff in the press and in fund-raising departments expressed concern about Oxfam's lack of profile, which they felt undermined the overall credibility of the organization in relation to journalists with whom they wanted to build long-term relationships. But others saw this as a bid for personal or organizational profile. A further factor was that the security situation in Somalia was worse than anything Oxfam had previously encountered, and this become an issue in itself. Should Oxfam work in such circumstances? But then – the argument went – how could we fund others to do what we would not do ourselves?

In the end, a particularly harrowing TV documentary in July 1992 impelled the deputy director to demand an immediate assessment. He made no secret of the fact that he was responding emotionally, but said that this was necessary in order to break the logjam of delay and uncertainty that he felt had undermined Oxfam's reputation. Others thought he was simply reacting to the fact that other agencies were getting all the publicity. I was given the job of making an assessment and left for Somalia within a few days, along with a colleague who was a specialist in health and nutrition.

On arrival in Mogadiscio, I found that although security was still a serious problem, agencies had adapted by paying hired gunmen who were quite likely to be the same people who had looted aid convoys. I wrote: 'To see an ICRC vehicle mounted with a heavy machine gun and a bunch of gunmen is a sign of flexibility and compromise that has characterized their operations in Somalia.'

I think I had already decided that Oxfam must intervene and was making light of things. I had experienced an incident in which we were stopped by our own armed guards on a side-road 80 kilometres from Mogadiscio. The guards demanded to be paid double, using the ends of their Kalashnikovs to emphasize their argument. We had no choice but to agree. I found Oxfam's position of arriving late very humiliating after so many situations where we had not only been the first to arrive, but had the best local knowledge, based on our presence there for many years. The competitive environment in Somalia made it especially difficult to operate because aid agencies kept secret their information about areas of need where they planned to operate. Because Oxfam had no field staff, I had to rely on other agencies even for transport. Fortunately, we still retained links with another international organization, Euro-Action Acord, which had stayed on after Oxfam left, and they provided invaluable support.

Various subjective factors combined to make my Somalia visit traumatic. There was the shock of the violence and the need to pay people who might have been responsible for the famine. There was the humiliation of Oxfam being so poorly placed and not respected. There was the lack of support from local staff, whom I had always relied on for my insight into such situations; without it I felt unable to operate. And then, there was the famine itself, which was worse than anything else I had seen. I wrote:

> It is impossible to overstate the extent of human misery and suffering in Somalia. The worst stories of the journalists are true. People die in front of you, and in every centre you know that there are many who will be dead within a week. There is a moral imperative to respond to the very extent of our ability.

The phrase 'people die in front of you' was my only reference then to an event that I felt unable to describe and did not talk about for many years. In a village, an old woman, skeletally thin, was carried out of her house to take part in a meeting. I had called the meeting to find out more about the famine from the villagers themselves. At the end, as I walked away thinking about what I had been told, I saw her being wrapped in a sheet ready for burial. She had died of starvation while we were talking.

The event made it impossible to be objective, and my own actions thereafter were driven purely by an emotive desire to stop the famine. Whether this was right or wrong, the problem was that other people had not seen what I had seen and therefore did not understand my motive. They might think that the deputy director had been worried about 'profile' and had sent me out to get things moving. I simply did what I was told. The whole response, they thought, was based on organizational interests, dressed up as a sudden rush of emotive commitment. My own view of what I was doing and why was, of course, entirely different. I felt angry that Oxfam had been talking for so long and was still doing so little. On my return, I confronted colleagues with accusations of moral failure.

The decision to intervene was approved by Oxfam's director, finally stepping in to end the interminable discussions. It was agreed that Oxfam should immediately re-establish its office, examine how it could help other agencies in the water sector, examine a possible role in feeding, and distribute goods that other agencies had overlooked. In addition, an agricultural rehabilitation programme that had been started by outside funding would now become a part of Oxfam's local response. We were late, and it would be an uphill task, but if everyone pulled together we could make a credible response which reflected Oxfam's resources and capacities. But the senior technical adviser, who controlled the staff specializing in emergency water supply, refused to participate. He said he was concerned about safety. I had drawn up security guidelines that had been endorsed officially, but Oxfam still operated largely as an association of individuals rather than an organization. He insisted on having his own view and there was insufficient organizational will to overrule him. After some weeks of letting the issue cool down, one of his staff who disagreed with his stance slipped quietly out to Somalia; but by that time it was too late for Oxfam to make a significant response in that sector. Moreover, the famine was already easing and by the time Oxfam was ready for action other organizations were beginning to close down.

The staff member who had been requested to go to Somalia to set up feeding programmes also deliberated about safety and other issues for a long time and finally refused to go, again on grounds of security. Under Oxfam's procedures staff have the right to choose not to work in a dangerous situation. But the issue of security could easily be used to cover other doubts. Most crucially, when managers were asked if they could spare an experienced person to run the new office in Mogadiscio, there were no offers. One person even objected to being asked on the grounds that it amounted to 'poaching' staff. There was no sense of an agreed organizational purpose. Order had collapsed.

This is not typical of Oxfam. The organization found itself without a firm base in agreed policy to cope with a changing world. Cold War developmentalism had not only created an optimistic mode, but also an organizational style based on individualism in which the predominant management style was consensus. If management stepped in, this was seen as dictatorial and might elicit poor cooperation – as had happened when the deputy director stepped forward to resolve the

Somalia question in July 1992. The Somalia case was a moral tangle and Oxfam was late. Only strong, decisive action could succeed. But this was contrary to the organizational culture that had developed during the Cold War years. As Oxfam's evaluation says, it also reflects a situation in which emotions take precedence over judgements:

> *The decision to go back to Somalia was an emotive one. Feelings were running high and decisions were personality-led rather than based on measured judgement. Oxfam is too big an organization to be swayed by individual argument and needs checks and balances in place in order to ensure that decisions are made rationally.*

Four years later one of the managers involved in the original decision to withdraw from Somalia wrote: 'No attempt is being made here to deny the seriousness of the situation which existed in Somalia, and the fact that it may have been getting worse during 1992. But the pressure to move back into what was potentially a very dangerous situation, very fast, where other agencies were already established, was largely a result of media pressure and the need for Oxfam to raise its profile.'

The internal evaluation concludes that Oxfam actually attracted little media interest. Oxfam's presence remained too small and, without a long history, Oxfam could not generate the kind of insights in which journalists were interested. If publicity had been the intention, the relief programme could have been deliberately directed towards high-profile activities such as child-feeding; this did not happen. But who can tell what were the motives underlying people's actions? The problem for humanitarians is that altruism is simply a feeling, and others cannot know whether it is our real motive, or whether we are exploiting the altruistic ideal for selfish purposes. Those whose task it is to implement programmes but are not clear as to the motive find themselves in an especially difficult and distressing situation. The Oxfam evaluation concludes:

> *The first four months of Oxfam's return can be described as nightmarish for the people involved. There was no clear work and Oxfam was 'scrabbling about' trying to find a role for itself. There was no team spirit. People were under enormous stress from the living conditions, the anarchic situation they had to operate in and the constant fear for safety.*

Field staff were caught between those in Oxford who were dubious about the whole operation and those who felt that it should be Oxfam's top priority. In Somalia they were caught between the terrible needs and the disruption caused by the gangs of youths who made it almost impossible to offer help. Two years after the event Oxfam's internal evaluation finds that the effects on the staff were devastating: 'The majority of people spoken to who worked in Somaliland and Somalia were still experiencing distress and trauma as a result of their experience. The feelings varied from nightmares, a loss of confidence, a feeling of failure and dissatisfaction with the work achieved, and feelings of personal inadequacy to anger and disillusionment with aid work.'

The programme was almost unmanageable with staff resigning suddenly and others suspecting that they were victims of plots. Hours were spent on satellite telephones discussing personalities and personality clashes. I came to the conclusion that the underlying problem was lack of clear policy about such situations. I wrote a strong paper for management and trustees that pointed out that Oxfam still lacked a clear policy on whether it should intervene in cases like Somalia. I felt that Oxfam attracted public donations on the basis that it would respond wherever it could and certainly in any very poor country where people were dying in hundreds of thousands, as in Somalia. It was not an issue of 'profile' but of carrying out our legal mandate for the 'relief of poverty, distress and suffering'. I detected an underlying:

> ... bias towards the view that development is the natural state of mankind and that emergencies are temporary, and that the existence of emergencies should be downplayed in order to promote 'positive images'. Such attitudes contribute to an ambivalent and half-hearted response ... Managers tend to resist emergency involvement until late in the day.

It was an emotive piece of writing, hitting out in all directions. It might have produced defensive responses, and perhaps deserved to, but fortunately it did promote a realization that something was fundamentally wrong. Over the next few years various steps were taken to ensure that the likelihood of emergency interventions was considered when Oxfam decided whether to open and close offices. Development and relief were not to be divided and all staff had a responsibility for both, regardless of their designations. Individuals should be more disciplined when accepting organizational objectives. The next four years saw Oxfam undertake a complete revision of its purpose and methods.

* * *

I still regret our lack of local perspective in the Somalia response. We failed because we had lost touch with those local voices and lost their trust. It was not simply that we lacked direction from above, but we also lacked understanding of the person in need. We could not follow the principle of humanity.

After leaving the village where the woman died, I passed along the edge of a banana plantation that, to my amazement, was full of fruit. I asked why the people did not take the fruit and was told by my interpreter: 'It belongs to a powerful merchant who puts a guard on it. People are frightened.' In the circumstances, which we had all come to regard as anarchic and chaotic, this reflected a profound sense of order. Siad Barre's troops, and then Aideed's, had been through this area looting food from the villages, which was why they had starved. But none of the villagers had touched this lush plantation. Who had such power that no one could touch them, even in the middle of war?

I never found out the name of that person. But clearly there were systems that were not part of the chaos that outsiders saw. The state had failed but other systems remained. I now realize that Oxfam could have worked through merchants and the mafia to get things done. Instead of bringing food through the ports and having it looted by angry gangs, we could have run feeding programmes by paying merchants to deliver food, or even to hand out bananas from the plantation – provided that we paid for them.

Natsios, the USAID official, had realized that in some ways external relief was making things worse: 'The diversion of relief assistance was, in fact, exacerbating the violence and reinforcing the power of the warlords.' He proposed, instead, that merchants should be used to deliver food, basing his analysis on the work of one of the most influential figures in humanitarianism of the last two decades, Fred Cuny:

Cuny observed that food markets in several cities were receiving most of their food for sale from looted stocks. Merchants would actually request the local militia or bands of thieves to steal more food as their stocks diminished each day. The relief effort was the cheapest and nearest source of the commodity. The market demand was driving some of the looting,

*though it was difficult to quantify its proportionate effect on the disorder.
In more stable social orders the merchant class supports law, order and
stability because they are essential to commercial exchange. The precise
reverse of this inherent disposition towards order was operative in Somalia: markets were distorted by the unnatural increase in food value, the
interruption of transport lines, and the collapse of law and order. Merchants needed food, and the relief effort was the most efficient source of it.*

One of Cuny's great contributions to humanitarianism was his insight that market forces could be used for humanitarian purposes. He
advised Natsios to make relief aid an attractive business proposition.
I had been in touch with Cuny about internal food-purchase operations involving merchants in Tigray, northern Ethiopia. He sent me a
document entitled 'A short briefing about the market sales approach'
in which he explained the rationale behind his thinking about Somalia. Basically the idea was to sell food to local merchants at
'advantageous prices' in order to:

> *... provide food to those people who can afford to buy it so they won't seek
> relief food; and to drive food prices down to reasonable levels so that a
> normal market system can provide food to a greater number of people...
> This program is based on two premises. Firstly, experience from many
> conflicts and famines shows that there are always a large number of people
> who can buy food and many more who could buy food if prices were re-
> duced. The number of people in this group may vary but they are there.
> The approach is not designed to make the poorest of the poor buy food; it is
> designed to take those who can afford to buy food, if it is available, off the
> relief registers. Remember, famines – especially those that occur in war –
> represent a breakdown of the agricultural market as well as a food short-
> age. This programme addresses one part of the problem and reduces the
> burden on food aid.*
>
> *Secondly, there are always traders who are willing to take risks to make
> profits. Often these traders can organize transport and make security ar-
> rangements to carry cargoes to areas that are inaccessible to relief agencies.
> In north-west Somalia during 1989–1990s, private traders were able to
> move food by ship, truck, and camel to areas that were sealed off to UN and
> NGOs by warfare.*

For the time being, Cuny's ideas about 'monetization' in war went the
same way as all other good ideas in the political and ideological

vacuum of the Somali crisis. Oxfam never got itself sufficiently organized to consider such an imaginative option and lacked the local
staff to carry it out. Natsios tried to get support for the idea but was met
with disbelief:

> *The notion that humanitarian organizations would sell food in a famine
> mystified some and appalled others... The senior NGO and UN execu-
> tives understood the concept quickly; however, their field staffs split over
> it. The UN field staff of the World Food Programme and the UN Develop-
> ment Programme initially resisted the concept: they opposed the scheme
> because they thought it abusive to sell food to starving people (which, of
> course, was not what the plan proposed to do) and they were uncomfortable
> with the practical mechanisms for carrying it out. Because of these misgiv-
> ings, they slowed the implementation in its formative early months.*

Natsios concludes that apart from small experiments the idea was lost
because of: 'conflicting mandates and interests, and report[ing] to different headquarters. Getting agreement on a single strategy dealing
with a crisis is difficult, particularly in a short time. The market interventions attempted by USAID during the summer and fall of 1992,
however appropriate and innovative, fell victim to this complexity.'

If Oxfam had had local staff who pointed out such things, there
might have been a very different history of early and timely intervention, as well as innovative use of business systems in Somalia to
alleviate the famine. The ICRC did, indeed, begin to move in that direction.

In order to persuade Achilles to get out of his tent and take action,
Ulysses used the argument that the past is soon forgotten:

Time hath, my lord, a wallet at his back,
Wherein he puts alms for oblivion,
A great-sized monster of ingratitudes.
These scraps are good deeds past, which are devour'd
As fast as they are made, forgot as soon as done.

Somalia gave ideals a bad name. The trouble is that instead of seeing
this as a failure arising from post-Cold War confusion, people saw it
as a failure in the absolute. When ideals were needed in the form of
determination to stop the Rwanda genocide of 1994, the spectre of
Somalia frightened decision-makers. When 12 UN soldiers were killed,

the troops were pulled out and when there should have been military intervention there was not. Unfortunately, what should have been forgotten about Somalia – the dead GI dragged through the streets of Mogadiscio – was remembered; and what should have been remembered – the need for clarity in support of ideals – was forgotten.

The problem of 'ideal' altruism is that it so easily turns to cynicism and distrust. Why? Perhaps because our default position is selfishness; and knowing that, we find it hard to believe in others. But the result is to distrust others and distrust ourselves. It becomes a disease, destroying us from within.

Chapter 7

Azerbaijan and Bosnia: Responsibility and Rights

S hould aid workers feel guilty if, despite their efforts, people still suffer and die? Should we respond to more and more crises? What are the limits to personal responsibility? To put it most simply, can an aid worker ever be happy?

Aid workers learn quickly that it is not enough to respond to obvious crises such as flood and famine. The invisible daily poverty of hundreds of millions of people creates constant suffering, even though the TV cameras are not there to watch. Often a crisis occurs within a continuum of suffering as an event that is witnessed by the world's media. If resources are limited, we have to address one set of needs and not another – but how do we choose? Is it enough to respond – without objectivity – to the images that strike us most deeply? And is the issue simply starvation and physical need, or does it also extend to the suffering of the mind? What is poverty? What is suffering? Who decides?

The great Russian writer Leo Tolstoy spent many years trying to define his personal responsibility. During 1891 and 1892 he repeatedly visited the region of Toula in Russia to help with famine relief, concluding, as aid workers often do today, that 'crisis' is not crisis at all but only a small publicized shock within the general occurrence of extreme poverty:

> *Our two years' experience in distributing, among a suffering population, contributions that passed through our hands have confirmed our long-established conviction that most of the want and destitution, and the suffering and grief that go with them, which we almost in vain have tried to counteract by external means in one small corner of Russia, have arisen not from some exceptional temporary cause independent of us, but from*

general permanent causes quite dependent on us, and consisting entirely
in the unchristian, unbrotherly relations maintained by us educated people
towards the poor.

In short the people of Toula were struck by famine because harsh land-
lords oppressed them and left them vulnerable. They had no household
reserves, and so when crops failed they starved immediately. It is the
same in most famines today. If crises have their roots in poverty, relief
work will achieve only very limited results. A cyclone hitting the coast
of Bangladesh is likely to kill thousands of people, whereas a cyclone
of the same strength passing across Florida may cause no deaths at
all. In Florida, people receive warnings on TV, pack up their belong-
ings in their cars and drive away along motorways. After the cyclone
they can claim compensation from an insurance company or their
government. In Bangladesh, poverty forces people to live in dangerous and inaccessible places, such as the shoreline and on islands in
the rivers from which there is no escape from floods. Rich people do
not live there because it is too dangerous. There may be no warning of
disaster and no means of escape. Merely providing relief allows the
inequality to continue. Eradicating the risk of crisis means eradicating
poverty. But if crisis, poverty and human suffering are equal issues of
concern worldwide, then surely the task of the aid worker is impossible.

An example of the problem of limiting responsibility occurred during the early 1990s when communist governments crumbled and
collapsed in Eastern Europe and the former Soviet Union, leaving
hundreds of millions of people impoverished. Aid agencies were suddenly confronted with a new and massive problem. Throughout this
gigantic region, children begged on the streets, girls were forced into
prostitution and old people died of neglect in unheated flats. Conflict broke out in Georgia, Armenia, Azerbaijan, Moldova, Chechnya
and throughout the Balkans. Millions of people were displaced from
their homes. Families suddenly lost incomes that they had considered to be absolutely assured. In the first three years after the collapse,
over half a million 'extra' deaths were recorded in Russia compared
with the period before. This was not a crisis within a context of poverty, as aid agencies had often experienced, but the collapse of the
context itself. It was huge in scale, extending throughout Eastern
Europe and across Russia's 13 time zones. It was also totally unexpected, leaving people unprotected by a state that had been 'mother

and father' for more than 50 years. There were few effective 'survival strategies', and suddenly people were as vulnerable as in Tolstoy's day. Many aid agencies backed away, overwhelmed by the sheer scale of the problem, unable to assess these new needs in relation to established programmes in Africa and Asia.

It was not just the physical poverty that was so striking. People were in a constant state of shock and grief for a way of life that had so suddenly been lost. Physical aid was not an adequate human response to such grief and suffering. But was this because the people and the aid agencies belonged to a similar culture?

I found the experience deeply disturbing. However much we may try to be impartial, it is people most like ourselves who trigger the most intense reactions. In Eastern Europe, people were similar to people in my own village: they dressed the same way, experienced events with similar emotions, lived in the same kinds of rooms with the same electric light bulbs, and cooked food in the same kind of saucepans on similar stoves. They had never expected their lives to change and their disaster provoked fears about my own security. But was my compassion essentially selfish, triggered by concern for myself? To outside observers this might appear as a form of racism. Did I respond to suffering among white people differently from suffering among black people? I realized that 'concern for the person in need' has the limitation of being subjective. It is something we feel differently in different circumstances. But concern is the uncertain and subjective basis on which we build the edifice of humanitarianism. However much we strive towards rules and policies, it seems impossible to escape the underlying uncertainty of a subjective reaction.

Although ideally our concern should be impartial, usually it is not. An African woman working for Oxfam in Eastern Europe asked: 'Why did I see Western aid workers holding the hands of suffering people in Eastern Europe when they never did in Africa?' Western aid workers in Eastern Europe were often deeply shocked to see white people in refugee camps. It reversed their normal sense of what humanitarianism was about, and forced them to ask difficult questions about themselves and their perceptions. African staff members working in Europe also said that they found the situation profoundly shocking. The same woman said: 'I could not cope with the idea of white people as victims. We had never seen that in Africa.'

Underlying all this is the question of whether our concern for others is really a disguised form of concern for ourselves. If we say that some feelings are good and some are not, how do we choose between them without the benefit of Tolstoy's fixed Christian morality? To some extent, we can train and discipline ourselves through self-awareness. On the basis of experience in Eastern Europe, we might ask: 'Why were we not sufficiently moved to hold the hands of adult Africans?' But ultimately, even in our post-moralist world, we cannot act collectively without some principles of morality. Acting alone, I can decide whether to help a beggar according to my mood. Acting collectively, I need rules. The lesson from Eastern Europe is that these rules are not reflections of reality – they are arbitrary defences against the chaos of human feeling. We need a rule of impartiality precisely because we are not impartial.

* * *

Inevitably, it is people's suffering that evokes our human response. We convert that concern for suffering by attending to physical needs. Oxfam's legal mandate is 'the relief of poverty, distress and suffering'. But does this mean that poverty, distress and suffering are separate issues, each demanding its own response? Or is Oxfam's purpose to address situations in which all three issues exist together? How can we define distress and suffering? It appeared that there was an extraordinary level of distress and suffering in Eastern Europe, but rather less poverty. How was the response to be measured? Did people actually suffer more in Eastern Europe, or were we, the aid givers, more sensitive to the suffering of white people? Was the difference outside or inside?

The debate made non-religious Oxfam consider questions that were usually the preserve of religion. We faced the fundamental question: Does man live by bread alone? But firstly, who is 'man'? Can we compare needs between one person and another regardless of their own expectations and culture? Do we measure the calorific requirement of welfare recipients in the UK, and the number of litres of water they need for survival, in the same way that we do for people in African refugee camps? To do so would be considered an affront to human dignity within the context of British society. But what is dignity except a set of culturally specific expectations? And if we say that people in Eastern Europe, like welfare claimants in the UK, seem to have much greater needs than individuals in Africa, is this racism?

Part of the problem is that the word 'racism' is impossible to use without strongly pejorative overtones. In some cases, its meaning is difficult to distinguish from the word 'patriotic' (signifying that we support our country in preference to other people's nations), which has the opposite connotation. Aid workers find themselves caught in a trap of cultural perception, helping other races for whom Western society feels deeply ambivalent. Beneath this lies the central ambivalence of humanitarian concern. Is it an expression of selfishness, as in the case of removing a feeling of guilt, or an altruistic concern for another person?

People in Eastern Europe had enjoyed stability for 50 years, and they were now deeply distressed because they had lost not only their possessions but also a way of life. In 1993 I wrote:

Displaced people expressed to us an angry sense of betrayal that not a hand was lifted when they were driven from their homes, nor now – when they are helpless and destitute – does the government do anything for them. In other parts of the world people rarely expect much from their government, but this is a country where the state had been father and mother. Social support, religion and philanthropy had been practically forgotten because they were unnecessary. Now people are finding themselves unable to cope physically and emotionally.

This, we would be inclined to think, is rarely the case in African disasters where people are supposed to have 'survival strategies' precisely because they are used to such tragedies. The physical effects may be terrible but we do not see the main issue as 'distress'. But are these assumptions based on a racist stereotype caused by our greater ability to empathize with the peoples of Eastern Europe? Do we subconsciously deny the existence of emotion among Africans?

The collapse of communism had parallels with the collapse of employment in the West. Jobs had been assured and were the defining factor in personal identity, especially for men, who therefore found it hard to cope with the psychological consequences. In both the East and West, alcoholism became rife and the life expectancy of men fell dramatically. Fathers lost their identity as head of the family. They lost the basic capacity to send children to school and hospital. Now the 'head of the family' was unemployed, purposeless, likely to be depressed and lacking in self-confidence because he was unable to support his family or pay for children to go to the (now privatized) schools and clinics. Several Oxfam visitors to Eastern Europe found themselves moved by the stories of professional people, such as university lecturers, who

had suddenly become destitute and might have to make a living sell-
ing cabbages in the market. The image struck deeply into their own
fears.

The problem with compassion and concern is that our feelings are
shaped culturally and by our own experience. As Oxfam's global emergencies coordinator I found myself becoming more and more perplexed
about my own response to scenes such as the one I described after
visiting Azerbaijan in 1993:

*A huge man in a tattered suit came forward when we were at a government
office and insisted on telling us how his land was seized – he fled for his
life and his brother disappeared. He wanted us to know how many sheep
and goats he had lost, how fine his home had been, with grapes and fruit
trees. When he finished, he relapsed into silence, unable to explain why he
had felt so compelled to speak.*

*It seemed almost like this was a whole society on the verge of collapse. In
a technical institute occupied by refugees a man constantly pulled me by
the sleeve and insisted that we come to his room. We walked around, re-
viewing sanitation and other issues, but still the man was there, darting
forward from the crowd. At last we plodded up a dark staircase, he threw
open the door of a room and began to shout crazily, with his arm pointing
to a woman who was crying on the bed. Then he shouted at a much older
woman who seemed to ask him to stop, but he snatched from her an embroidered bundle and, pulling down the flap, revealed a perfect, dead baby.*

*Suddenly he stopped talking as if he had lost interest in us. We left the
room, unable to ask any more about this unexplained tragedy of a homeless
despairing man.*

The man looked like someone I might meet on the streets of Oxford,
outside my office. His suit was old fashioned like those worn by the
older generation of working men in Britain as a mark of respectability.
He reminded me of an uncle (the same one I had thought of in
Mozambique), and this memory triggered a strong sense of compassion. This feeling might easily be converted into emotive language
when writing reports, such as 'appalling suffering' or 'extreme human need'. The real reason for the strong reaction, I suspect, was that
his experience was highly personal and specific. The immediate impact was different from what I usually felt in African crises, but this was
not, I realized, simply because of the historical perspective. The difference was really that this man had demanded my personal attention

when telling his personal story in a way that no African had ever done. He had recognized the person in me, not just the aid giver. He had the confidence from the recent past that I should stop and listen. There was no colonial or racial barrier between us.

One solution to this problem of bias would be to avoid personal encounters, but it is often those personal encounters that yield the greatest insights. The alternative is to objectify our emotional reactions by compensating for cultural difference. The implication is that in Africa, or in any other more distant culture, we have to work much harder in order to achieve the same result in terms of emotional contact. The question is whether we attempt a deeper understanding (at great personal cost) or limit ourselves to a more comfortable view from a safe distance. Should aid workers actually get emotionally involved?

I am not saying that this never happens in Africa. On reflection, I recalled cases where individual people in Africa had deeply affected my sensibility. But it was less common than in Eastern Europe. The administrator in Mozambique who took me to see the rebels being killed had also become a person with whom I felt a deep sympathy, but this was partly a retrospective feeling developed from a number of special factors that made the whole visit emotional. An old Ethiopian man who reached through the window of my Landrover, and touched my head in thanks for a gift, had broken through the social barrier represented by my position in the vehicle. His was a time-honoured and traditional gesture from the poor literally reaching out towards the rich. Furthermore, he reminded me of an old man I had known 20 years before with whom I had enjoyed walks in the countryside. It was not that the same feelings could not be evoked by people of very different appearance, but that the 'connections' were just a little less likely in Africa. The equation of white with power and black with suffering had created a barrier. It was a two-way process, involving Africans' perceptions as much as my own. We stereotyped each other and remained distant. As my African colleague observed, it was only when she saw a white person's vulnerability that she could react to him as a person rather than as a symbol.

* * *

Does any of this help with the problem of defining human responsibility? While emotive responses might be misleading, objective intellectual methods also seem to yield no useful results. It was extremely difficult to define who were the poor people. Apart from the mafia, politicians and a few business people, everyone was sinking into poverty, but some were doing so much faster than others depending upon their specific circumstances. Many people hid their problems out of personal pride. No outsider could tell who was going down fastest or how far they had to fall. It depended on past assets, social connections and chance events such as illnesses and funerals. Who knew how has much money someone might have under the bed, or what relatives were sending in sealed envelopes.

The main recipients of external aid were those who had been displaced from their homes by conflict. But among them were people who had travelled with tractors laden with goods, combine harvesters and trucks. They filled their rooms with TV sets, glass chandeliers and even grand pianos. Regardless of wealth, some seemed to abandon all interest in life. Others tried to maintain their former dignity, wearing their suits and ties, sitting down to play cards or chess. However, underneath many suffered severe depression. External aid was not simply a source of goods, but a reassurance that the suffering was acknowledged. As the man who took me to see his dead child had shown, his grief was as much an issue as anything else. He wanted me to know. Surely to respond to such distress and suffering was within the scope of humanity?

But how was this extraordinary combination of poverty, distress and suffering (with all its subjective and objective uncertainties) to be compared with other humanitarian needs in other parts of the world? Could money be taken out of African and Asian budgets to fund new programmes in Eastern Europe? Many people, especially those in charge of budgets for the traditional areas of work, argued that Oxfam was already overextending itself and should not take on more.

But Oxfam did not have clear criteria for choosing where it worked. This was not for lack of trying. Over the years Oxfam had commissioned several attempts to rationalize the allocation of its resources between different parts of the world according to need. The legal mandate was 'relief of poverty, distress and suffering' but there were no clear definitions of what poverty, distress and suffering were. Oxfam commissioned a 'fundamental review', completed in 1998, which examined the problem in some depth but ultimately expanded the meaning of the words rather than limit them to something precise and measurable. The only 'shortening' was the conclusion that distress and suffering were similar concepts as far as Oxfam was concerned – suffering was more physical and distress more psychological. The report also concluded that suffering and distress could not be separated from poverty: 'People suffer because of many factors. The pain endured by victims of torture in prison constitutes suffering, as does the distress endured by those who lose loved ones ... Oxfam's remit does not extend to all of these. Oxfam responds to the suffering of the poor.'

No measures of suffering and distress were proposed. In studying poverty, the report examined several definitions, concluding that they all had some validity. The most basic was sheer lack of resources or income: 'Income–consumption poverty starts from the premise that it is the level of resources which people command that determines whether they are poor. The World Bank, for instance, defines those that live on less than one [US] dollar a day as poor.'

But this 'dollar a day' definition obviously failed to reflect differences in the purchasing power of the dollar or the needs of the person in varying circumstances. It fails to address the problem of the refugee in the UK compared with the African relief camp. The 'dollar a day' measurement had never been applied to Western countries and the World Bank now accepted that it was also impossible to use it in the post-communist states where warm clothing and heating are essential to life and prices are higher. A minimum of US$4 was eventually agreed for the post-communist states, but the exception then raises the question of whether other countries should be given a US$2 or US$3 rating. In fact, following global debate, the East Europe figure was later reduced to US$2. If the 'dollar a day' measurement was a vague approximation, was it useful for Oxfam in deciding where it worked? Moreover, if poor countries were defined as those with the highest proportion of poor people, did this necessarily mean that they should be the focus of aid rather than countries such as China and India, which had the highest absolute numbers of poor people? Moreover, this purely physical method of measurement seemed to overlook the question of whether people live by bread alone.

The second definition of poverty gives this much greater prominence. Poverty is defined as the absence of basic 'capabilities', 'freedoms' or 'rights', such as education, health, life expectancy, gender equality, etc, rather than simply deficits of food and water: 'Capability-based poverty springs from the premise that what people are able to achieve is important. Poverty is therefore a deficit of capabilities.'

This is the 'development as freedom' approach favoured by Nobel economist Amartya Sen. It became the basis for the UN's Human

Development Index, in which countries are ranked according to a combined measure of incomes and capabilities. Although it may seem rather remote from poverty as it is normally conceived, this index does reflect a wider concept of humanity. It sees people in a social context.

The problem with applying the Human Development Index (HDI) to Eastern Europe, as with many other countries, was that the figures were not reliable. During the communist period, officials were instructed to make the statistics fit the plan. During 1993–1994, when people were plunged into sudden poverty, the HDI rankings for ex-communist countries were still extraordinarily high and only began to fall much later. Decisions about aid budgets that were made on the basis of the HDI would have been inaccurate. The deeper and more lasting problem was that, as with all aggregate figures, the index failed to reflect the rapid polarization of wealth and opportunity and the fragmentation of society. It was not a static society but one in such rapid transition that nothing could be measured. Studies by UNICEF in the former Soviet Union indicated that categories such as 'old', 'children' and 'women' were not a reliable guide to poverty. Some people in each group did very well while others from a similar background failed. The problem does not lie so much in the concept of 'development as freedom' as in the concept of the state as the usual measure of aid budgets. The logical answer, which Oxfam began to consider, was to tie budgets to 'freedoms' or 'rights' rather than to countries.

The third measure of poverty looks directly at inequality, but has only been applied to economic inequality. It compares the incomes of the poorest with those of the richest:

Marginalization is, at some levels, a question of relative poverty or inequality... To some extent, analysts who rely on measures of 'income poverty' already accept the premise that their definition of poverty is based on a perception of where individuals should stand in relation to a social average. Income inequality measures, however, go further. In their purest form, they purport to say that, whatever the standard of life of individuals, what matters is solely their relative income. This approach, therefore, is not only concerned with poverty, but also social justice and morality.

But again, there were problems of measurement. In Eastern Europe there was now conspicuous wealth alongside appalling poverty. Much of the wealth was held by the mafia and their associates who were unwilling to provide figures for government statistics. The 'black' economy in Russia has been estimated to be equal to the 'white' or official economy. Measures of inequality for the region, such as the Gini-coefficient, failed to reflect the extraordinary gaps that were so obvious to anyone visiting the region. But was inequality and indicator of poverty? There was a distinction between absolute poverty, meaning lack of the means of life, and relative poverty: a person might consider themselves poor in relation to the society in which they lived, and yet seem well off from the perspective of someone in a much poorer society. Was poverty simply a matter of perception?

Oxfam now considered a fourth measure – social exclusion:

> *The fourth approach, used among others by some departments of the UK government, suggests that poverty is also a deficit of integration. As the strength of community ties, household-support structures and relationship with the state are crucial to avoiding suffering, those excluded are vulnerable or poor. It is these unequal relationships that are often at the heart of other types of deprivation.*

Although it is really not much more than a variant of the 'capabilities' measure, this approach is quite helpful for aid agencies because their task is to define an extreme which justifies human concern. It describes aptly the particular sort of poverty experienced by many women in India, for example, or by disabled people where access to community assets or places of employment may be impossible. In Oxfam, exclusion emerged as probably the best single description of the kind of poverty it sought to address in the post-communist world. As state services disappear, some people can afford to buy health and education but others are excluded.

The problem was that all these definitions, except the first, ultimately involved subjective judgements about human needs. The question that followed was: 'who defines them?' The analysis added: 'Some argue that there is a fifth approach to defining poverty: by asking those living in poverty... This presupposes, however, that we can independently ascertain who "the poor" are, before we try to seek their assessments.'

Of course, this is not a measure in itself but a method of getting to a measurement. Yet it reflects the persistent problem that issues of poverty, distress and suffering are fundamentally subjective and involve different perceptions by different people, most notably the aid giver and the aid recipient. The report concludes: 'When asked to define their poverty, even those living in income poverty describe a range of deficits, ranging from lack of resources to exclusion from the rest of the community. Different aspects affect people at different times. Poverty in its lived experience, therefore, does not conform to the strait-jacket of one single approach.'

In the end, Oxfam found no magic formula, and still has no rationally justified method of allocating resources between different areas of the world. While the objective remains 'the relief of poverty, distress and suffering', all three as much subjective as objective; we guess their extent according to our own feelings. Another way of putting this is that values, such as 'relief of poverty, distress and suffering, are little more than conglomerations of specific feelings.

* * *

Despite all these uncertainties, aid managers have to make decisions, but they can do so in a participatory manner. In practice, the fifth method is quite widely used, especially by Oxfam. In the collective centres of Eastern Europe the people themselves proved able to draw up a list of the most needy. A list would be drawn up by a group of representatives and would then be tested in public, offering the chance for people to challenge it if they wished. Oxfam staff would cross-check a small sample in order to ensure that the system was not being abused. It rarely was. But it must be said that there were no outside interests capable of distorting the process. Left to themselves, people were able to find the definition of poverty that best fitted their feelings and values. But if aid agencies are responding to distress and suffering as well as more physical forms of poverty, what sort of actions should they undertake?

I remember one of our women staff who visited a home for the mentally ill in Montenegro, a distressing place where patients were chained to the walls or forced to live in cages. She had the ability to touch another person and immediately make them smile. I saw a woman weep for joy within seconds of meeting her. Such a gift is surely part of our humanitarian response? In situations where people are highly distressed, the way we work counts as much as what we give. Yet, how does this match with the advertising slogans used in the West? Feed a family for £5. Save a granny's sight for £10. Plant a forest for £100. The reality is that aid itself is not so much a solution as a symbol. But who are we, the people who give aid? And what do people want from us?

Srebrenica in Bosnia had been designated as a 'safe area' by the UN Security Council, but despite this assurance and the presence of UN troops, the town fell to Bosnian Serb forces. Calls for external support from the UN were turned down and the UN soldiers were instructed to offer no resistance. Muslim men and boys who had fought for many months against the Serb attack were now helpless. They were separated from their families, taken away in buses and trucks to different places and massacred a few days later. Unaware of this, but fearful because the men and boys had been taken from them, women, girls, the elderly and the very young were put on buses that took them to Muslim areas, not knowing what was going to happen to them or those they had left behind.

After several hours of travelling the buses arrived at the town of Tuzla in Muslim territory, where Oxfam had its base. People had been given no food or water and most had not been able to take more than a few possessions with them. Oxfam quickly distributed clothing but staff realized that the main issue was distress about the fate of the men and boys left behind. Those who offered clothes found themselves criticized for offering such useless assistance. Gradually, they found that what people actually wanted (or at least those who were open to help at all) was guidance in adapting to the new conditions. The UN was running a reception camp with great precision, but it generally failed to explain to people what was happening or to provide practical help. Oxfam's report states:

In Tuzla, Oxfam played an unforeseen, and unseen role in this emergency, which served a crucial purpose not covered by any other agency. The movement from the access road to the tented area by the runway began at 6.00 pm on the second day. Small groups of people (approximately 20–25) were taken to the registration area and then moved to the first group of tents. Many of the refugees were carrying one or two large bags and also babies, young children, and helping elderly relatives. It was a natural response to help an elderly woman, carry a young baby or a heavy bag, and talk to the people as they moved to the tents. Clearly, many people were distressed and disorientated, but glad to have arrived at the air base and to be moving to a place where they could sleep. Once they arrived at the first group of tents the UN soldiers accompanying them tried to give them instructions in English; we quickly realized that there was no interpreter present, and no officer directing the soldiers. While they were very moved by the plight of the refugees, there was no organization or system, and nobody to give basic information.

So began Oxfam's most immediate intervention by giving refugees information about the location of water supplies and toilets, and how many people should be accommodated in each tent... Blankets were dropped onto the runway to be collected by those already in tents. The blankets were tightly tied together with strips of plastic. In order to collect the blankets, the people had first to know that they were there (grey lumps on a dark runway at night), find something with which to cut through the plastic, and then carry the blankets through the grass criss-crossed with guy-ropes. For a young mother with four small children, an elderly couple already exhausted and confused, it was simply too much. Here again we were able to assist by filling up our Landrovers with blankets. We were also able to help people who were unable to collect water, a group of amputees, elderly people, or the many harassed young mothers trying to calm their children, carry their bags, spread a ground sheet and feed their baby simultaneously!

In retrospect, many of the staff felt that their greatest contribution was simply to be there. But this raises some further questions: 'Can I, a person, be independent of my role in Oxfam, and Oxfam's role within the West?' Is Oxfam itself an agent of the West, which, in this case, failed to save Srebrenica?

Aid workers often talk about 'demanding' situations. However, the greatest demands are not for goods but for emotional sympathy – first because the demands are limitless and second because such feelings may be tinged by a sense of hypocrisy. There are different ways of coping with, or limiting, the response. Some concentrate their emotional energy in short bursts. Others try to remain detached. Short-term staff tend to overwork, but sometimes hide themselves from the emotional consequences of what they are dealing with. Aid staff tend to overwork – work becomes a drug to quiet the human response.

Aid workers are beset by a constant sense of failure. If organizations claim to save lives, this implies that they can fail to save them too. For an organization, this is a theoretical question that can be lightly dismissed, but for aid workers in the front line it is a serious worry. They can become more and more embedded in the problem of limiting their own sense of responsibility. Like Tolstoy, they may hate the idea of compromise and yet find that neither complete commitment nor complete detachment are actually possible. They must learn to live with a constant sense of having never quite reached the ideal.

At different points during the experience of aid workers, human suffering becomes an issue in its own right, rather than as an intellectual problem. Yet, such a process can involve too much introspection.

An organization tends to push the issue of personal responsibility away from the centre and out to the 'edges'. Canteen helpers sometimes end up as counsellors. In aid organizations the field workers are left with the full emotional impact of problems that central managers only dimly perceive. This is not necessarily bad, but is rarely recognized. As a result, no one knows when the limit is reached or what personal sense of responsibility, including inevitable failure, people build up inside themselves. Most expatriate staff members working for Oxfam in Bosnia during the war sought counselling on their return. For local staff, the stresses may have been greater. But their employers knew very little about it, and perhaps preferred not to know.

Aid managers need to recognize that stress is a constant factor in humanitarian work and that a supportive system is important. Stress-driven activity is dysfunctional. Those who are unable to cope may rush around in pointless activity, taking on more and more responsibility and becoming suspicious of the efforts of others. Such people often hide their anger, only to let it out when least expected and causing the most confusion. They can build mistrust of their colleagues, and seek to undermine them. They can show a cynical disregard of those whom they are trying to help, treating them as incapable victims rather than as people whose greatest wish may be to recover their capabilities. Failed idealism easily turns to bitterness.

It may be helpful to recognize that these problems arise from deep contradictions in the notion of humanity – which is, in a sense, a selfish desire to assuage our own feelings of compassion for those in need as well as a desire to be altruistic. It involves a combination of personal emotions and societal norms. Organizations cannot fully resolve these uncertainties. In the end, they are dealing with public emotion that varies according to a host of factors. The more they try to impose or develop norms, the more they risk the possibility of losing the emotive force that underlies the human response. The results of this tension are felt by those who have to translate the overall confusion into actions that may involve life and death. In other words, distress and suffering are the outcome of aid work, as well as its inspiration.

* * *

Oxfam's work in Eastern Europe began with the distribution of clothing and blankets collected from Oxfam's second-hand shops. But gradually, Oxfam staff members in the region came to realize that women would much rather knit their own garments than be given them as charity. In these circumstances, their dignity and sense of self-worth were arguably as important to them as the gift of a jumper. Aid that undermines confidence can add to the suffering and distress. It can easily make people feel helpless and useless, perhaps leading to an unwillingness to find schools for children or to look after themselves. In extreme cases, people turn to drink or fall into deep depression and other psychological disorders. It is not enough to hand out more and more clothes, and judge success by numbers and statistics. Oxfam provided wool for people to knit their own clothes. This process turned into a formal project in which women gathered together in centres, knitting and talking. By providing goods for relief distribution, the women were able to feel that they were contributing and were therefore empowered to take on other initiatives. Their incomes and capacities increased. The exclusion of despair was diminished.

But was self-confidence something that Oxfam should support for itself? A difficult question was raised when a knitting group in Bosnia asked Oxfam to fund a fashion show. The group argued that it would be a wonderful way to boost the confidence of the young women, many of whom felt their lives had been made pointless by war. After much internal debate about whether fashion shows were an appropriate use of Oxfam funds, a small grant was allocated and the show took place in the full glare of floodlights. The representative at the time recalled: 'Senior Oxfam staff, visiting from Oxford, were invited as guests of honour. One later remarked, "While appreciating the invitation, we almost begged them not to send a copy of the video to Oxford! Who knows what people at home would have made of Oxfam funding a women's fashion show".'

As the 'senior Oxfam staff' at the show I was not entirely sure that I could justify it because the connection with poverty appeared to be so tenuous. However, another staff member, Fiona Gell, described the event with unequivocal enthusiasm:

It was incredible and fantastic, a sort of glittering parade, in total contrast to all the gloom outside. Shells still pounded the wrecked city intermittently. But inside Hotel Tuzla something else was going on. In the crystal ballroom, which had seen no gathering or celebration since the start of the bombardment, the Oxfam-funded fashion show was underway. Young refugee women, ground down by bereavement and violence, their futures bleak and hopeless, were striding up and down the catwalk, tripping up and

down playfully in silken evening dresses and gorgeous woolly jumpers.
The atmosphere was bursting with self-confidence. They were lovely, ex-
citing, sexy, had the audience rapt.

Would Oxfam have supported such an event in Africa, I wonder?

The distress of people in Bosnia was so visible, and so resonant with European wartime experiences and even with the day-to-day grief of normal European life, that 'psycho-social' projects had become a focus for much of the Western humanitarian response. These projects aimed to address distress and suffering; they became a recognized sector of the aid response and increasingly sophisticated. A directory produced by the European Economic Community (EEC) described nearly 300 such projects in Bosnia, many of them concerned specifically with counselling rape victims. They involved expatriate psychologists, psychiatrists and other experts. Various therapies and treatments were experimented with in areas where there was no effective government regulation. As well as youth camps and children's play projects, there were projects that defined and addressed post-traumatic stress disorder (PTSD). Western aid managers were told that as many as 50 per cent of the people in the region were suffering from PTSD, and they were urged to allocate huge budgets to deal with it. The whole issue of human need became obscured by medical and scientific jargon. As commentator Paul Stubbs says, this meant that people were not being treated as people but as illnesses. Instead of people with stories and troubles, there were:

'Depressive mothers', 'psychotic mothers usually in acute PTSD', 'con-
fused mothers with a high level of anxiety' and 'well-adapted mothers'.
Using, apparently, object relations theory, these 'types' are renamed 'dead
mother', 'part-object mother', 'absent mother' and 'loving mother'.

Although some 'experts' try to claim otherwise, it is difficult to distinguish PTSD (devised during the Vietnam war) from 'stress', and there is much debate about whether it is a useful term at all. In Bosnia, it was presented as a known fact and gave entry for professionals to take over. Stubbs considers that it: 'is a cruel irony that the form in which various kinds of concerns have tended to be distilled has led, yet again, to a silencing or disempowering of those who have suffered, and an aggrandisement of various professionals, notably psychologists.'

I asked psychiatrist Derek Summerfield of the Medical Foundation for the Victims of Torture to travel with me in Bosnia and advise Oxfam on psycho-social responses in Bosnia. He observed:

Fundamental to the human processing of atrocious experience is the subjective meaning it has, or comes to have, for those affected, the understandings and attributions they draw on in the struggle to encompass what has happened. These understandings, and the adaptations that flow from them, are drawn from society, its history and politics. People who have not been able to generate an interpretation of what has happened, and who find events incomprehensible, are likely to feel the most helpless and unsure what to do.

The process of grief may have universal characteristics but it is also intensely social and therefore relates to culture, such as the youth culture that gives fashion very high status. In Bosnia aid agencies imported psychological norms from different cultures and applied them unchanged to the people of Bosnia as if they were Scandinavians, Americans or Israelis. Summerfield advised Oxfam not to 'medicalize' the projects but to keep them firmly rooted in Oxfam's normal social approach, responding to felt needs. He recommended that Oxfam develop community support for those experiencing stress rather than hand over the issues to professionals. In a paper for Oxfam he wrote that:

Most people endure war and recover from it as a function of the extent to which they can regain a measure of dignity, control and autonomy over their immediate environment. They will seek to reconstitute what they can of their family and other networks, so often splintered in modern conflict. Anything that generates a sense of solidarity or community, and bolsters the viability of local organizations and structures, must be helpful.

Women in the social centres would sometimes recall painful events and perhaps burst into tears. Staff members at the centres were trained to recognize the difference between grief and signs that a person might benefit from external help. They received support sessions themselves in order to cope with distressing situations. But cases of mental illness that required professional input were extremely rare. In general, Oxfam simply learned to revalue its traditional approaches of listening respectfully to those in need. Projects with much greater levels of medical expertise often failed. A major Scandinavian evaluation of 'psycho-social projects' in Bosnia and the Caucasus concludes that the recognition of 'the psychological and social aspects of human suffering' was 'a landmark in the history of human rights', but the projects themselves were often unsatisfactory: 'Little evidence of real participation, representation of the contribution from beneficiaries in the projects was found... The general perception of the staff in projects carrying out psycho-social work with groups and individuals was that the people attending the groups were helpless and too traumatized to take any part in the "ownership" of the projects.'

Oxfam's experience had shown that where people were given the chance to take the initiative, they did so enthusiastically. A number of local organizations were formed. But the huge inequality between Western funding and the possibility of finding resources locally meant that any such initiative was likely to be taken over and converted into a 'success story' for one of the donors. The organization that formed around the knitting centres in Bosnia chose to call itself Bosfam as a tribute to Oxfam for encouraging its start. It went on to attract World Bank funding for computer training courses and several other major projects. But it now required sophisticated and centralized management rather than the small group of women who ran the social centres. Donors needed to spend money on success, and Bosfam was the ideal local project run by women. Oxfam's attempts to advise against rapid expansion were ignored. A review of Bosfam concluded in 1996:

> The international donor sector has also played a strong role in setting its own agenda in defining needs, to which local NGOs respond... This has set up a largely lethargic sector that is to a great extent donor-led, and has primarily been created by the international community... It is unrealistic and unfair now to expect the local NGO sector to be anything other than what we created.

The Scandinavian evaluation of psycho-social projects concluded that the real problems lie far outside the capacity of aid agencies, not only in individual suffering but in the breakdown of social relationships:

> The most pernicious aftermath of long-lasting civil war based on ethnic conflicts is the loss of trust in, and sense of betrayal by, people whom before one regarded as close friends, neighbours, valued teachers. There are continual expressions of resignation and loss of hope in a common future, as

well as difficulty in creating new meaning in life, reflecting a crisis of values and beliefs.

The issue is that aid workers can only cope to a limited extent with distress and suffering, and must avoid exaggerated expectations. During my visit to Azerbaijan in 1993, I wrote:

When asked what were their priority needs, people invariably replied:
'Stop the war. Stop the war.'
'Yes, but that is beyond our power', we replied. 'What is your next priority?'
'Stop the war and let us go back, that is all. There is nothing else.'

I felt badly because I could do so little to help. But ultimately the aid worker cannot solve all of the problems he encounters. In Armenia I visited rooms in abandoned factories where people were living amidst the rubble of their former lives, with plastic bags nailed across the windows to keep out the cold, and a door made out of flattened tins. Inside, over a cup of coffee or a glass of vodka, they would tell me about the houses where they used to live. In one case I simply asked an old woman where she came from. She looked back at me, surprised by my question, thinking of her home, forming the name of the place on her lips but unable to utter it. Suddenly her face became contorted with grief. She lost control of herself, pulling out her hair and beating her head against the wall. She pulled out photographs of her dead son from under the bed, and pushed them at me as her grief became wilder and wilder. A man put his arm on her shoulder, and pulled her away as I walked out of the room.

Conventional aid can be an insult to people's feelings. It implies that the donors care for nothing except food and water. But what really matters to people in need may be beyond our reach. We may not be able to help the distressed woman to deal with her grief, but we can at least provide some warm clothes for her grandchildren. Perhaps that would give her some pleasure, indirectly relieving her suffering and distress.

Do aid workers ever find satisfaction in their work? It pleased me to discover, by listening and learning, that there was a special need for children's boots. It had been overlooked by practically every other organization – rather like the need for women's clothes in Mozambique, which I had 'discovered'. When people fled from their homes, the children might have had only one pair of boots which they would have quickly outgrown. In the deep snow of the Caucasus, it was a pleasure to see the children in their brightly coloured Noddy-boots, yellow and red. Even though the adults were huddled inside with their unreachable grief, the children would be out playing. But was the pleasure in the children playing or in my own sense of achievement?

* * *

From these experiences I learned that managers in emergency operations have an obligation to set limits for their staff. Staff must know what they are supposed to be doing so that they are not accused – or do not accuse themselves – of failing to respond. This boils down to dull but accurate job descriptions and clear instructions, good briefings before the job and excellent debriefings afterwards, and listening to the painful experiences of staff. One of the worst scenarios for an aid worker is to return from a stressful situation for a serious discussion or a final debriefing, only to find that the manager has rushed out because of some new crisis. The impression given is that no one cares about aid workers, even though the truth may be that people are concerned, but busy. Because they do not have time and are stressed themselves, they cannot always fully understand another person's experience or needs. They may feel undervalued themselves and therefore unwilling to support anyone else.

Humanitarian organizations have a tendency to be inhumane. It is so easy to put the cause, or crisis, above the people who serve. If we treat ourselves in an inhumane way, as if we need only food and water, we may be more likely to think that other people can make do with the same. Instead of expressing concern about human capabilities, we may become involved in problems of our own guilt and self-esteem. Summerfield's words about people in distress apply equally to aid workers:

It is important to allow intense emotion to be expressed without a sense of shame. Issues around helplessness and low self-esteem may emerge, as well as anger and guilt, which are inherent in grieving processes. People may need realistic assurances that their feelings are normal responses to extraordinary events beyond their control and do not reflect personal weakness.

The word 'ritual' has become debased by its application to ostentatious religious ceremony or primitive anthropological rites. But humanitarians working in a non-religious environment without universal norms have begun to realize that rituals are important. The distribution of shrouds and payments for burial is not a wasteful diversion of resources from food and water, but can be essential to recovery and happiness. Rituals are also important within the process of humanitarianism because we are trying to come to terms with the infinite, although in our case it is not the infinitude of God but of human need.

Rituals act as the markers of our intentions. The grandest ritual of the humanitarian sector is the 'strategic planning meeting'. This is the gathering of the entire team to exchange experiences and work together to define future tasks. Although people are working in official roles, they also act socially and personally, forming boundaries to their own sense of responsibility. Of course, envy can play a role and result in competition. Love of power can distort the process, and some people may be tempted to control the weak rather than to help them. All the temptations described in this book play out in such a meeting. Overall, however, people are glad to share and define their sense of awe at the task they have taken on. Ideally, staff leave such a meeting with a sense of having come to terms with their limitations and their role within the wider group. They see more clearly where they end and where others begin. It defines the self and adds to self-esteem. But the document itself is not the real product. It is the process, the ritual, that creates the right psychological atmosphere in which aid workers can do their job without the interference of personal distortions.

It may be better to set arbitrary goals than to have no goals at all. Thus, in a globalizing world, a convergence of views around 'rights', 'capabilities' or 'freedoms' would be desirable, and is something that humanitarians should work towards. International humanitarian law may be based upon a strange set of compromises between politics and cultures, but it provides an escape from the pressure of individual responsibility.

For many years Tolstoy pondered whether he should give away all of his possessions and became obsessed with the need for moral compromise. Eventually, it was only the influence of his family that prevented him from renouncing worldly goods. For many aid workers the interaction with their family is what ultimately restrains their aspiration to a universal humanity and defines a limit which keeps them content. But to be happy requires a further abandonment of self – an ability to rejoice in other's success and in the formation of their altruism. It lies, as Sen has said, in developing other people's capabilities. For aid managers, it lies in finding local people, even from among the victims of disaster, who have the greatest understanding and sympathy, and in building that short sturdy bridge to those in need rather than sending our own space-mission directly to those we do not understand.

Chapter 8

The Rwanda Genocide: Man's Inhumanity

T he Rwanda Genocide of 1994 shook the confidence of aid workers and left many feeling deeply unsettled. There was an unseemly scramble of aid agencies to respond to the genocide after the worst had happened. This evoked such revulsion that codes of conduct were revived and standards of professional behaviour were proposed. Aid agencies realized that unless they put their house in order there would be a loss of public confidence. But for many aid workers, there were two other troubling questions. How did it happen that after decades of intensive development, 800,000 people in a population of five million were systematically slaughtered? And second, after the genocide, can we continue to believe in human nature? The genocide seemed to deny everything that humanitarians stood for.

Evidently, the majority of people in Rwanda took part. Many of the killers had participated in aid projects – they were the same people we believed in and with whom we worked. They were 'partners'. How do we explain their actions? Do we dissociate them from the rest of the human race?

My own small involvement was to have visited Rwanda several times before the genocide and again long afterwards. I met many people and liked or disliked them in the usual way, but found them perfectly normal. If I now regard them as inhuman, I must have a logic for separating them from others. If they are like others, then do I also have the same capacity for murder? Would I have become a murderer if I happened to live in Rwanda in April 1994?

There is some evidence that I and others would have. Genocide, broadly speaking, is the systematic murder of one definable group of people by another. It is not perpetrated by a small group of psychotic individuals but by large numbers of people acting together, and is organized with the support of authority. It is a rare event. During the

20th century, there are three plausible cases of genocide. The first was the massacre of Armenians in Turkey, but this is poorly recorded. There is a huge body of literature about the second, the Nazi Holocaust. Inevitably, for such an emotive subject there is a great deal of controversy and it is beyond my competence to comment on the detail. However, it appears that hundreds of thousands of people were involved in creating the process of mass murder and that very few did anything to dissociate themselves from it or to stop it. One of the abiding puzzles is why so many 'civilized' people condoned the massacres while others were merely bystanders, aware of what was happening but doing nothing to stop it. Genocide is not limited to particular types of people or nations. The chilling reality is that, in certain circumstances, any person and any society can perpetrate crimes of a similar sort. Where does this leave humanitarians?

Genocide is such a frightening subject that it is difficult to focus on it for long. In writing this chapter, I fear the smallest deviation from the truth, and yet know it is impossible to be truthful because the moment I think of genocide – and the possibility that I too could be a killer – my pulse rate increases, and I am not the detached person I was earlier. I know that the 'me' who might have been a Rwandan Hutu or a Nazi officer who committed such crimes is not 'me', but someone with a different set of values. Indeed, I may even be tempted to define 'me' as someone who would not commit such crimes and say that my culture is separate and superior in that respect. But genocide arises out of the warping of a culture and I am very aware that my own culture is changing all the time. Could it be heading towards some eventual genocide, in which the circumstances of mass murder are created?

* * *

Joseph Conrad's *Heart of Darkness* is a famous exploration of whether what we fear lies outside ourselves or within. At one level, it is a story about the savagery of Africans. At another, it is a story about the Western myth about the savagery of Africans. The objective and the subjective move in and out of each other.

The story is set on the Congo River, downstream from Rwanda, and the narrator travels by boat to rescue the mysterious Kurtz who has 'gone native' in ways that are not entirely clear, but involve horrific tribal rituals. When the narrator finally meets Kurtz, the man he has been seeking for so many months, Conrad's normally measured language becomes disjointed, reflecting the narrator's irrational fear:

I tried to break the spell – the heavy, mute spell of the wilderness – that seemed to draw him to its pitiless breast by the memory of gratified and monstrous passions. This alone, I was convinced, had driven him out to the edge of the forest, to the bush, towards the gleam of fires, the throb of drums, the drone of weird incantations; this alone had beguiled his unlawful soul beyond the bounds of permitted aspirations.

In Conrad's writing, Africa becomes the imaginary world of the white man's horror. At no point does the narrator ever see what he fears, nor is it clear what Kurtz did, but fears have become part of his perception. Conrad's narrator himself becomes obsessed with Kurtz's dying words: 'The horror, the horror.'

This is the reason why I affirm that Kurtz was a remarkable man. He had something to say. He said it. Since I have peeped over the edge myself, I understand better the meaning of his stare, that could not see the flame of the candle, but was wide enough to embrace the whole universe, piercing enough to penetrate all the hearts that beat in the darkness. He had summed up – he had judged. 'The Horror'.

Why else do we watch horror films like *Silence of the Lambs* and *Hannibal*, except to enjoy the discovery of horrific tendencies inside ourselves? Journalist Fergal Keane describes his book about the genocide as a 'diary of an encounter with evil' (*Season of Blood*, 1995). But can it be dismissed in such an easy way. Surely we must stare genocide in the face and find out what it is?

For those who had worked in Africa for many years and spent much of their time defending Africans against racist stereotypes, the genocide seemed to confirm the worst prejudices of others. We knew they were wrong but we could not find a proper explanation. As Fergal Keane said about his feelings when he started to write his book: 'How can I best describe it? It is a mixture of dread fascination, sorrow for what we learned and lost in the short weeks of chaos, a mind weariness that feeds itself by replaying the old tapes over and over. We reach for the off-switch but in the darkness we cannot find it.'

There is no 'off-switch' for genocide. It pursues us with frightening questions. Our thoughts are not necessarily programmed for humanitarian concern and can be programmed for the systematic destruction of individuals. We have a great capacity for concern and compassion in certain circumstances, but the opposite is also true. There is uncomfortable evidence that the killers enjoyed their task and became addicted to it. How else were so many people killed with machetes, hoe-heads and hammers in such a short time?

How could humans like ourselves be so brutal? But then, how could the rest of the world have done so little about it? Is there a clue as to how we can be so indifferent to such horrors?

At different times we see things in different ways, and our perceptions shift according to varying experiences. As a result, all of us may find ourselves in circumstances where we despise, hate or kill other people, although we may not be able to fully explain why. We have the capacity for major changes in our personality. The alternative is that Rwandans are fundamentally different from the rest of humanity.

Humanitarians tend to be idealists and have what I have already called an overoptimistic outlook on human behaviour. For them, the impact of an event such as the Rwanda genocide is particularly severe, although potentially salutary. Many aid workers became deeply troubled by their experiences and some lost faith in their work. Many sought counselling after their involvement and some found it difficult to adapt to normal life. Such experiences undermine the ability to laugh because we can see only the one overwhelming event, and all else loses perspective. We are unable to see the smaller shifts of perception that are the basis of humor. Without the benefit of a fixed morality, including its helpful notions of good and evil and its rituals of absolution, humanitarians can be plunged into despair by the smallest failure in human nature. Like believers who lose their faith, we wonder if humanity exists at all. Are we no more than the 'bare fork'd animal' of King Lear's description, shivering in the rain. We may have reached equality with the Africans we seek to help, but is this the equality of nothing? Is the meaning of the genocide that all of us are equally 'evil'?

* * *

I was also one of the bystanders too busy with other things to pay much attention to the genocide when it occurred. My first reaction was one of annoyance that the focus of world attention was shifting away from Bosnia. Oxfam did well to alert the world to the true nature of the genocide, but in the end no one can say that they did enough. Even those in Oxfam who wrote letters to the newspapers, rightly labelling the event as genocide when it was denied by others, must still question whether they could have done more. The possession of that knowledge carries a heavy responsibility. The awful fact is that the genocide could have been stopped, and there was an international obligation to stop it under the international convention on genocide of 1949. The UN had been warned, the US was well aware, but there was just not enough public or political will. Rwanda was a small country of no strategic importance. A very modest international force could have prevented the genocide. Instead, the small number of UN troops already there was withdrawn.

We are left with the guilt of the survivor. We are all tainted by what happened and the more capacity we have the greater our sense of guilt. If I had not become involved in Eastern Europe, I would have continued with responsibility within Oxfam for Rwanda, a position I held until 1993. If I had retained that role perhaps I might have managed to get the world to notice. But I had become deeply involved in the problems of Eastern Europe and the former Soviet Union, and had passed on the responsibility of Africa. It is not a very rational guilt but it exists nevertheless.

The genocide lasted three months, from April to July 1994, and was over almost before the world was aware of it. People were hacked to death at a rate faster than achieved by the Nazis with gas in their extermination camps. The world's great powers did nothing significant to stop it and the genocide came to an end only when Rwandan exiles in Uganda invaded and pushed the murderers into 'refugee' camps beyond the borders.

Rather than the word 'evil', I find the word 'disgust' represents the situation more precisely. The Western world was characterized by an unwillingness to react – a withdrawal from events that we, as Westerners, were unwilling to contemplate. Just before the genocide, the influential American writer Robert Kaplan published an article that predicted for Africa: 'the withering away of central governments, the rise of tribal and regional domains, the unchecked spread of disease, and the growing pervasiveness of war'.

Kaplan's message to the US was not just 'keep separate' but also 'keep out', and his article has been cited as a powerful influence in the United States' decision not to intervene in the genocide. It was circulated among officials and embassies at the time. Among policy-makers there was also the fear of a new Somalia. The issue was decided not on its real characteristics, but on the basis of prejudice.

Even when donor agencies finally poured in money after the genocide, there was an unwillingness to actually understand, to engage or to analyse. Very little of the aid went to the victims of the genocide in

Rwanda and far more to the killers in the camps. Some aid agencies apparently did not even realize that the people in the camps were killers rather than victims. They sent out aid workers who suddenly discovered that they were helping murderers. The survivors of the genocide were asked to show reconciliation and forgiveness. The blame was shuffled on to 'the Hutus' and attributed to 'evil'.

* * *

The Rwanda genocide was particularly shocking for longer-term aid workers because it happened in a country where development had once appeared so successful. Rwanda had been a place where aid agencies congregated in the hundreds, with flags waving in almost every village to proclaim the activity of a donor from abroad. Many Rwandan children had been sponsored or even 'adopted' by people abroad who sent a few pounds or dollars every month to help them through their school. They wrote to the children, asking how they were getting on and telling them about events in the lives of their own families. We, the Western world, sent textbooks and constructed water supplies, suggested new crops and introduced technical solutions to the problem of poverty. Oxfam's own programme, during the time that I was involved with it, acted mainly through the 'commune' officials or local government authorities, who turned out to be among the worst perpetrators of the genocide. I wonder now what hands I have shaken.

Gradually, after 1994, we learned that the genocide had been planned carefully within the government. In response to international pressure mounted on the Rwandan president to sign a peace agreement, hardliners within the government saw that their position was being undermined, arranged for his plane to be shot down and then blamed 'the opposition' or 'the Tutsis' and used the event to start the process of massacre. Many of those who organized the genocide were government officials – the same people to whom we had given money to construct roads and plant trees. We, the aid community, had also helped the government, under 'villagisation' programmes, to move people from their homes on scattered hillsides to smart new villages with gleaming steel roofs. There, as we thought, they could be supported by more services. But the new villages were places where surveillance was easier and ultimately facilitated the genocide.

As veteran aid worker Peter Uvin says:

The development community considered Rwanda to be a well-developing country. Rwanda was usually seen as a model of development in Africa, with good performance on most of the indicators of development, such as growth in gross national product (GNP), manufacturing, or sevices; the more social indicators, such as food availability or vaccination rates; and the new bottom-up indicators, such as the number of non-governmental organizations (NGOs) and cooperatives in the country.

In the 1980s President Habiyaramana was widely regarded as a benevolent father of the people, one of Africa's most reasonable leaders. In France he was especially popular as a personal friend of President Mitterand. He was said to have a deep and sensitive understanding of French culture and, in the French-speaking world at least, was the symbol of African progress.

Outsiders saw danger mainly in terms of ethnic conflict rather than the misuse of power. They were too ready to view the Hutus and Tutsis according to the Western concept of a 'tribe' with a fixed culture and set of symbols like football teams, constantly competing. The reality is much closer to the ethnicity that exists in the West where traditional definitions such as Welsh, Irish and Scots are constantly modified by location and intermarriage, and immigrant groups assimilating within other cultures. But a Western stereotype of Africa demands something different: the monolithic, indivisible tribe, liable to fight other such tribes as a matter of custom. Christine Umotomi Nyinawumwami entered Rwanda with the Rwanda Patriotic Front (RPF) forces as a 'Tutsi' to bring an end to the genocide. She became a vice-minister in the new government. Her account of Rwandan ethnicity is as follows:

The Banyarwanda [Rwandan people] are made up of three social groups – Bahutu, Batutsi and Batwa [Hutu, Tutsi and Twa] – and for a long time before colonialism they lived in relative harmony. The Batutsi were mainly cattle keepers, while the Bahutu were cultivators and the Batwa were hunters and craftspeople. This did not mean that there were no Bahutu with cattle or Batutsi involved in cultivation, but generally people were categorized according to their economic occupation. Bahutu, Batutsi and Batwa are not tribes or ethnic groups as they have been misrepresented in the Western sense.

They occupy the same land – no Hutu, Tutsi or Twa land and no separate district exists for a particular social group. They live together on the different hills of Rwanda and speak the same language, Kinyarwanda. The different groups needed each other and complemented each other's needs. However, because cattle multiplied faster and provided more wealth, the cow was a symbol of wealth. Those who did not own a lot of cows were in an inferior position and this created a kind of class structure. However, the Bahutu, Batutsi and Batwa who did not own enough cattle would go to work for rich Batutsi who would, in return, reward them with cattle, thus providing a mechanism for social mobility.

There was an up and down movement of people from one class to another. Batutsi, Bahutu and Batwa who would acquire wealth would move in the upper class and vice versa. Class division, in general, created some tension among the different social groups, although it was not big enough to result in genocide if no other factors had influenced Rwanda's evolution.

Ethnicity, power and class were interrelated, but for their own purposes, the Belgian colonists converted the more class-based set of divisions into a rigid ethnicity by deciding that a Tutsi was someone who owned more than ten cows. People were given cards that determined their ethnic status. Thereafter, any issue tended to split along ethnic lines. After independence in 1962, the Tutsis who had been favoured by the Belgians lost their support and found themselves victim of retribution and an organized attempt to seize power by Hutu politicians. The first massacres in 1963 created the refugee problem that was to cause Habiyaramana such fear. In the 1980s, behind the mask of development, he turned Rwanda into a repressive and secretive dictatorship. During the apparently peaceful developmental years of the 1980s, the government used external aid to increase its ability to control the people. Peter Uvin noted that: 'The process of development and the international aid given to promote it interacted with the forces of exclusion, inequality, pauperization, racism, and oppression that laid the groundwork for the 1994 genocide.'

Uvin states that the causes of the genocide were multiple, but for the sake of clarity emphasizes three issues:

The anomie and frustration caused by the long-standing condition of structural violence; the strategies of manipulation by elites under threat from economic and political processes; and the existence of a socio-psychological, widespread attachment to racist values in society. It is the specific interaction of these three processes that allowed the genocide to occur in Rwanda.

Four further factors are of secondary importance; they contributed to the genocide but did not cause it directly. Foremost among them is the occurrence of past violence, both in Rwanda and Burundi. The others are opportunism, the absence of external constraints and the colonial legacy.

But this list of causes still leaves a gap. Many other countries might experience internal oppression and widespread racism but mass murder is extremely rare. We have to come back to the fact that genocide is the systematic extermination of an entire group of people by another entire group. It goes beyond ethnic cleansing, which would have simply pushed the undesirable population out of Rwanda, and becomes a desire to exterminate for its own sake. What started in Rwanda as an attempt to hold onto power, and to eliminate a specified list of potential opponents, gathered an internal momentum of its own. People joined in enthusiastically, killing almost indiscriminately because someone was tall or because they had a grudge. The extraordinary spread of killing throughout Rwandan society was recorded in detail by the organizations African Rights and Human Rights Watch. Further records were gathered by Philip Gourevitch in his book *We Wish to Inform You that Tomorrow We Will Be Killed with Our Families* (readers are referred to the Notes on Sources for publication details). All three volumes describe the events in a matter-of-fact style. But, especially for humanitarians who have to consider returning to Rwanda and working there again, these records require explanation. What view of human nature can encompass the facts recorded in these reports?

One of the most significant attempts to explain the genocide itself is the work of André Sibomana, *Hope for Rwanda* (1999). Sibomana was a Rwandan priest who lived through and survived the genocide but died in 1998. His views were recorded as dialogues with two French journalists. He points out that even for Hutus the political system was deeply oppressive, and life in Rwandan villages deeply depressing. The rural people were: 'completely stripped of any responsibility and follow orders blindly, whatever they might be, without any detachment and without the slightest thought of criticism. You cannot imagine the power of submission of Rwandan peasants.'

It is worth noting that this behaviour is not limited to Rwandan peasants. Humans have an extraordinary capacity to obey orders rather than to express their concern for another human. In the classic experiments originally performed by American psychologist Stanley Milgram, the following results were observed:

He set up a laboratory situation in which subjects thought they were teach-
ers in a learning experiment. If the 'learner' made a mistake, the 'teacher's'
task was to administer an electric shock. And if the learner continued to
make mistakes, the teacher was instructed to increase the power of the shock
until the learner was in considerable pain. In fact, there were no shocks at
all, the whole experiment was simulated, sometimes even with actors play-
ing the learner roles and giving every evidence of being severely hurt by
the shocking punishments. The subjects knew nothing of this, however,
and were told by those running the experiments only that they were to obey
all instructions without question and that by doing so they would be mak-
ing an important contribution to science.

A few subjects refused to go through with the procedure, but most proved
surprisingly willing to inflict severe pain on complete strangers, 'for the
sake of science'. And everywhere the experiment has been repeated – in
Italy, Germany, Australia and South Africa – the results have been the
same. We tend, as a species, to be remarkably obedient to authority, and
perfectly capable, depending on the context of the situation, of doing hor-
rible things to others.

Sibomana goes on to describe the alienation of youth. But here again,
surely, we can recognize a universal tendency:

There were many, especially young people from poor districts of the capi-
tal, whose lives were completely empty, who had no family, no religion, no
work and no hope. They saw no future for themselves in the world. They
turned upside down the value system to which they no longer had access:
instead of taking advantage of their youth to build themselves a life, they
used their energy to destroy the lives of others. These young people denied
others not only the right to live, but also the right to die in dignity and to
have a proper burial.

Sibomana describes an orgy of violence:

Others acted under threat or under the influence of drugs, or else agreed
to go along with the killers out of weakness or opportunism. The geno-
cide saw looting on an unbelievable scale. Whole families were killed for
a foam mattress, which is worth less than 50 francs in France. Then the
looters killed each other. After several days of this horrific blood bath, the
killers went completely mad. Politics, ethnic divisions, the war, none of
this even entered their minds. They killed for a crate of beer, for a look

which may have been too insistent, or just because they did not know
what else to do.

The violence may have started with a political objective, but then became an objective in itself, and it spread: 'It would be an exaggeration to say that the entire population took part in the massacres, but those who resisted were rare and those who had conceived the genocide left no stone unturned to involve as many Rwandans as possible in their crime.'

How did people justify such actions to themselves? One aspect of the killing was, as Sibomana describes, an expression of disgust for something unclean:

> *In the countryside, the upkeep of the yard is a hard task: as soon as you have swept away the dirt it comes back. You should not spare any effort to cleanse the place where you live. The authorities compared Tutsi to dirt that had to be eliminated. So peasants threw Tutsis into latrines, without it troubling their conscience. Why into latrines? Not only because it might be 'convenient'. All houses have latrines; it was easy to get rid of a body by throwing it in. There is another explanation: latrines are full of excrement, the most revolting aspect of human life. Throwing Tutsis into latrines was an additional way of denying them that essential quality: belonging to the human species.*

The phrase 'ethnic cleansing' conveys a similar sense of disgust. It is worth remembering that 'ethnic cleansing' was a phrase coined in the West for what happened in Bosnia. The Holocaust, the greatest genocide in history, was perpetrated by Europeans. We are not dealing with an African evil but a universal aspect of human nature.

Another link with universal experience is the fact that the majority of killers were men and that this fits a general human pattern. Sociobiologist Stephen Pinker tells us that:

> *Maleness is by far the biggest risk factor for violence. Daly and Wilson report 35 samples of homicide statistics from 14 countries, including foraging and preliterate societies and 13th-century England. In all of them, men kill men massively more often than women kill women – on average 26 times more often.*

Pinker points out that the woman serial killer is virtually unknown. Britain's best-known 'serial killer', Myra Hindley, did not actually perpetrate the violence herself but created the opportunity for a man. Similarly, the instances of women perpetrating extreme and systematic acts of violence in Rwanda seem to be exceptional. Sibomana gives an example of a woman who killed others with a hammer but ascribes to her a motive (apparently from talking with her) which seems unlikely in a man. This was to eliminate the women who would otherwise give birth to the oppressors of her own children. It is a different motive from the 'cleansing' motive characteristic of men.

What Sibomana clearly finds most difficult to explain is the pleasure in gratuitous violence exhibited by men during the act of killing:

> *I don't explain it. You can't explain everything or understand all forms of human behaviour. It is a fact: during the genocide, not only were hundreds of thousands of people killed, but many were victims of cruelty, torture and forms of ill-treatment which defy imagination.*
>
> *I can't explain the cruelty, but I think it was an integral part of the genocide. Such cruelty isn't the result of individual 'excesses'; it belongs to genocide. The gratuity of the crime, its careful planning, the passionate desire to destroy not only the body but the soul of the victims before ending their life are elements which characterize genocide.*
>
> *The killers took the trouble to invent the worst kinds of cruelty. There were militiamen who travelled long distances to go and kill a person – a Tutsi whom they knew. I mentioned that some people were forced to kill under threat. But others revelled in it. They inflicted horrific injuries without going as far as killing the victims, simply to intensify the cruelty of death and to prolong the suffering. They did it just like that, without any worries, in complete indifference. They stood around drinking beer calmly, watching their former friends literally dying in agony at their feet.*

I come back to my earlier question. Why do people enjoy films about horror and violence? The killer who kills without any compunction and then sips a beer could easily be a hero in a film. Perhaps that was exactly how those young men saw themselves. They were playing out, in reality, what for the rest of us is a fantasy.

But what exactly makes violence pleasurable and addictive? In his famous description of the fall of the Bastille in *A Tale of Two Cities*, Charles Dickens offers a way of entering the mind of the person who is excited by violence. The mob kills anyone it suspects of being members of the 'aristocracy', and in order to keep their knives sharp, people have to keep rushing back to the grindstone:

The grindstone had a double handle and, turning at it madly, were two men whose faces, as their long hair flapped back when the whirlings of the grindstone brought their faces up, were more horrible and cruel than the visages of the wildest savages in their most barbarous disguise. False eyebrows and false moustaches were stuck upon them, and their hideous countenances were all bloody and sweaty, and all awry with howling, and all staring and glaring with beastly excitement and want of sleep. As those ruffians turned and turned, their matted locks now flung forward over their eyes, now flung backward over their necks, some women held wine to their mouths that they might drink; and what with dropping blood, and what with dropping wine, and what with the stream of sparks struck out of the stone, all their wicked atmosphere seemed gore and fire. The eye could not detect one creature in the group free from the smear of blood. Shouldering one another to get next at the sharpening-stone, were men stripped to the waist, and with the stain all over their limbs and bodies; men in all sorts of rags, with the stain upon those rags; men devillishly set off with spoils of women's lace and silk and ribbon, with the stain dying those trifles through and through. Hatchets, knives, bayonets, swords, all brought to be sharpened, were all red with it. Some of the hacked swords were tied to the wrists of those who carried them, with strips of linen and fragments of dress: ligatures various in kind, but all deep of the one colour. And as the frantic wielders of these weapons snatched them from the stream of sparks and tore away into the streets, the same red hue was red in their frenzied eyes: eyes which any unbrutalized beholder would have given 20 years of life, to petrify with a well-directed gun.

For me it comes as a shock when Dickens suddenly reminds us that the 'unbrutalized beholder' should be thinking calmly about morality and not getting excited his description: the 'strips of linen and fragments of dress', the men 'devillishly set off with spoils of lace and silk and ribbon'. This is not a dreadful act that we feel shocked by, so much as an orgy in which we want to take part. The sharpening of knives on the grindstone itself becomes a metaphor of sexual excitement. Pleasure in violence is pleasure in sex, Dickens tells us, because he knows it is true of himself. Dickens confirms through our own feelings how sexually 'male' violence can be.

Having entered the mind of the killer through Dickens's description, perhaps it becomes just a little easier to sympathize with murderers or at least to find a link between their humanity and ours. When the excitement has worn off, Sibomana describes the killers:

Many of them are living, or rather surviving, in a state of complete dejection and loss... They live together in warehouses or schools just a few kilometres from their houses. But they are afraid of going home and don't have the psychological strength to rebuild their lives. They have been destroyed.

As Macbeth said, after he committed many murders:

I have liv'd long enough: my way of life
Is fall'n into the sere, the yellow leaf.

All other aspects of life are emptied of significance compared with the appalling recognition of pleasure in violence and the self-doubt that follows. For Sibomana, the overwhelming question is: 'Where did it come from, this hatred of others? I can only explain it by insurmountable hatred of one's self. Indeed, some killers committed suicide after they had killed.' He continues:

These people who are alive today have not been able to rekindle a desire to live: the earth has opened up under their feet. Those who have survived often speak of a kind of emptiness inside, into which they keep falling. 'After the killings, there were only a few of us who survived. We couldn't even cry, we couldn't feel sadness any more, we were broken inside', explains one survivor... They are still filled with this sense of existing somewhere between the world of the living and the world of the dead.

The Rwanda genocide seems to show a circle of self-hate – of authoritarian government, oppression, low self-esteem and self-disgust – that both causes and results from genocide. There is also a cycle of violence and sexuality. Both seem to be universal characteristics, and it seems conceivable that both combine in certain circumstances to produce frenzies of killing.

The Rwanda genocide has relatively little to do with African forms of ethnicity. It has a great deal to do with human life. The real issue for us today is that false conclusions can so easily be drawn from the massacre and that it promotes a sense of alienation and disgust. Here was a society needing external restraint. The capacity was there to step in, but we, in the West, did not do so. Rather than blame the killers and express disgust, we should feel a sense of tragedy for the human race, an awesome sense of what is inside ourselves.

* * *

Can aid workers come to terms with their own special sense of guilt?

When I visited Rwanda again in 1999, I found that the huge majority of aid agencies and churches had returned to Rwanda much as if nothing had happened. Churches are being reconstructed, and the flags and signboards of aid agencies once again proclaim the same happy and hopeful messages. But as Oxfam's representative at the time of the genocide, Anne Mackintosh, concluded: 'Despite their reputation within the region as a substantive force in civil society, and notwithstanding the courage of individual staff in attempting to combat ethnic hatred, Rwandese NGOs as a body – along with every other institution in the country, including the churches – completely failed to provide any moral leadership or counterforce to the violence, prior to or during the genocide.'

What had we been doing in Rwanda? Our aim was community development, yet this seemed to be the ultimate case of communities falling apart. For those who spoke of religion, it was the ultimate case of religious collapse. Senior church figures, including a bishop, were accused of horrific crimes. Rwanda had received more aid than almost any other country in Africa, and had as many churches as anywhere else. Was something wrong with the aid and the church, or with the people? It was tempting to conclude that it was the latter and to limit the guilty to a few scapegoats. But the truth is that the Belgian colonial system created the ethnicity that became the focus of genocide. Outsiders from many countries supported the genocidal regime, and when the killing started, countries with the power to intervene, and the obligation to do so under the 1949 convention, did not do so.

One of Oxfam's senior local staff in Rwanda, Esther Mujawayo, lost 31 members of her family:

Her invalid, bedridden mother was taken from her bed (which was looted), stripped of her clothes and left to die of thirst and exposure amid the bodies of those who had already been hacked to death – including her husband, Esther's father. Before he retired, he had for many years served the community as a primary schoolteacher: a much-respected man, gentle, generous, compassionate, with a strong religious faith and great integrity – he too was slaughtered.

Esther Mujawayo said: 'I'm ready to forgive, but no one has said they're sorry.'

No one has said they are sorry because it is easier to blame a few scapegoats. The onus of guilt falls more on those who tried to help than those who did nothing at all. Oxfam representative Anne Mackintosh was evacuated from Rwanda after being caught up in some of the earliest killings:

At around half past four in the afternoon, a crowd of about 100 young men armed with spears, machetes and clubs stormed the mission and swept through the compound. Several of them were wearing the black, red and yellow caps of the CDR (Coalition for the Defence of the Republic), the Hutu supremacist party that had done so much to whip up suspicion and hatred towards the Tutsi minority. They flushed out and killed seven members of the Tutsi nurse's family who had, unbeknownst to us, been hiding in the mission buildings. The victims included a three-year-old boy, his skull split open by a machete blow, and a pregnant woman whose belly was slit open by a machete blow, and the unborn baby exposed. We heard the groans, and later the death rattle, of the elderly mission cook who had been clubbed to the ground.

Anne Mackintosh and a priest tried to reason with the leaders of the crowd:

They explained their mission – the Tutsis had murdered the president and were trying to take over the country by force, so had to die. While we were talking two little girls aged about five and seven ran through the garden towards us, and begged to be hidden. They had obviously witnessed the killings and were terrified and distraught. 'Surely you are not going to kill these children!' protested Father Richard. 'No, no', the two replied. 'We have an honourable cause.' They waved aside the armed men, who had seen the girls, and allowed us to take them inside the main building; then they strolled away down the road, leaving their companions to continue the killing and looting.

But when the expatriates had to leave they could not take the little girls with them; there was no chance at all that they would have been allowed through the numerous road blocks. Mackintosh expressed a sense of guilt: 'Much later I learned that the girls had escaped to Goma with some of the mission nuns and were being cared for in an orphanage there – but little thanks to us.'

She blames herself, unjustifiably but inevitably. In a couple of days practically all of the expatriate aid staff were evacuated, leaving behind their own local colleagues, many of whom were certain to be killed.

What of the UN, which was given clear warnings and ignored them? The troops that might have stopped the genocide were evacuated at the first sign of trouble. The guards protecting people from an atrocious death were ordered to push away the people clinging to him and to drive away. After the death of ten Belgian soldiers, troops that could have stopped the genocide were flown out and officials in the US and other governments were given instructions not to use the word 'genocide' because it would entail the obligation to respond under the 1949 convention. It was a deliberate and calculated cover-up. The UN forces in Rwanda were not allowed to intervene. Its commanding officer, General Dallaire, later suffered seriously from a personal sense of guilt. He wrote:

> *The fact that nearly 1500 highly capable troops from France, Italy and Belgium landed in Kigali within days, with several hundred US marines standing by in Burundi, to evacuate the expatriates and a few hundred selected Rwandans, and then left in the face of the unfolding tragedy and with full knowledge of the danger confronting the emasculated UN force,* is inexcusable by any human criteria.

Unfortunately, African tragedies have become horror films under another name. This is not just because we enjoy horror, but because the media exploit that tendency in their ratings wars. As Fergal Keane says, commercialism has become an inherent characteristic of the media, especially of TV:

> *Where television is concerned, African news is generally only big news when it involves lots of dead bodies. The higher the mound, the greater the possibility that the world will, however briefly, send its camera teams and correspondents. Once the story has gone 'stale', ie there are no new bodies and the refugees are down to a trickle, the circus moves on. The powerful images leave us momentarily horrified but largely ignorant.*

Africa provides the horror stories for the new channels. Being horrified is a form of pleasure. We are all part of the genocide.

But does this inevitably lead to self-hatred and bitterness? Aid workers need an inner confidence which is proof against all shocks. This comes from a sense that the tendencies of human nature, the driving forces of the gene, are not all that make us human. We have a sense of space still left, an ability to challenge and protest, to fight against the cycles of oppression and impoverishment. We draw our inspiration from others who think the same way, and those – however few – who, in the midst of genocide, resisted.

Chapter 9
The Selfish Altruist

I wrote this book because the Kosovo crisis was a warning to me that in the New World Order humanitarianism itself might become a victim of 'spin'. Indian academic Professor B S Chimni has suggested that:

> *Humanitarianism is the ideology of hegemonic states in the era of global-ization marked by the end of the Cold War and a growing North–South divide… It mobilizes a range of meanings and practices to establish and sustain global relations of domination. In particular, it manipulates the language of human rights to legitimize a dubious range of practices, in-cluding its selective defence.*

In the course of my researches I discovered that the 'spin' in Kosovo had been even greater than I thought. In the last stages of the negotia-tions over Kosovo, with a peaceful solution in sight, the West imposed conditions that made a military confrontation inevitable. The incon-gruously-named Appendix B, setting out the Western demands at the Rambouillet peace talks, 'Status of Multinational Military Implemen-tation Force of the Western Demands', stated: 'NATO personnel shall enjoy, together with their vehicles, vessels, aircraft and equipment, free and unrestricted passage and unimpeded access throughout the Federal Republic of Yugoslavia.'

As Noam Chomsky wrote, 'It is hard to imagine that any country would consider such terms except in the form of unconditional sur-render.' Further, the West demanded that there should be a referendum on the future of Kosovo, with the implication that Yugoslav sover-eignty was negotiable. Bombing ensued, and ethnic cleansing followed the bombing. Little was known of these demands at the time. But why should the West be so keen, apparently, to go to war?

In Washington, they called it 'Madeleine's war'. They said that the leader of the US, or Western, delegation, Madeleine Albright, had gone beyond the national interest. We do not know what was happening in Albright's mind during the negotiations; but why did she impose conditions that were so obviously unacceptable? Why were the new conditions kept so secret? Her motive might have been vindictive, and it might equally have been based on deep sympathy for Kosovo's suffering people or on a commitment to human rights. Perhaps, with memories of her roots in Eastern Europe, Madeleine Albright acted according to different motives at different times. She may not even be aware of them. But there is a warning. Political leaders must now grapple with the slippery morality of humanitarianism which they left to aid agencies in the past. Even for politicians such issues evoke emotional responses. The self muddles into our altruism without our being aware.

An increasing sense of profound uncertainty about the motivation for the Kosovo intervention made me ask whether everything I had done was similarly tainted with 'spin'. The value of my life's work suddenly seemed fragile and brittle. Was there any purity in humanitarianism at all?

In this book I have tried to explore some of the ways in which our responses interact with our feelings, and end with the view that humanitarianism is what scientists might call a singularity – a situation in which the tools of analysis themselves break down. We use our mind to analyse our mind.

Humanity is subjective. The degree and nature of concern that I feel for a person in need reflects my personality and mood. In analysing the context in which that person lives, I have to choose from innumerable possibilities, and I may choose those which reflect my prejudices rather than the person's interests. I remain in my world – he or she in his or her own.

Humanitarianism therefore rests on shifting sands of subjectivity, but more so for politicians than for aid agencies. Tony Blair intervenes in Kosovo when his government is in a confident and idealistic mood after a huge election victory. Would he have been quite so enthusiastic if his margin of political support had been smaller? Perhaps like John Major during the Bosnian war, he would have hesitated. Ultimately, both personality and context affect the decision.

The humanitarian 'imperative' is not an imperative at all but a bundle of feelings. The public sees images of a particular event on TV but not another. The way those images are presented may strike a particular chord at a particular time, as Michael Buerk's documentary on Ethiopia did in 1984. By looking at past experience, I hope that I have illustrated some of the subjective forces that influence supposedly objective decisions. In the world of humanitarian response the subjective and the objective merge; objectivity is simply an analysis that follows subjective values.

As individuals we still cannot know exactly what other people are thinking or why they take a particular view any more than we can understand other people's suffering, or know whether our feelings of sympathy correspond to what they are feeling. Imagination alters our morality.

Looking at situations such as the famine in Ethiopia, we may conclude that humanitarianism, even when left primarily to independent aid organizations, has not always been as altruistic as it should. Ideological prejudices clouded the judgement of aid workers in Ethiopia and they did not see the imminence of famine. Aid workers in Sudan battled against a war mentality but overlooked the marginalization of women. In Mozambique an obsession with white South African power deafened us to the roar of our own power. In Afghanistan personal and organizational interests masqueraded as principle. In Somalia we were too self-righteous about our good intentions and did not listen enough. In the post-communist world we could not rationally limit our response. In Rwanda we hid from the fallibility of our own humanity. And in Kosovo we let our human concern be swept away on a political tide.

Some of these outcomes may not have been inevitable. They may reflect who we are as humanitarians rather than the situation in which we worked. Not all of us made the same mistakes at the same time and in the same place. Nor is there anything to be ashamed of for what we are in humanity. The pattern tells us much about ourselves. It also tells us about a changing world.

Now, in the New World Order, Western governments are stepping forward to take the lead. No longer inhibited by the Cold War, they can force Milosevic to stop abusing human rights, whereas in 1984 they let Mengistu get away with it. But they ignore what Russia does in Chechnya or the way Turkey treats the Kurds. With such power and such possibilities come risks and obligations, dangers and temptations. As well as the distortions of personal selfishness they are altered by political self-interest. But political interest is the more powerful element and it is more transparent. On the whole aid is far more accountable today than it was in the past. The responsibility is taken from individuals like myself and thrust back into the hands of the public, the voters.

The simplest and most important lesson from the past is that we need to keep our focus on the person in need, trying as hard as possible to understand his or her whole being, as well as the social and cultural context, without the interference of our own prejudice. If we do not, and respond on the basis of our own superficial knowledge and personal interests, we will find ourselves doing harm as well as good. In Mozambique we will inadvertently undermine local capacities by assuming that there are none. In Afghanistan we will withhold aid in pursuit of our own principle. In an increasingly politicized and changing world, humanitarians will need even greater levels of understanding and analysis.

Aid agencies today are becoming contractors for governments. Those governments have much greater powers of analysis and much greater capacities than the aid agencies. Governments have the power to take over aid agencies and use their supposed independence for their own ends. The aid agencies should therefore cling more tightly to the fundamental principle of humanity with impartiality. Governments have not, and cannot, espouse these principles. Governments put national self-interest first. As Tony Blair said in the case of Kosovo, it makes a difference to them where human suffering occurs. Much depends on how close it is to home. Bill Clinton had to persuade Americans that involvement in Kosovo was an issue of national self-interest. No other argument would do. Such humanitarianism, tagged along with Western strategy, will lose credibility in those parts of the world where the West is least impartial and will be seen as a 'tool' of Western interests and culture. The pursuit of altruism will be lost. Aid will become a tool of self interest.

* * *

But the real threats to humanitarianism today come from 'spin' – and here I mean spin not just in describing events but also in underlying values. In this last section I will examine seven types of spin that seem to me particularly characteristic. To an extent they correspond to the Seven Deadly Sins of medieval theology.

1 GREED

There is a view that it is good to pursue wealth selfishly, and even that the more ruthlessly selfish we are the more it will ultimately benefit the poor. The values of this perspective are efficiency and competition. Often referred to as 'market ideology' it draws heavily from the work of Adam Smith, who is quoted selectively for his argument that greed is good for society as a whole: 'Each intends his own gain but in the end promotes that of society although this was no part of his intention.'

Mixed with neo-Darwinian ideas about the 'survival of the fittest' as the 'natural' mechanism of life, market ideology has become a creed which seems to give a rational and altruistic basis for selfishness. Smith himself qualified his statement by saying that he did not seriously recommend anyone to rely on his precept without moral considerations. But it is such a convenient view that it remains a powerful force long after the excesses of the Thatcher and Reagan administrations have been forgotten. Strangely enough it is international speculator and philanthropist George Soros who is one of its strongest critics:

> We are left with the impression that people are guided by their self-interest as isolated individuals. In reality, people are social animals. The survival of the fittest must involve cooperation as well as competition. There is a common flaw in market fundamentalism, geopolitical realism, and vulgar social Darwinism: the disregard of altruism and cooperation.

Without any restraint, market forces can lead to terrible poverty for some and such uncertainty for many that their lives are blighted by distress and suffering. Matching his words with actions Soros chose to use his wealth to tackle the problems of the post-communist world.

2 SLOTH

We can be adept at finding reasons for inaction. Descriptions of Africa and other poor countries as places of a 'new barbarism' allow us to sleep peacefully with the view that it is nothing to do with us. The American writer Robert T Kaplan has been particularly influential in creating a sense of disgust with regard to poverty. But examined in more detail Kaplan stirs the mind with hints of a threat. He imagines seeing the world from space:

> From the perspective of space, where there is no gravity, there is also no up or down. The maps of the world that show north as up are not necessarily objective. Scan the map with the South Pole on top and you see the world entirely differently. The Mediterranean basin is no longer the focal point, lost, as it is, near the bottom of the globe. North America loses its continental width – and thus its majesty – as it narrows northward into the atrophied limb of Central America toward the centre of your field of vision. South America and Africa stand out.

Kaplan's new barbarism replaces traditional areas of civilization such as the Mediterranean and North America with Latin America and Africa, which he describes in disease-related language such as the 'atrophied limb'. He trades on an issue very familiar in the UK, the fear of immigration. According to *The Economist* the demography of the US is undergoing a dramatic change:

> In the 1950s census, America was 89 per cent white and 10 per cent black. Other races hardly got a look-in. Now Latinos account for around 12 per cent of the population. Within the next five years, they will overtake blacks to become the largest minority group. If current trends continue, they will be a majority in Los Angeles County in ten years. In 20 years, they will dominate Texas and California. By 2050, one in four of the 400 million people who will then be living in the United States will be Latino – and if you add Asians, their joint share will be one in three.

Although Western countries face severe problems because of their ageing workforce, they seem inclined to tighten up rules concerning refugees. There is even talk of redrafting the 1951 Refugee Convention to restrict rights of asylum. All this is part of a general tendency in the West to close its doors to outsiders, to avoid responsibilities, to stay at home and be ideologically slothful.

3 ANGER

A third tendency is to imagine a threat, even from the poor, and respond with anger and aggression. A very distinguished American academic, Samuel P Huntington, sanctions these fears by dividing the world into huge cultural groupings – the West, Africa, Latin America, Islam, and Orthodox, Sinic and Hindu groups – and then proposing that there will be a 'clash of civilizations', especially between the West and Islam.

Huntington asserts that there is an inherent tendency of Islam towards violent conflict. As Edward Said has repeatedly pointed out, Islamic fundamentalism is more a product of poverty and confusion than of power and confidence. But Huntington's arguments have proved useful to military 'hawks' and arms dealers. Unfortunately, by identifying the threats specifically with Islam, the West makes an enemy of poverty. As in the case of the Israeli conflict, it finds itself on the side of the rich and reacts with anger against the poor.

4 COVETOUSNESS

A fourth line of argument is that humanitarianism does not exist because aid agencies are selfish. Alex de Waal has made increasingly exaggerated criticisms of aid agencies, especially in his book *Famine Crimes: Politics and the Disaster Relief Industry in Africa* (1997). He makes the very reasonable point that international aid often fails to take account of political realities. He also argues that aid agencies have failed to take a principled stand on human rights issues, such as the forced resettlement in Ethiopia. But, as I indicated in Chapter 2, de Waal becomes too concerned with the supposed power of aid agencies. It is something he seems first to covet and then to want to destroy. All of this is justifiable. Where de Waal loses credibility is in speculating that such failures simply reflect an attempt to maximize income. In his view, 'There is, in fact, a tendency towards systemic duplicity. The language that relief agencies use to their peers, donors and constituents is a systematic distortion of the realities of their work on the ground.'

The words 'systemic' and 'systematic' emphasize de Waal's view that the process is deliberate. He assumes that the viewpoints of fundraisers always prevail in aid agencies: 'Within a single agency, fund-raisers and those adept at grabbing media attention will prosper at the expense of those who grapple with the problem of making aid a genuine service to its target group.'

De Waal offers no evidence for this. He quotes no memoranda or case studies that might prove his point, nor does he attempt to distinguish between types of agencies in which such tendencies might be stronger or to analyse the perspectives of the aid agencies themselves. De Waal simply asserts that the process is inevitable, following what he calls the 'humanitarian Gresham's law'. This describes: 'the decoupling of aid agencies' hard and soft interests (their institutional interests versus their stated aims). It states: in a situation of unregulated private humanitarian activity, "debased" humanitarianism will drive out the "authentic" version.' Behind de Waal's attacks lies public scepticism of the high-profile do-gooder. To an extent people covet the certainty of the humanitarian, and not being able to reach it, they may be tempted to destroy it.

Aid agencies are also to blame. They must let go of the argument that any criticism of them is an attack on the world's poor. Too often they argue that in a context of falling aid budgets their reputation must be kept sacrosanct at all costs. What is lost in this emotive exchange of attack and defence is public awareness of the erosion of power in the voluntary sector and the increasing dominance of the state in humanitarian issues.

5 LUST

In medieval theology lust entailed the subjection of the soul to the desires of the body. In our modern world there is a parallel in the subjection of truth to commercial interests, especially in the media. In April 2000 *The Observer* reported that:

> *An* Observer *survey has confirmed what discerning viewers have long suspected: current affairs, documentaries and dramas are being replaced by chat shows, quizzes and docu-soaps. Despite claims by BBC and ITV bosses that 'dumbing down' is a myth dreamed up by ageing, out of touch broadcasters, the study shows the main channels are serving up more and more trivia.*

Western television viewers today see fewer programmes on poorer countries than they did during the Cold War. Research conducted by the Third World and Environment Broadcasting Project (3WE) concludes that television remains the primary medium through which the British public is informed about the developing world, but that:

The total output of factual programmes on developing countries by the four ongoing terrestrial channels has dropped by almost 50 per cent since 1989... There is substantially less non-news/current affairs factual programming output filmed outside the British Isles than at the beginning of the decade. The gap between commercial television, which is subject to the economics of audience ratings, and the public service strongholds of BBC1 and BBC2 has widened. In 1998–1999 almost 60 per cent of programming on developing countries concerned travel (20 per cent) and wildlife (38 per cent).

At the risk of caricature, media coverage of poorer countries is directed towards wildlife and holiday programmes, rather than people. Reflecting the ability of the global media to produce shock-horror images, public donations to emergency appeals constantly break new records. But this response is very variable because it does not rest on any objective understanding but only on a subjective response to selected images. The public response to the earthquake in India was almost three times greater than to floods. Why should this be except for 'images'?

We have lost the old certainty of the days when the BBC educated citizens as part of a process of responsible government. The concept of 'public information' is being consigned to the museums, along with the 'nanny state'. Journalists have to compete to attract the attention of busy editors and may be tempted to go for sensational stories rather than accurate reports. Commercial pressures and the influence of the ratings determine when the news is shown and what it shows us.

The Kosovo crisis of 1999 was by no means the greatest humanitarian tragedy of its time and yet it attracted by far the greatest response – in fact, the highest ever recorded. A refugee from Kosovo received as much as fifty times the aid given to a refugee in Africa. Is this real human concern – or token gestures directed by the politics of the time? After a visit to Bosnia early in 1993 I wrote:

The difference between what the European public believes and what happens on the ground is extraordinary. Kate Adie seems to have persuaded everyone that the 'Cheshires' are indispensable. But although they are certainly the best element of the UN Protection Force, and heroic in carrying out their task, most relief workers consider their presence as a protection force to be irrelevant. What lorry drivers value is occasional assistance with bridge-mending and some help with recovery of broken-down trucks.

It seemed to me extraordinary that UK forces should be praised for such a tiny role and not criticized for failing to stop the war. But Adie, as she told me herself in 1999, was doing what her editors wanted – focusing on UK involvement with Bosnia rather than on Bosnia itself. The focus was not on 'the person in need' but on ourselves, or our representatives. By this process of exaggerating the importance of what UK forces were doing, the editors reduced public demands for a full military intervention. Many people imagined, from Adie's reports, that the British response was already massive and effective. In fact what they were seeing was only a few isolated incidents. A journalist might feel that they had an obligation to compensate for this tendency by being 'committed', as veteran BBC reporter Martin Bell has argued. But the trend seems to be to give the public what they want. The customer, like the voter, is supreme.

The problem with telling the public what they want to hear is that we give a falsely reassuring, and therefore pleasurable, experience. After our holiday programmes about the gorillas of Rwanda (with the genocide conveniently forgotten), we watch news in which British soldiers save the world from crazy black people and the stupidities of the UN bureaucrats. The public pay to be told that it is not their fault – so they get what they pay for. Editors who do not follow the ratings will lose their jobs.

6 PRIDE

But the argument that underlies all the other attacks on humanitarianism is a deep-seated belief, encouraged by popular science, that we are selfish by nature. We are all the product of our genes, and because genes are selfish, selfishness is natural and therefore right. Advertisers want us to lose our inhibitions about buying, and so they tell us that what we want is what we should have. What is natural is good; 'because I am worth it', and so on. It is almost impossible to dissociate ourselves from this crackle of commercialism in the airwaves of our intellectual environment.

Richard Dawkins' *The Selfish Gene*, published in 1976, virtually created a new morality of selfishness justified by science. The fact that Dawkins himself had ruled out a connection between genetics and morality was ignored. In the same book he had stated:

I am not advocating a morality based on evolution. I am saying how things have evolved. I am not saying how we humans morally ought to behave. I stress this because I know I am in danger of being misunderstood by those people, all too numerous, who cannot distinguish a statement of belief in what is the case from advocacy of what ought to be the case. My own feeling is that a human society based simply on the gene's law of universal ruthless selfishness would be a very nasty society in which to live.

Darwin also had similar worries about 'the survival of the fittest' and delayed publication of his *Origin of Species* for many years, partly because he was uneasy about its misuse in the moral sphere. In a little-known passage Dawkins tries to compensate:

Let us try to teach generosity and altruism, because we are born selfish. Let us understand what our own selfish genes are up to, because we may then at least have the chance to upset their designs, something that no other species has yet aspired to.

What lingers in public perception from *The Selfish Gene* is the idea that altruism is just a form of selfishness. Again, it is worth looking more closely at what Dawkins had written:

An entity, such as a baboon, is said to be altruistic if it behaves in such a way as to increase another such entity's welfare at the expense of its own. Selfish behaviour has the opposite effect... In practice, when we apply the definition to real behaviour, we must qualify it with the word 'apparently'. An apparently altruistic act is one that looks superficially as if it must tend to make the altruist more likely (however slightly) to die, and the recipient more likely to survive. It often turns out on closer inspection that acts of apparent altruism are really selfishness in disguise.

This does not mean that there is no such thing as altruism. Dawkins concluded:

It is possible that yet another quality of man is a capacity for genuine, disinterested, true altruism... We are built as gene machines and cultured as meme machines, but we have the power to turn against our creators. We alone on earth, can rebel against the tyranny of the selfish replicators.

7 PRIDE

Coming to the last of the Seven Deadly Sins I find that much of what I have written emphasizes the need for self-awareness, and this can only be built on self-respect. We actually need pride in ourselves as humans if we are to promote the values of humanity. And what I find lacking is exactly that confidence. We do not believe in ourselves as a species – we are just naked apes that can be studied and experimented with as if we were chemicals or atoms. Indeed, we live in an atomized society in which values are individual and separate. But can we reconcile pride in the capacity of our species, altruism and science? What does Dawkins mean when he says 'we are cultured as meme machines'? He explains:

> We need a name for the new replicator, a noun that conveys the idea of a unit of cultural transmission, or a unit of imitation. 'Mimeme' comes from a suitable Greek root, but I want a monosyllable that sounds a bit like 'gene'. I hope my classicist friends will forgive me if I abbreviate mimeme to meme.

As examples of memes, Dawkins suggested: 'tunes, ideas, catch phrases, clothes fashions, ways of making pots or of building arches.'

If such scientific verification is needed, humanity could be described as a meme that is passed down through generations by imitation, as when children imitate the values of their parents.

The value of the concept of the meme is that it can explain altruistic behaviour in a way that does not require an external deity or a metaphysical set of beliefs. We can view ourselves, driven largely by genes, switching intellectually between different memes that we perceive as morals. The meme of altruism is not tied to a specific morality or religion but our cultural heritage – to what we took from the behaviour of our ancestors and our society. It is the social response to our individual selfishness. This helps us to make some sense of the interaction of selfish and altruistic influences.

But essentially the concept of humanity remains outside the preserve of both the gene and the meme. It is not determined by our biological or our cultural heritage. There exists an element of choice or free will – an ability to select knowingly between selfishness and altruism. In the exercise of that choice lies the clue to what we are, and a justification for pride in our species.

Notes on the Sources

INTRODUCTION

The Introduction draws on R Rorty, *Contingency, Irony and Solidarity* (Cambridge, 1989). Literary references in this book owe something to Rorty's use of them as an entry into philosophy. *Development as Freedom* (Oxford University Press, 1999) is the title of Amartya Sen's summary and simplification of many of his earlier writings. Nicholas Leader's account of where humanitarian principles have got to is published by the Overseas Development Institute (ODI) as *The Politics of Principle: The Principles of Humanitarian Action in Practice*, HPG Report 2, March 2000. The *Code of Conduct for the International Red Cross and Red Crescent Movement and NGOs in Disaster Relief* was published by ODI's Relief and Rehabilitation Network as Paper 7, September 1994. The Oxfam policy referred to is *Oxfam and Disasters* approved by the executive committee in September 1985. Rembrandt's portrait 'Belshazzar's Feast' is in the National Gallery, London, and the account of it being turned in the frame is from Kelch Brown and Pieter van Thiel, *Rembrandt: The Master and his Workshop* (Yale, 1991). The description of 'Ubuntu' comes from Desmond Tutu's *No Future Without Forgiveness* (Rider, 1999, p35), which is mainly about the Truth and Reconciliation Commission in South Africa. For the most recent comprehensive account of Oxfam's history, see Maggie Black, *A Cause for our Times – Oxfam the First 50 years* (Oxfam/Oxford University Press, 1992), and for more up-to-date information see the Oxfam website at www.oxfam.org.uk.

CHAPTER 1

I would like to thank Roy Gutman, Lukas Haynes, Maurice Herson and Marina Skuric-Prodanovic for help with my explorations of different perspectives on Kosovo and recent Balkan history. They disagreed with aspects of what I wrote in earlier drafts, and may still disagree with the outcome.

I have been obliged to use the phrase 'new world order' because I have not found a better one for what has come after the Cold War. I realize that no such thing has yet emerged. A few writers refer to a 'new agenda', but this is not a widely recognized description and rather parochially limits analysis to a Western perspective.

The description of NATO's bombing of Gordana Rajkov's flat is from an internal Oxfam communication dated 30 April 1999 from Marina Skuric-Prodanovic, Oxfam representative in Belgrade. The Belgrade emails passed around during the bombing were from the same source. For the analysis of ethnicity, I particularly acknowledge Michael Ignatieff's *Blood and Belonging* (Vintage, 1994) and David Turton's introduction to *War and Ethnicity: Global Connections and Local Violence* (University of Rochester Press, 2000). For the full ethnic treatment of the conflict, see Robert Kaplan's *Balkan Ghosts: A Journey Through History* (Vintage, 1993). Laurence Silber and Alan Little's BBC film that was also published as a book is *The Death of Yugoslavia* (Penguin, 1995). My own account draws particularly from James Gow's *Triumph of Lack of Will – International Diplomacy and the Yugoslav War* (Hurst, 1997). For an account that puts heavier blame on the Serbs, see, for example, *Yugopslavia's Bloody Collapse – Causes, Course and Consequences* by Christopher Bennett (Hurst, 1995). Some of the questions about NATO derive from Noam Chomsky's *The New Military Humanism – Lessons from Kosovo* (Pluto, 1999). Slavenka Drakulic's account of loss of identity is quoted from *Balkan Express* (Random House, 1993, pp50–51).

On the figures for rape in Bosnia, the ICRC's Urs Boegli is quoted from the transcript of a Reuter Foundation conference on 'Bosnia and the Media', held at Green College, Oxford, October 1999. The expert committee conclusions are from Gutman and Rieff *Crimes of War* (Norton, 1999) under the headings 'Sexual Violence: Systematic Rape' and 'Bosnia', in which the percentages of blame are quoted (p56). Zarkov's article is 'War Rapes in Bosnia – On Masculinity, Femininity and Power of the Rape Victim Identity' from the journal *Temida*, vol 1, no 2, May 1998, published in Belgrade by the Victimology Society of Serbia and the European Movement in Serbia. Toby Porter's Oxfam report is *Final Report – Emergency Programme Coordinator, Oxfam GB Albania Programme*, 16 August 1999, Oxfam.

CHAPTER 2

I would particularly like to thank Marcus Thompson, Oxfam's emergencies director and my boss during this period, for unfailingly wise counsel. My thanks are also due to Aregawi Hagos for feedback on the draft of this chapter.

Mark Duffield's critique of developmentalism comes from 'The Symphony of the Damned', *Disasters*, vol 20, no 3, 1996. See also *Complex Emergencies and the Crisis of Developmentalism*, IDS Bulletin, vol 25, no 4, 1994. My report on reasons why the response was slow is *The Ethiopia Famine 1984 – Oxfam's Early Involvement*, February 1985. My *Tour Report April 1986* and *Tour Report November–December 1997* gives evidence obtained from various sources and direct interviews of the serious effects of taxation in Ethiopia. My worries about the profile of the war were published as 'A Public Relations Disaster' in *The New Internationalist*, no 148, June 1985.

Alex de Waal has strongly criticized the aid agency silence about resettlement in his *Famine Crimes – Politics and the Disaster Relief Industry in Africa* (James Currey, 1997). Before de Waal, the main critique of aid agencies was Graham Hancock's *Lords of Mercy* (The Atlantic Monthly Press, New York, 1989), which focused on the lifestyles of UN and other aid agency staff.

A major source for my analysis in this chapter, especially regarding supplementary feeding programmes, is Oxfam's official evaluation, *Oxfam's Response to Disasters in Ethiopia and Sudan 1984–1985* by Robert Dodd, September 1986, described by Oxfam's current director as the most important evolution ever done for Oxfam. Dodd continued to provide new insights into humanitarian work until his recent death.

The manual referred to is Oxfam's *Practical Guide to Selective Feeding Programmes* by the Oxfam Health Unit, published in a revised version in 1984. Hugo Slim's analysis of the moral dilemma about resettlement is from *Doing the Right Thing – Relief Agencies, Moral Dilemmas and Moral Responsibility in Political Emergencies and War* (Nordska Afrikainstutet, 1997). The discussion of lobbying against resettlement comes from my *Ethiopia Visit March 1988* and is supplemented by personal communication from Nick Winer. The validity of this account was recently confirmed verbally by Will Day and Nick Southern, who worked for Oxfam at that time and brought the report of human rights violations to Addis Ababa and were actively involved in mobilizing support from the ambassadors.

I have drawn also on Barbara Hendrie's 'Knowledge and Power: A Critique of an International Relief Operation' in *Disasters*, vol 21(1), 1997, which made me think about the issue of power relationships.

CHAPTER 3

Melvyn Almond died on 7 November 1989 and the booklet he was writing at the time of his death is called *Pastoral Development and Oxfam in the Sudan*. It was edited by his partner, Dr Linda Small, and published by Oxfam as a tribute to Melvyn. Some information used in this chapter is based on personal conversations with Linda Small, as well as her report *Mundari Food for Work Tree Nursery Project*, 14 April 1988 (Oxfam archive). The description of the cattle camp is by Nigel Walsh, Oxfam's field secretary, in his *Tour Report – South Sudan*, October 1985 (Oxfam archive). David Turton's account of the attack on the Mursi is from 'Mursi Political Identity and Warfare: The Survival of an Idea' in K Fukui and J Markakis (eds) *Ethnicity and Conflict in the Horn of Africa* (James Currey, 1994). The debate between Duffield and Mary B Anderson is from *New Routes*, March 1998.

For an overall analysis of the war in Sudan I have drawn heavily on Nicholas Stockton's *Oxfam: Sudan Programme November 1984–July 1986*. Stockton's paper 'From Relief to Development' caricaturing the 'boneheads and pinkoes' debate was presented at the Oxfam Emergencies Conference in Kampala October 1989 (papers and minutes are in Oxfam archive). Alex de Waal's book on the Darfur famine is *Famine That Kills: Darfur, Sudan 1984–5* (Clarendon Press, 1989), and the study for Oxfam is *Famine Survival Strategies in Wollo, Tigray and Eritrea – A Review of the Literature* (Oxfam, 1990; unpublished internal report). David Keen's *Famine, Needs Assessment and Survival Strategies in Africa* was published by Oxfam as research paper no 8, 1993. The book by David Keen referred to here is *The Benefits of Famine – A Political Economy of Famine and Relief in Southwestern Sudan 1983–1989* (Princeton, 1994). Alex de Waal's critique of aid agencies is quoted from 'Compassion Fatigue' in *New Statesman and Society*, March 1995 and on the views of Africans from his book *Famine Crimes* (see references in Chapter 2).

The problems of information-gathering among pastoralists are described by Jok Madut Jok in 'Information Exchange Between Aid Workers and Recipients in South Sudan' in *Disasters*, vol 20, no 3, September 1996. The extrapolations concerning gender are my own.

CHAPTER 4

I would like to thank Oxfam's recent representative in Maputo, Kate Horne, for help and advice with this chapter. The account of missionary Ellie Hein is from K Austin, *Invisible Crimes – US Private Intervention in the War in Mozambique* (Africa Policy Information Centre, Washington, 1986). The Oxfam case study is from the booklet *Chicualacuala: Life on the Frontline* (Oxfam, 1987). The reports quoted are *Tony Vaux – Mozambique Tour November–December 1986*; *Tour to Maputo, Harare etc, February–March 1988*; *Mozambique – The War Continues February 1990*; and *Mozambique – July 1992*. I wrote a parable about my disillusionment with Mozambique and my struggle with the issue of private enterprise, published as 'Meditation on a Bucket of Lugworms' in *The New Internationalist*, no 228, February 1992. Ken Wilson's description of RENAMO's better side comes from M Hall and T Young, *Confronting Leviathan – Mozambique Since Independence* (Hurst, 1997). In the 1980s, Ken Wilson greatly assisted me in the long process of learning about Southern Africa. The 'solidarity mode' in Mozambique was articulated by Joseph Hanlon in a series of influential books. His classic attack on apartheid was *Mozambique – Who Calls the Shots?* (James Currey, 1991). More recently he has criticized the IMF in *Peace Without Profit – How the IMF Blocks Rebuilding in Mozambique* (James Currey, 1996), and continues to question the role of South Africa and big business in the Mozambican economy.

Charles Dickens's description of Mr Bumble in *Oliver Twist* (1837) caused a serious shift in public policy. It made the running of workhouses impossible, and accelerated reforms. But in a little-known description of a visit to a real workhouse (*A Walk in a Workhouse* from *Household Words*, 1859) Dickens portrays a very different reality. The person in authority who shows him round is 'humane and compassionate' and the nurse in charge of the 'paupers' bursts into tears at the thought of their suffering; she comes from a poor background herself. There is temptation, but this does not always mean that there is a fall. In the nature of things, Mr Bumble is well known and the other workhouse supremo remains nameless.

CHAPTER 5

I am extremely grateful to Oxfam's representative in Afghanistan, Chris Johnson, for a very stimulating dialogue, including a long letter dated 23 May 2000 from which I have drawn many of the quotations. The other quotations primarily come from her booklet *Afghanistan – A Land in Shadow* (Oxfam Country Profile, Oxfam, 1998). Another major contributor to this chapter was Marcus Thompson, who condensed his familiar detached and measured judgements into a personal communication dated 4 May 2000 from which I have quoted. Oxfam's programme manager for Afghanistan, Fiona Gell, also sent me a detailed personal communication dated 11 August 2000, which I have also quoted from.

My experiences are recorded in *Afghanistan Visit 4–27 July 1989* (Oxfam archive). The Oxfam representative at the time of the Taliban capture of Kabul was Nancy Smith, but I have had to rely on accounts taken from an article written by her immediate successor, Sue Emmott. It was published by Oxfam as 'Personnel Management in Crisis: Experience from Afghanistan' in P Porter, I Smyth and C Sweetman (eds) *Gender Works – Oxfam Experience and Practice* (Oxfam, 1999). This book also contains several articles about the history of Oxfam's gender policy and the evolution of the gender unit, which I have drawn on. The full name of the Oxfam policy is 'Gender and Development – Oxfam's Policy and its Programme', agreed by Oxfam Council in May 1993.

The evaluation of the water programme is 'Making Omelettes with Other People's Eggs – An Evaluation of the Logar Water Project in Kabul, Afghanistan' (quoted from a draft version) by John Cosgrave, unpublished. The UN gender report is *Report of the United Nations Interagency Gender Mission to Afghanistan 12–24 November 1997*, from the Office of the Special Adviser on Gender Issues and Advancement of Women, United Nations, New York. For a wider context on Western attitudes to Muslim fundamentalism I have drawn on Edward Said's work, notably *Covering Islam – How the Media and the Experts Determine How We See the Rest of the World* (Vintage, 1997; original publication 1981). Specifically on Afghanistan, I read William Maley (ed) *Fundamentalism Reborn? – Afghanistan and the Taliban* (Hurst, 1998), and Peter Marsden's *The Taliban – War, Religion and the New Order in Afghanistan* (Zed, 1998). For the best and latest account of the problem of proliferating principles, see Nicholas Leader's *The Politics of Principle:*

The Principles of Humanitarian Action in Practice, HPG Report 2 (ODI, London, March 2000).

Jane Austen's *Pride and Prejudice* (1903) is quoted from the Penguin edition of 1996. Joseph Conrad's *Heart of Darkness* (1902) is quoted from the Penguin edition of 1989. The source for my quotation from *Troilus and Cressida* is the Oxford University Press edition of the *Complete Works of Shakespeare* (1964).

CHAPTER 6

Roger Naumann's views are quoted from an internal paper, 'Oxfam's Learning on Conflict – Case Study from the Horn of Africa 1987–1995'.

I have drawn heavily on Walter Clarke's and Jeffrey Herbst's *Learning from Somalia – The Lessons of Armed Humanitarian Intervention* (Princeton, 1997), which includes the memoir by Andrew Natsios about the use of private traders. The account of Mohammed Sahnoun's experiences is from his article 'Mixed Intervention in Somalia and the Great Lakes' from Jonathan Moore (ed) *Hard Choices – Moral Dilemmas in Humanitarian Intervention*, published under the auspices of the ICRC by Rowman and Littlefield (1998). My assessment report on Somalia is *Somalia Famine Report on a Visit – 20–27 August 1992*, and the later report recommending extensive changes in Oxfam is misleadingly entitled *Strategic Plan – Emergencies Unit*, September 1992 (Oxfam archive). I have also referred to the *Evaluation of Oxfam's Emergency Work in Somalia and Somaliland May 1991 to December 1993* by Alison Lockhead, May 1994 (Oxfam archive). The use of local business people to assist in the delivery of humanitarian aid has been given the title 'smart relief' and is elaborated by Paul Richards in his fascinating study *Fighting for the Rainforest – War, Youth and Resources in Sierra Leone* (James Currey, 1996, p157).

Fred Cuny's papers 'Alternative Food Distribution Schemes for Conflicts and Famines' and 'A Short Briefing about the Market Sales Approach' were attached to a private letter to the author dated 24 February 1993. Cuny was a very great humanitarian, and his death in Chechenya has left a serious lack of intellectual leadership to take forward the concept of 'smart relief'.

CHAPTER 7

The quotation from Tolstoy is from *Essays and Letters* in the World's Classics series (Grant Richards, London, 1903): 'An afterword to an account rendered of relief supplied to the famine-stricken, in the Government of Toula, in 1891 and 1892'. The essay was suppressed during Tolstoy's lifetime because it was considered unacceptable to say that the famine arose from chronic poverty.

My report is *Azerbaijan: The Karabakh Emergency*, October 1993 (Oxfam). The Oxfam Fundamental Review is entitled *Setting Course for the Twenty-First Century – Oxfam Strategic Review 1998* (Oxfam, 1998). Quotations by Derek Summerfield are from 'Assisting Survivors of War and Atrocity: Notes of Psycho-social Issues for NGO Workers', published in S Commins (ed) *Development in States of War* (Oxfam, 1996), and from 'The Psycho-Social Effects of Conflict in the Third World – A Short Study', internal Oxfam paper, November 1990. For the full account of knitting projects and fashion shows in Tuzla, see Usha Kar, 'Much Ado about Knitting: The Experiences of Bosfam (Bosnia)' in P Porter, I Smyth and C Sweetman (eds) *Gender Works – Oxfam Experience in Policy and Practice* (Oxfam, 1999). The critique of psycho-social projects follows P J Bracken, and C Petty, *Rethinking the Trauma of War* (Save the Children/Free Association, 1998). The evaluation referred to is Norwegian Ministry of Foreign Affairs, *Evaluation of Norwegian Support to Psycho-Social Projects in Bosnia-Herzegovina and the Caucasus*, March 1999. The local NGO set up by Oxfam in Tuzla was called 'Bosfam' (at the request of its members and rather to Oxfam's embarrassment), and the *Bosfam Review* was conducted by Rachel Hastie, August 1996 (Oxfam archive).

CHAPTER 8

This chapter draws on two articles by Anne Mackintosh, Oxfam representative for Rwanda, Burundi and Kivu (Zaire) from 1991–1994. The first is 'International Aid and the Media' in *Contemporary Politics*, vol 2, no 1, South Bank University, spring 1996. This included Anne's description of being surrounded at Gisenyi and trying to protect local people from violence. The second article reflects on the process of reconciliation: 'Rwanda: Beyond "Ethnic Conflict"', published in *From Conflict to Peace in a Changing World* by Deborah Eade

(Stylus Publishing, Sterling, VA, 1998). Anne was awarded an MBE in 1995.

No one can be proud of their record in Rwanda, but Oxfam comes out of it better than most, in so far as that provides any satisfaction. Oxfam's international director, Stewart Wallis, wrote to the newspapers several times while the genocide was happening and called it a genocide, demanding international intervention under the terms of the 1949 Genocide Convention. In 1992 Oxfam had presciently commissioned a regional study of increasing tensions in the region. This paper by Peter Wiles is called 'Rwandese Refugees and Migrants in the Great Lakes Region of Central Africa'. In 1993 a former representative, David Waller, wrote a general profile of Rwanda, published by Oxfam in 1993, as *Rwanda, Which Way Now?* This book warned that the path to violence lay open.

I have drawn heavily on Peter Uvin's brilliant book *Aiding Violence – The Development Enterprise in Rwanda* (Kumarian, 1998) and also on Andre Sibomana's *Hope for Rwanda – Conversations with Laure Guilbert and Herve Deguine*, which is quoted in the English translation from French by Tertsakian (Pluto, 1999). Stanley Milgram's experiment is described by Lyall Watson in *Dark Nature* (Hodder and Stoughton, 1995). The UN commander, Lieutenant General Romeo Dallaire of the Canadian army, is quoted from 'The End of Innocence – Rwanda 1994' in Jonathan Moore (ed) *Hard Choices – Moral Dilemmas in Humanitarian Intervention* (Rowman and Littlefield, 1998). Fergal Keane's short account of his experiences in Rwanda is *Season of Blood – A Rwandan Journey* (Viking, 1995).

There is an increasing body of Rwanda genocide literature. The international evaluation was edited by David Millwood and published by the Steering Committee of the Joint Evaluation of Emergency Assistance to Rwanda in 1996. It has been available from ODI London as *The International Response to Conflict and Genocide from the Rwanda Experience*. An early historical account is Alain Destexhe's *Rwanda and Genocide in the Twentieth Century* (Pluto, 1995). A set of eyewitness accounts has been published as *We Wish to Inform You that Tomorrow We Will Be Killed with our Families – Stories from Rwanda* by Philip Gourevitch (Picador, 1998). A huge collection of similar accounts was collected by Rakiya Omaar and published by Africa Rights as *Death, Despair and Defiance* (London, 1995) and there is a similar collection by Human Rights Watch.

For the methods of literary analysis used in this chapter and elsewhere, I owe a debt to Professor John Carey of Oxford University, my former tutor. In using Dickens's description from *A Tale of Two Cities* (1859) I have drawn on the spirit, but not the word, of Carey's *The Violent Effigy – A Study of Dickens's Imagination* (Faber, 1973).

CHAPTER 9

The detailed Western demands over Kosovo are quoted from Noam Chomsky's *The New Military Humanism* (Pluto, 1999). Jonathan Dimbleby's documentary for ITV, *A Kosovo Journey*, was shown in Britain in March 2000, raising similar questions.

My conclusions reflect Richard Rorty, especially *Moral Universalism and Economic Triage* found at www.unesco.org/phiweb/uk/2rpu/rort/rort.html.

I would like to thank Oxfam's director, David Bryer, for being generous with his time in discussing the overview. For his views on the increasing importance of global advocacy and international alliances, see David Bryer and John Magrath, 'New Dimensions of Global Advocacy' in *Non-Profit and Voluntary Sector*, quarterly vol 28, no 4, September 1999. I also owe a general debt to Michael Ignatieff's reflections on humanitarianism in *The Warrior's Honor – Ethnic War and the Modern Conscience* (Chatto and Windus, 1998).

Professor B S Chimni's remarks were made in the Barbara Harrell-Bond lecture 'Globalization, Humanitarianism and the Erosion of Refugee Protection' at the Refugee Studies Centre, Oxford, March 2000 (to be published). For the shenanigans around the creation of international law and the United States' refusal to sign up, see Geoffrey Robertson's *Crimes Against Humanity – The Struggle for Global Justice* (Allen Lane/Penguin Press, 1999), especially p167 onwards on the 1997 Geneva Protocols.

In the section on market ideology, I refer to Anthony Giddens, *The Third Way – The Renewal of Social Democracy* (Polity Press, 1998). George Soros is quoted from *The Crisis of Global Capitalism – Open Society Endangered* (Little Brown, 1998). A full critique of market ideology is given by John Gray in *False Dawn – The Delusions of Global Capitalism* (Granta, 1998).

The book by Robert D Kaplan referred to here is *The Ends of the Earth – A Journey at the Dawn of the 21st Century* (Papermac, 1997). His influential article about Rwanda was 'The Coming Anarchy' in the *Atlantic Monthly*, February 1994. Samuel P Huntington's book is *The Clash of Civilizations and the Remaking of World Order* (Simon and

Schuster, 1996). *The Economist* is quoted from a supplement on 'The New Americans' (11 March 2000).

Martin Bell has written about committed journalism in his autobiographical book, and how it arose in Sarajevo, in *In Harm's Way* (Hamish Hamilton, 1995). Kate Adie's remarks were made at a Reuter Foundation Conference on 'Bosnia and the Media' held at Green College Oxford, October 1999.

My report referred to here is *The Bosnia War, January 1993* (Oxfam archive). The survey of UK media coverage is *Losing Perspective: Global Affairs on British Terrestrial Television 1989–1999*, Third World and Environment Broadcasting Project 2000. *The Observer* survey by Rosalind Ryan and Ellen Bennett is described by John Arlidge, media editor, on 17 April 2000, giving email john.arlidge@observer.co.uk.

Alex de Waal's critique of aid agencies is *Famine Crimes – Politics and the Disaster Relief Industry in Africa* (James Currey, 1997).

The Selfish Gene by Richard Dawkins was first published in 1976, and my quotations are from the 1989 paperback version published by Oxford University Press. For elaboration on memes see *The Meme Machine* by Susan Blackmore published in 1999, also by Oxford University Press.

Index